BRADY

WORKBOOK
Alyson Emery

First Responder
A SKILLS APPROACH

Seventh Edition

Daniel Limmer, EMT-P

Paramedic, Kennebunk Fire-Rescue
Kennebunk, Maine

Adjunct Faculty,
Southern Maine Technical College
South Portland, Maine

Keith J. Karren, PhD

Professor, Department of Health Sciences
Brigham Young University
Provo, Utah

Brent Q. Hafen, PhD

Late of Brigham Young University
Provo, Utah

Medical Editor
Edward T. Dickinson, MD, NREMT-P, FACEP

PEARSON

Prentice
Hall

Upper Saddle River, New Jersey

The Active Learning activities in this workbook were provided by textbook author Daniel Limmer.

Publisher: Julie Levin Alexander
Publisher's Assistant: Regina Bruno
Executive Editor: Marlene McHugh Pratt
Senior Managing Editor for Development: Lois Berlowitz
Project Manager: Eileen Clawson, Triple S Press
Associate Editor: Monica Moosang
Director of Marketing: Karen Allman
Executive Marketing Manager: Katrin Beacom
Marketing Coordinator: Michael Sirinides
Marketing Assistant: Wayne Celia, Jr.
Managing Production Editor: Patrick Walsh
Production Liaison: Julie Li
Production Editor: Sarvesh Mehrotra
Manufacturing Manager: Ilene Sanford
Manufacturing Buyer: Pat Brown
Senior Design Coordinator: Cheryl Asherman
Composition: Techbooks
Printing and Binding: Bind Rite Graphics
Cover Printer: Lehigh Press

NOTICE ON CARE PROCEDURES

It is the intent of the authors and publisher that this workbook be used as part of a formal First Responder education program taught by qualified instructors and supervised by a licensed physician. The procedures described in this workbook are based upon consultation with First Responder and medical authorities. The authors and publisher have taken care to make certain that these procedures reflect currently accepted clinical practice; however, they cannot be considered absolute recommendations.

The material in this workbook contains the most current information available at the time of publication. However, federal, state, and local guidelines concerning clinical practices, including, without limitation, those governing infection control and universal precautions, change rapidly. The reader should note, therefore, that new regulations may require changes in some procedures.

It is the responsibility of the reader to familiarize himself or herself with the policies and procedures set by federal, state, and local agencies as well as the institution or agency where the reader is employed. The authors and the publisher of this workbook disclaim any liability, loss, or risk resulting directly or indirectly from the suggested procedures and theory, from any undetected errors, or from the reader's misunderstanding of the text. It is the reader's responsibility to stay informed of any new changes or recommendations made by any federal, state, and local agency as well as by his or her employing institution or agency.

Pearson Prentice Hall™ is a trademark of Pearson Education, Inc.
Pearson® is a registered trademark of Pearson plc.
Prentice Hall® is a registered trademark of Pearson Education, Inc.

Pearson Education LTD
Pearson Education Singapore, Pte. Ltd
Pearson Education Canada, Ltd
Pearson Education—Japan

Pearson Education Australia PTY, Limited
Pearson Education North Asia Ltd
Pearson Educación de Mexico, S.A. de C.V.
Pearson Education Malaysia, Pte. Ltd

10 9 8 7 6 5 4 3 2 1
ISBN 0-13-195811-9

CONTENTS

1 | Introduction to the EMS System

Key Ideas

This chapter provides an overview of the EMS system and the roles and responsibilities of the First Responder in the EMS system. Key ideas include the following:

- The EMS system is a network of resources linked together for the purpose of providing emergency care and transport to victims of sudden illness and injury.

- The public has access to the EMS system through 9-1-1 and non–9-1-1 phone numbers. With enhanced 9-1-1, the EMS dispatcher is able to see the street address and phone number of the caller on a computer screen.

- There are four levels of EMS training: First Responder, EMT-Basic, EMT-Intermediate, and EMT-Paramedic.

- The First Responder is the first person with emergency medical training on the scene of a sudden injury or illness.

- First Responders are the designated agents of the medical director, who is the physician responsible for out-of-hospital emergency medical care.

Exam Warm-up

1. The emergency medical services (EMS) system is organized to
   a. deny non-emergency personnel access to the scene.
   b. provide care to victims of sudden illness or injury.
   c. upgrade 9-1-1 phone systems all over the U.S.
   d. coordinate extrication and rescue operations.

2. First Responders are the first
   a. law enforcement officials on the scene of an emergency.
   b. people on scene with emergency medical training.
   c. EMS rescuers who can administer medications.
   d. people to notice that an emergency exists.

3. A _____ is a medical facility that is devoted to the treatment of infants and children.
   a. trauma center
   b. pediatric center
   c. poison control center
   d. local hospital emergency department

4. Your most important responsibility as a First Responder is to guard your own health and safety. Identify the item(s) below that are consistent with that responsibility.
   a. Drive safely at all times.
   b. Do not enter high traffic areas.
   c. Use a seat belt whenever you drive or ride.
   d. Enter a crime scene after you see the criminal leave it.
   e. Remove yourself from gas leaks and other such hazards.
   f. Always wear the appropriate personal protective equipment.

5. The EMS medical director is responsible for the clinical and patient-care aspects of an EMS system.

   _____ True

   _____ False

6. An EMS medical director is a physician who oversees EMS care of patients in the field in two ways:
   a. directly and indirectly.
   b. internally and externally.
   c. out of hospital and in hospital.
   d. informatively and educationally.

7. Maintaining a clean, professional appearance is NOT a realistic goal for a First Responder.

   _____ True

   _____ False

8. It is the First Responder's responsibility to meet the standard of care with all patients, no matter what their gender, age, culture, or socioeconomic background.

   _____ True

   _____ False

Short-Answer Review

9. The National Highway Traffic Safety Administration recommends that every EMS system include 10 basic components. Write a brief description of each component:

a. Regulation and policy:

b. Resources management:

c. Human resources and training:

d. Transportation:

e. Facilities:

f. Communications:

g. Public information and education:

h. Medical oversight:

i. Trauma systems:

j. Evaluation:

10. List the four levels of out-of-hospital emergency care providers.

a.

b.

c.

d.

11. What is your role as a First Responder? List eight tasks you should be able to perform.

a.

b.

c.

d.

e.

f.

g.

h.

12. Write an example for each type of medical control listed below.

a. Direct medical control:

b. Indirect medical control:

Vocabulary Practice

Across

4. Standing _____ are a type of indirect medical control.

6. A _____ center specializes in high-risk pregnancies.

9. Each EMS system must have a _____ as a medical director.

11. First Responders are the designated _____ of the medical director.

14. Second highest level of EMS training.

19. Short for U.S. Department of Transportation.

21. Most advanced level of EMS training.

22. Hour immediately after an accident.

Down

1. A _____ center offers injury treatment that exceeds that of a general hospital.

2. Short for cardiopulmonary resuscitation.

3. EMS is meant to care for the suddenly _____ or injured.

5. A rescuer's first and most important priority.

7. With _____ 9-1-1, the dispatcher can see a caller's address and phone number.

8. A _____ center focuses on treating infants and children.

10. Short for National Highway Traffic Safety Administration.

12. One First Responder role is acting as a _____ with other public safety personnel.

13. An EMT- _____ may staff and drive ambulances.

15. The National _____ of EMTs offers exams for certification.

16. Short for emergency medical services.

17. Short for emergency medical technician.

18. Another name for indirect medical control.

20. One way for a medical director to provide direct medical control.

21. Short for personal protective equipment.

The Call: First on Scene

Read this scenario and answer the questions that follow. Focus on your role/responsibilities as a First Responder.

You and your partner have just completed the evening check of your equipment, when the dispatcher sends your unit to a man having "difficulty breathing" at a restaurant. When you arrive in front of the small restaurant, there is a group of very worried patrons at the curb. They tell you that the patient, Mr. Gianelli, must be having a heart attack. They say he cannot breathe well and is clutching his chest and neck. When you determine that it is safe to do so, you leave your vehicle, enter the restaurant, and approach Mr. Gianelli.

At Mr. Gianelli's side, you assess that he is awake, that he cannot speak or breathe, and that this happened while eating steak and laughing. Your partner performs abdominal thrusts on Mr. Gianelli, immediately expelling the bit of food that was blocking his airway. Mr. Gianelli can now breathe. His voice is very hoarse.

1. What are your roles/responsibilities now? Name at least three.

2. The EMTs arrive to continue patient care and transport. What are your roles and responsibilities now? Name at least three.

Active Learning

To help you learn more about your EMS system, as well as other EMS systems around you, find the answers to the following questions. Call or visit your local EMS station or interview a person from that station. Remember that members of fire and EMS agencies may need to respond to calls before and during the time you need to talk to them. If you visit a fire station, be aware that you are in a place which doubles as the "house" of the people on duty. Be respectful of their station and privacy.

1. Which fire, police, and EMS agencies respond to your home, workplace, and school?

2. Is the EMS agency that responds to you paid, volunteer, or a combination of both?

3. What level of EMS provider (First Responder, EMT-Basic, EMT-Intermediate, or EMT-Paramedic) can you find in the agency that will respond to you?

4. What would happen if that EMS agency was out on another call and you needed medical assistance?

5. What hospital or hospitals would you be transported to if you were ill or injured?

2 | Well-Being of the First Responder

Key Ideas

This chapter outlines the basic steps you should take to maintain your well-being as a First Responder. It discusses how to protect yourself against infection. It introduces you to scene safety, and how to anticipate and handle the emotional aspects of emergencies. Key ideas include the following:

- First Responders must protect themselves in the field by preventing infection by disease. In order to do that successfully, you must practice a strict form of infection control—body substance isolation (BSI)—with all patients. You also must clean, disinfect, or sterilize your equipment properly. Also follow your physician's orders regarding immunizations.

- It is imperative that you do not fall victim to the same problems that affect your patients. Therefore, do not enter the scene of an emergency until you have determined it is safe to do so. If the scene is unsafe, request additional resources, if necessary, to make the scene safe before you enter.

- Death and dying are inherent parts of emergency medical care. When your patient is dying, you must care for his or her emotional needs as well as the injury or illness. If the patient dies suddenly, help the family or bystanders deal with their grief.

- The five stages of the grieving process are denial, anger, bargaining, depression, and acceptance.

- Stress related to EMS work can have a negative impact on First Responders. Be aware of the warning signs. Lifestyle changes—including keeping physically fit and maintaining a balance between work and family—can help you deal with stress effectively.

- Critical incident stress requires aggressive and immediate management. One way to meet that need is through a critical incident stress debriefing, a process by which a team of peer counselors and mental-health professionals help rescuers deal with their feelings.

Exam Warm-up

1. Identify the items below that describe high-stress situations.
   a. A patient in your care stops breathing.
   b. A hit-and-run involves an eight-year-old boy.
   c. You hear that a coworker has died on the job.
   d. You suspect physical abuse of a patient in your care.
   e. A two-car collision results in injury to four adults.
   f. A factory worker just had part of his hand amputated.
   g. You hear loud, angry voices in the apartment to which you were called.

2. Dying patients—and those close to them—experience what is called the "grieving process." This process includes five stages, which are
   a. anger, acceptance, sorrow, shock, despair.
   b. shock, silence, acceptance, anger, mourning.
   c. denial, rage, blame, forgiveness, acceptance.
   d. denial, anger, bargaining, depression, acceptance.

3. One way a First Responder can help a dying patient's family is by
   a. keeping them away from the dying patient.
   b. allowing them to cry and get angry, even at you.
   c. gently assuring them that everything will be all right.
   d. saying as little as possible about the patient's condition.

4. Which one of the following strategies is NOT acceptable for dealing with dying patients?
   a. Provide reassurance, even if it's false.
   b. Maintain the patient's dignity.
   c. Show respect for the patient.
   d. Use a gentle tone of voice.

5. Any event that causes unusually strong emotions, that interfere with your ability to function either during an emergency or later is called a
   a. burnout.
   b. critical incident.
   c. mental breakdown.
   d. crisis of conscience.

6. A critical incident stress debriefing may include:
   a. anyone involved in the critical incident.
   b. disaster support services personnel only.
   c. only EMS workers who were at the scene.
   d. the rescue workers, but not the commanders.

7. One CISM technique is called "defusing." It is _____ than a debriefing.
   a. shorter and more formal
   b. shorter and less formal
   c. longer and more formal
   d. longer and less formal

8. A critical incident stress debriefing is usually held _____ the incident.
   a. 30 to 45 minutes after
   b. 30 to 45 minutes before
   c. 24 to 72 hours before
   d. 24 to 72 hours after

9. A pathogen is a(n)
   a. type of protective equipment.
   b. disease-causing organism.
   c. vaccine for hepatitis.
   d. antibacterial soap.

10. Which one of the following is NOT true of hepatitis B?
    a. It directly affects the liver.
    b. It can last for months, and it can be fatal.
    c. It is contracted through intimate contact only.
    d. An infected person may not know he or she has it.

11. The letters "OSHA" stand for
    a. organizational safety and health act.
    b. occupational standards and health act.
    c. organizational standards for healthy action.
    d. occupational safety and health administration.

12. When you are caring for a patient who might have tuberculosis, protect yourself against infection by
    a. wearing an OSHA-approved respirator.
    b. avoiding any kind of artificial ventilation.
    c. having contact only with the patient's clothing.
    d. turning your face away when the patient coughs.

13. A device used for protection against tuberculosis is the
    a. surgical mask.
    b. K-20 face mask.
    c. N-95 respirator.
    d. forehead-to-chin face shield.

14. Transmission of HIV, the AIDS virus, requires intimate contact with the body fluids of an infected person. That means infection may occur in all of the following circumstances EXCEPT which TWO?
    a. changing an infected baby's diaper
    b. using infected blood in a transfusion
    c. during pregnancy, from mother to child
    d. injecting an infected needle into your skin
    e. sharing a warm drink with an infected person
    f. sexual contact involving the exchange of semen

15. The single most important thing you can do to prevent the spread of infection is to
    a. get vaccinations and booster shots.
    b. wash your hands after caring for a patient.
    c. wear gloves with all patients no matter what.
    d. clean, disinfect, or sterilize your equipment.

16. The term "body substance isolation" refers to a strict form of infection control in which you assume that
    a. where there's smoke there's fire.
    b. all patients who seem to be ill are ill.
    c. only blood can transmit fatal diseases.
    d. all blood and body fluids are infectious.

17. For patients with diseases for which you have been vaccinated, you do NOT have to take BSI precautions.

    _____ True

    _____ False

Short-Answer Review

18. What are some immediate strategies you can use to lessen the effects of an emotional response to a high-stress situation?

19. Dealing with chronic stress may require a First Responder to make some lifestyle changes. List four examples of what those changes might be.

    a.

    b.

    c.

    d.

20. As a First Responder, your family members may suffer from stress related to your job. Describe four of their possible stress factors.

    a.

    b.

    c.

    d.

21. List six circumstances for which a First Responder would initiate CISD.

    a.

    b.

    c.

    d.

    e.

    f.

22. Describe the personal protective equipment appropriate for each of the following emergencies.

    a. An unresponsive elderly man is lying on a bed wet with urine.

    b. A 16-year-old girl has been stabbed in her thigh. The blood is spurting out with force.

    c. A 24-year-old male is complaining of a painful, swollen ankle after tripping over a curb. No blood or other body fluids are present.

    d. A 72-year-old woman on her living room floor is not breathing and has no pulse.

    e. A six-year-old has a shallow two-inch cut in his lower leg. A moderate amount of bleeding is present. The blood is oozing, rather than spurting.

23. Listed below are descriptions of five emergency scenes. Decide whether or not you would enter each one. Write "yes" or "no" in the space provided.

_____ **a.** You happen across an auto wreck and find two moderately injured patients trapped in a sedan. Right beside the car is a downed power line. It does not appear to be "hot."

_____ **b.** You are out one Saturday night catching a show at a nightclub when a fight breaks out just outside the front entrance. A woman screams that somebody has been stabbed. You step outside to find a large group of people gathered a short distance away. There is much screaming and shouting. The patient appears to be at the center of this group.

_____ **c.** You are waiting on a customer in your hardware store when a passerby runs in and shouts that the office building next to yours is on fire. You run out to investigate and find that smoke is billowing out of open windows and doors.

_____ **d.** You arrive at the scene of an assault. The assailant has reportedly fled, and law enforcement officers state that they have secured the scene. They want you to look at the assault victim.

_____ **e.** A chemical tanker has overturned on the interstate. You arrive and are told that a small amount of the chemical has spilled. The local fire department has begun to contain the spill. There is one critically injured patient who is lying on the ground about 10 feet from the spill.

Vocabulary Practice

Across

3. Assume that all _____ and body fluids are infectious.

7. Chronic _____ can lead to exhaustion and irritability.

8. Garment that resists penetration by bullets.

14. What a disease is when it can spread from one person to another.

15. Short for U.S. Occupational Safety and Health Administration.

16. Second stage of grieving process.

18. Do this with health, family, recreation, and work.

22. Short for Centers for Disease Control.

23. Skin test for tuberculosis.

24. Microorganisms such as bacteria.

26. Short, informal type of debriefing.

27. Short for human immunodeficiency virus.

Down

1. To wash a soiled object with soap and water.

2. Always _____ your hands after patient care.

4. A _____ incident can cause unusually strong emotions.

5. Short for body substance isolation.

6. Short for tuberculosis.

9. First stage of the grieving process.

10. Disease for which annual immunization is recommended.

11. Type of respirator.

12. Short for personal protective equipment.

13. With a dying patient, do not give false assurances, but allow for this.

17. Wear these with a patient who has minor bleeding.

18. Result of long-term, chronic stress.

19. Transmission of this requires intimate contact.

20. Listen to your patients with this.

21. Short for critical incident stress debriefing.

22. Short for hepatitis B.

The Call: An AIDS Patient

Read this scenario and answer the questions that follow. Focus on strategies you can use to protect yourself and your coworkers from infectious exposure.

It's late on a Tuesday night, and you are responding in your private vehicle to a "man down" at a residence. You arrive at the scene and note that another First Responder unit is parked on the street. You enter the home and find them assessing the patient in a back bedroom. The patient is 42 years old. He states that he was diagnosed with AIDS 15 months ago and was recently prescribed some medication that has been making him nauseous. This evening he threw up four times, and then may have passed out. He states that his vomit looked "a little bloody." He is pale and sweaty. Small amounts of vomit cling to his bathrobe. He also states that he is moderately short of breath, a problem associated with a recent "flu."

1. What specific sources of infectious exposure are you concerned about with this patient?

2. What personal protective equipment will you wear when managing this patient?

As you begin to assist the other First Responders, you notice that one of them is not wearing protective gear. You have the opportunity to question her about this a short while later, and she states, "Look. I know that this guy has AIDS, but it's not like there's blood everywhere. I'm watching where I put my hands, so relax."

3. Critique her argument. Do you agree with her rationale? Disagree? Explain your answer.

4. You assist paramedics in transporting this patient to the hospital. En route, he vomits twice more and you see it contains a small amount of blood. After turning the patient over to the emergency department team, what steps would you then take to eliminate possible contamination?

Active Learning

The following exercises will help you explore chapter topics, using resources such as your newspapers, the Internet, and a local EMS provider/instructor.

1. Look back over your local newspapers, a national newsmagazine, or a news website. Find a report of an incident that involved violence. Picture yourself at the scene of this incident providing First Responder care.
   a. What safety measures would you have taken?
   b. What BSI precautions would have been appropriate?

2. Speak to a local EMS provider or your instructor. Find out where he or she carries or keeps BSI equipment when responding to a call.
   a. Ask why the equipment is kept there.
   b. Ask what BSI equipment is used the most and what is used the least.

3. Imagine this scenario: You are home one Sunday morning and an upset neighbor comes to your house, saying he can't wake up his wife. He knows you are a First Responder and asks for your help. You arrive to find his wife obviously deceased. It would be futile to perform CPR. Using a family member or another student from class acting as the man, tell him that there is nothing you can do for his wife.

3 | Legal and Ethical Issues

Key Ideas

This chapter describes your scope of practice and what it means to have a duty to act. It defines patient consent and explains advance directives. It also gives you an overview of various other legal issues that will affect you in the field. Key ideas include the following:

- First Responders must keep their practice within the scope of care as defined by the state.

- Among a First Responder's ethical responsibilities is to serve the physical and emotional needs of the patient with respect for human dignity and with no regard to nationality, race, gender, creed, or status.

- Before providing emergency care to any patient, a First Responder must determine the patient's competency and get either expressed or implied consent.

- A competent adult has the right to refuse treatment or to withdraw from treatment for himself or herself or for his or her child. Follow state law and local protocols in regard to advance directives.

- As a First Responder, you have a duty to act. That is, you have a legal obligation to provide care to a patient who needs it and consents to it. If there is a breach of duty, you could be charged with abandonment or negligence.

- A patient's history, condition, and emergency care are confidential. You must have a written form signed by the patient or legal guardian before you can release this information, unless you are required by law to share it.

- When you are called to a potential crime scene, the police must be notified. Do not enter a crime scene until it has been secured by the police and they tell you it is safe to do so. Once on scene, your priority is patient care. However, take all necessary precautions to preserve any potential evidence.

- Special reporting situations in your state may include reporting child, elder, or spouse abuse; injury that is the result of a crime including sexual assault; and infectious disease exposure.

Exam Warm-up

1. As a First Responder, you are allowed to perform only certain defined skills. These skills are called your
   a. duty to act.
   b. scope of care.
   c. standard of care.
   d. ethical responsibilities.

2. A competent adult is one who is
   a. any person over the age of 18 or 21.
   b. lucid and able to make an informed decision.
   c. married, a parent, or a member of the armed forces.
   d. seriously ill or injured, which could affect judgment.

3. The patient must be _____ and the consent must be _____ in order for consent to be valid.
   a. alert, understood
   b. informed, written
   c. competent, informed
   d. persuaded, expressed

4. Expressed consent may be any of the following EXCEPT
   a. oral.
   b. a nod.
   c. implied.
   d. an affirming gesture.

5. Whose responsibility is it to make sure the patient understands the First Responder's plan for emergency care, including the risks?
   a. First Responder
   b. patient's lawyer
   c. patient's physician
   d. EMS medical director

6. An example of an advance directive is a(n)
   a. emancipated minor.
   b. prehospital care report.
   c. refusal-of-treatment form.
   d. DNR order.

7. You arrive at a scene where you find a 22-year-old woman who has apparently overdosed on heroin. She is unresponsive. You begin to initiate treatment based on the idea of _____ consent.
   a. actual
   b. implied
   c. substituted
   d. mandatory

8. If a First Responder forces care on a patient who refuses it, the First Responder may be charged with
   a. assault and battery.
   b. abandonment and assault.
   c. battery and attempted rape.
   d. negligence and breach of duty.

9. The word _____ is defined as terminating care of a patient without making sure that care will continue at the same level or higher.
   a. assault
   b. battery
   c. negligence
   d. abandonment

10. If a First Responder's care deviates from the accepted standard of care and results in further injury to the patient, the First Responder may be guilty of
    a. assault
    b. battery
    c. negligence
    d. abandonment

11. A medical identification tag is meant to inform health care personnel of
    a. the preference for private over public hospitals.
    b. physical characteristics such as a limp or stutter.
    c. a medical condition such as an allergy or diabetes.
    d. the patient's medical insurance company ID number.

12. In general, _____ includes the patient's history, condition, and emergency care.
    a. assault and battery
    b. preservation of evidence
    c. confidential information
    d. the public's right to know

13. Under "Good Samaritan" laws, a person suing an emergency care provider must prove that care was markedly below the
    a. duty to act.
    b. standard of care.
    c. reasonable standard.
    d. negligence threshold.

14. The term "standard of care" refers to the care that would be expected to be provided to the same patient under the same conditions by
    a. someone who has taken care of other patients.
    b. a fair, reasonable, and unbiased family member.
    c. the standards as outlined in the Hippocratic oath.
    d. another First Responder who has the same training.

15. When you respond to a crime scene, which one of the following rules of thumb would NOT be true?
    a. If the crime is in progress, do not try to provide care.
    b. Do not move the patient, even if an emergency move is needed.
    c. You may be required to report injuries caused by suspected abuse.
    d. As you provide emergency care, try to preserve all possible evidence.

Short-Answer Review

16. List six of a First Responder's ethical responsibilities.

    a.

    b.

    c.

    d.

    e.

    f.

17. As a First Responder, how might you go about getting a responsive, competent adult's expressed consent?

18. You are at the scene of a terminally ill patient who has gone into respiratory arrest in your presence. The patient's daughter arrives on scene and insists that you withhold treatment. How should you proceed? Explain your answer.

19. List six actions you should take before leaving the scene of a moderately injured adult patient who has refused your treatment.

a.

b.

c.

d.

e.

f.

20. A First Responder with the fire department arrives on scene just in time to see a woman being carried away from a fire to safety. The woman's clothes are still smoldering. Very quickly, the First Responder realizes this patient needs more help than he can provide. Does the First Responder have a duty to act? Explain your answer.

21. Jake works in a factory on an assembly line. He is also one of three employees who were trained as on-site First Responders. One day on the way to work, Jake spots a car crash along the highway. Does he have a duty to act? Explain your answer.

22. List three examples of emergencies you may be legally required to report to law enforcement or another appropriate authority or agency.

a.

b.

c.

Vocabulary Practice

Read the definition. Then write the term in the blanks provided. Hint: There is a box for each letter in the correct answer.

1. Permission to provide medical care.

2. Legal term that means discontinuing medical care without making sure that another health care professional with at least equal training has taken over.

3. A patient's instructions about medical care, written in advance of an emergency.

4. An adult who is lucid and able to make an informed decision about medical care.

5. Legal obligation to provide emergency care to a patient who needs it.

6. Care that would be expected to be provided to the same patient under the same circumstances by another First Responder who had received the same training.

7. Emergency care that deviates from the accepted standard of care and results in further injury to the patient.

8. Actions and care legally allowed to be provided by the First Responder.

9. What a First Responder assumes in an emergency when a patient is unable to grant permission for medical care.

10. Permission that must be obtained from every competent adult patient before medical care may be provided.

The Call: The Patient Who Will Not Go to the Hospital

Read this scenario and answer the questions that follow. Focus on the rights that adult patients have regarding consent to medical care, as well as the obligation of First Responders to encourage patients to go to the hospital should they appear to need medical care.

It is two o'clock in the morning. You are working on the engine at your volunteer fire department when you are paged out to respond to a possible heart attack. You arrive to find an elderly patient, Mr. Boyd, sitting on the edge of his bed. During your initial assessment, you notice that he appears to be slightly sweaty and pale. He tells you that he had a bout of chest pain that felt the same as the heart attack he had one year ago. He took three of his nitroglycerin pills, which relieved the pain. He says he is feeling much better and does not wish to go to the emergency room. The paramedic ambulance, which is coming from the next town, has yet to arrive. His wife says he really needs to be taken to the emergency room and that his last heart attack "almost killed him."

1. Does this patient need to go to the hospital? Explain your answer.

2. Describe two strategies you might use to convince the patient that he should go with the paramedics to the hospital.

   a.

   b.

Mr. Boyd is still refusing treatment and transport even after the paramedics arrive and complete their assessment. By now his skin has dried and he appears less pale. He states that he is pain-free, has no other symptoms, and that he will follow up with his doctor in the morning. His vital signs appear stable, and he is fully alert. The paramedics have by now become frustrated with Mr. Boyd's reluctance to go to the emergency room with them. In exasperation, they tell him that if he will not go voluntarily, they will force him to go against his will. A wrestling match ensues, with Mr. Boyd finally restrained on a wheeled stretcher.

3. Do you agree with the paramedics' strategy? What rights does an alert adult patient have to refuse treatment and transport?

Active Learning

Fortunately, lawsuits, crime scenes, and ethical dilemmas are not common occurrences. However, when they happen, you must be prepared. The following exercises will help you be ready for the out-of-the-ordinary experiences you may face. All you need is a journal, possibly an Internet connection, and your imagination.

1. Look in an EMS professional journal or website for an ad selling malpractice (liability) insurance for EMS providers.
    a. What does this insurance protect against?
    b. Why would someone in EMS want this type of insurance?

2. You have given First Responder care to a patient who was stabbed. The patient is conscious while in your care but dies at the hospital before talking to an investigator. The police come to the station later to talk to you.
    a. Think of three questions the investigator may ask you.
    b. If you knew these questions in advance, how would it affect your next similar call?

3. You are on a serious trauma call with another First Responder. You arrive to see her panicking and straightening the badly twisted leg of the patient. Afterwards, she denies this when talking to the EMTs. You later see the EMTs on another call.
    a. Should you tell the EMTs? Why or why not?
    b. Should you tell the director or your organization? Why or why not?

4 | The Human Body

Key Ideas

This chapter introduces you to basic anatomy and physiology. Key ideas include the following:

- An understanding of key anatomical and topographic terms is important for describing a patient's position, as well as the location of injuries and other physical findings.

- The body is divided into three main cavities: thoracic, abdominal, and pelvic.

- Major body systems are the skeletal, muscular, circulatory, respiratory, digestive, urinary, endocrine, reproductive, nervous, and integument (skin) systems.

- Understanding the anatomy and physiology of these systems is critical if you are to understand your patients' injuries and illnesses.

Exam Warm-up

1. The location of the injury to the patient's abdomen is _____ to the sternum.
   a. inferior
   b. superior
   c. anterior
   d. posterior

2. The _____ thorax includes the chest and abdomen.
   a. inferior
   b. superior
   c. anterior
   d. posterior

3. The patient suffered a _____ injury, which was less than an eighth of an inch deep.
   a. deep
   b. medial
   c. lateral
   d. superficial

4. The entrance wound from the bullet was _____ to the left nipple. It almost looked as though it had entered through the patient's left side.
   a. deep
   b. medial
   c. lateral
   d. superficial

5. The bruise to the patient's chest was _____ to the right nipple, along the right border of the sternum.
   a. deep
   b. medial
   c. lateral
   d. superficial

6. The patient was experiencing _____ neck pain where the back of her neck impacted the headrest during a collision.
   a. posterior
   b. anterior
   c. proximal
   d. distal

7. The fracture of the patient's leg was to the lower thigh, just _____ to the knee.
   a. posterior
   b. anterior
   c. proximal
   d. distal

8. The patient had a forearm fracture. The First Responder was able to feel a strong pulse _____ to the injury, at the patient's wrist.
   a. posterior
   b. anterior
   c. proximal
   d. distal

9. The swelling to the patient's face was isolated to the cheek, just _____ to the left eye.
   a. inferior
   b. superior
   c. anterior
   d. posterior

10. The abdominal cavity is separated from the thoracic cavity by the
    a. ribs.
    b. lungs.
    c. stomach.
    d. diaphragm.

11. The lungs and heart are found in the _____ cavity.
    a. pelvic
    b. cranial
    c. thoracic
    d. abdominal

12. The intestines are found in the _____ cavity.
    a. pelvic
    b. cranial
    c. thoracic
    d. abdominal

13. The borders of the _____ cavity are bounded by the lower part of the spine, hip bones, and pubis.
    a. pelvic
    b. cranial
    c. thoracic
    d. abdominal

14. The largest part of the liver is located in the _____ quadrant of the abdomen.
    a. left upper
    b. left lower
    c. right upper
    d. right lower

15. The left kidney is located in the _____ quadrant of the abdomen.
    a. left upper
    b. left lower
    c. right upper
    d. right lower

16. The spleen is located in the _____ quadrant of the abdomen.
    a. left upper
    b. left lower
    c. right upper
    d. right lower

17. Ligaments connect
    a. bone to bone.
    b. muscle to bone.
    c. different layers of muscle.
    d. internal organs to bone and muscle.

18. The side impact from the car crash broke the patient's upper arm, or
    a. ulna.
    b. radius.
    c. humerus.
    d. patella.

19. The _____ is made up of the top, back, and sides of the skull.
    a. femur
    b. cranium
    c. mandible
    d. iliac crest

20. The _____ is made up of 33 bones called vertebrae.
    a. coccyx
    b. lumbar spine
    c. spinal column
    d. xiphoid process

21. The bones that make up the shoulder girdle are the
    a. clavicle and scapula.
    b. humerus and radius.
    c. ilium and ischium.
    d. tibia and fibula.

22. The passing of air into and out of the lungs is called
    a. exhalation.
    b. expiration.
    c. ventilation.
    d. inspiration.

23. All the following are related to breathing and the respiratory system EXCEPT
    a. alveoli.   f. ventricle.
    b. bronchi.   g. epiglottis.
    c. larynx.   h. oropharynx.
    d. pharynx.   i. bronchiole.
    e. trachea.   j. nasopharynx.

24. The area posterior to the mouth and nose is called the
    a. pharynx.
    b. diaphragm.
    c. costal cartilage.
    d. left main bronchus.

25. After air enters the mouth and nose, it passes through the _____, down through the _____, and into the _____.
    a. pharynx, larynx, trachea.
    b. trachea, larynx, pharynx.
    c. pharynx, nasopharynx, oropharynx.
    d. oropharynx, nasopharynx, pharynx.

26. The smallest vessels through which fluid, oxygen, and carbon dioxide are exchanged are called
    a. alveoli.
    b. venules.
    c. arterioles.
    d. capillaries.

27. The organs of the digestive system include all of the following EXCEPT
    a. pancreas.
    b. epidermis.
    c. esophagus.
    d. thalmus.

28. Which system consists of two kidneys, two ureters, one bladder, and one urethra?
    a. urinary
    b. endocrine
    c. digestive
    d. reproductive

29. Which one of the following is NOT true of the endocrine system?
    a. It influences behavior.
    b. It stimulates breathing.
    c. It influences reproduction.
    d. It affects physical strength.

30. Which system includes ovaries and fallopian tubes?
    a. urinary
    b. endocrine
    c. digestive
    d. reproductive

Short-Answer Review

31. Explain the difference between smooth and skeletal muscles and where each would be found in the human body.

32. Use words from the list below to complete the sentences. Not all the words in the list are utilized, and some may be used more than once.

    smaller   harder   more
    larger   softer   less

    a. Every part of an infant or child's airway is _____ than an adult's.

    b. In children, the tongue takes up _____ space than an adult's.

    c. In infants, the tongue is _____ likely to cause a blocked airway.

    d. The trachea of an infant or child is _____ flexible, narrower, and

       _____ than the trachea of an adult.

Vocabulary Practice

1. Draw a line to connect each body position term to its correct description.

anatomical •
               • face up, lying on the back

lateral recumbent •
               • face down, lying on the stomach

prone •
               • standing, arms down, palms out

supine •
               • lying on the side

2. Draw a line to connect each anatomical term to its correct description.

cervical vertebrae •
               • collar bone

clavicle •
               • bone of the lower leg

humerus •
               • bone of the upper arm

femur •
               • bone of the upper leg

fibula •
               • neck bones

3. Draw a line to connect each anatomical term to its correct description.

scapula •
               • bone of the forearm

patella •
               • hip bone

radius •
               • eye socket

orbit •
               • knee cap

ilium •
               • shoulder blade

4. Draw a line to connect each arterial pulse point to its correct location.

carotid •
               • upper arm

femoral •
               • wrist

brachial •
               • groin

radial •
               • foot

dorsalis pedis •
               • neck

The Call: Anatomy and Physiology Applied

Read the scenario below and answer the questions that follow. Focus on how knowledge of anatomy and physiology can help you to manage patients in the field.

You have just responded to an unhelmeted bicyclist who was hit by a car and thrown onto the pavement. She is complaining of pain to the upper right quadrant of her abdomen and to her right chest. She has suffered huge scrapes to her side and abdomen. She has a large bruise on her forehead. In addition, she does not remember the collision and continues to repeat the same confused questions over and over again. Her breathing appears rapid and labored.

1. Which abdominal organs may be injured?

2. An injury to which system is probably causing this patient to be confused?

3. Her rapid breathing is quite noticeable. It is obvious to you that this patient has a problem with her respiratory system. Would you treat this problem before or after treating her abdominal pain and scrapes to her skin? Explain your answer.

4. You examine the patient further and find that she has a leg injury. It appears that the large bone of her lower leg is fractured just below the knee. The fracture has caused the lower leg to be turned away from the midline of her body. Use the correct terms of direction and location to describe the position of the leg and its injuries.

Active Learning

Your knowledge of the human body is critical to patient assessment and care. The following exercise will help you learn and remember common body structures and functions.

1. Pair up with a friend or partner from class. On strips of paper, write the following bone names: humerus, radius, tibia, femur, mandible, scapula, tarsal, and clavicle. Tape each strip of paper on your friend's or partner's respective bones within 45 seconds.

2. Repeat this same exercise with other body structures you wish to learn and remember. You may want to include arterial pulse points and major organs in the abdominal quadrants.

5 | Lifting and Moving Patients

Key Ideas

This chapter provides an overview of how to lift and move patients and equipment safely, without injury to patients and without injury to you. Key ideas include the following:

- Incorrect lifting and handling of patients can worsen their injuries and cause career-ending injuries to rescuers.

- There may be instances in which you must move a patient prior to treating him or her due to hazards, inaccessibility, or other problems.

- Emergency techniques for moving patients include the shirt drag, blanket drag, and shoulder or forearm drag.

- Non-emergency, or non-urgent, moves include the direct ground lift and extremity lift.

- Equipment First Responders should be acquainted with and know how to use properly include standard stretchers, the stair chair, vest-type immobilization device, and backboards.

Exam Warm-up

1. The term "body mechanics" refers to methods of
   a. exercising to strengthen your back muscles.
   b. positioning the patient for safe extrication.
   c. using your body to gain a mechanical advantage.
   d. determining how a patient may have been injured.

2. Always try to reach _____ to lift a heavy object.
   a. up, not down,
   b. a long distance
   c. a short distance
   d. with a power grip

3. The key to preventing injury during lifting, carrying, moving, reaching, pushing, and pulling is
    a. correct alignment of your spine.
    b. balance, strength, and attitude.
    c. to keep your knees slightly bent.
    d. to lock your elbows, wrists, and knees.

4. In a power lift, you should _____ to splint your vulnerable lower back area.
    a. avoid excessive slouch or swayback
    b. take a long deep breath and hold it
    c. relax the muscles of your legs and buttocks
    d. tighten the muscles of your back and abdomen

5. Which one of the following describes good posture while STANDING?
    a. Knees are locked and pelvis is tucked back.
    b. Chin points out and shoulders are rolled forward.
    c. Chin, sternum, and knees are in vertical alignment.
    d. Ears, shoulders, and hips are in vertical alignment.

6. Which one of the following describes good posture while SITTING?
    a. Knees are locked and pelvis is tucked back.
    b. Chin points out and shoulders are rolled forward.
    c. Chin, sternum, and knees are in vertical alignment.
    d. Ears, shoulders, and hips are in vertical alignment.

7. Even when there is no immediate threat to life, you should move your patient to an area that is suited to the administration of emergency medical care.

    _____ True

    _____ False

8. The GREATEST danger to the patient during an emergency move is the possibility of making a spine injury worse.

    _____ True

    _____ False

9. Rescuers should use an "extremity lift" when the patient has injuries to his or her arms or legs.

    _____ True

    _____ False

Questions 10 through 13 may have more than one correct answer. Circle the letters next to all statements that are correct for each question.

10. Portable stretchers are usually used when there
    a. are multiple patients.
    b. are flights of stairs to navigate.
    c. is not enough space for a standard stretcher.
    d. is a spinal injury accompanied by unresponsiveness.

11. What type of stretcher can be used to lift a patient from a confined area where a larger stretcher will not fit?
    a. stair chair
    b. scoop stretcher
    c. standard stretcher with wheeled legs
    d. vest-type immobilization device plus wheeled stretcher

12. Which one or more of the following pieces of equipment should be used for moving a patient with a possible spine injury?
    a. backboard
    b. stair chair
    c. pole stretcher
    d. blanket stretcher

13. Identify all the items below that contribute to a balanced physical fitness program.
    a. cardiovascular conditioning
    b. flexibility training
    c. strength training
    d. good nutrition

Short-Answer Review

14. List four basic safety rules of lifting any object.

    a.

    b.

    c.

    d.

15. List five conditions under which you would consider utilizing an emergency move.

    a.

    b.

    c.

    d.

    e.

16. Below are the steps a rescuer must take to perform a "forearm drag." Number the following steps 1–5 to show the order in which they should be performed.

    _____ a. Drag the patient toward you.

    _____ b. Stand at the patient's head.

    _____ c. Grasp the patient's forearms.

    _____ d. Slip your hands under the patient's armpits.

    _____ e. Support the patient's head on your own forearms.

17. What materials can be used to improvise a stretcher?

Vocabulary Practice

Circle the words or terms that are related to lifting and moving and write them on the lines below the puzzle. Hint: There are exactly 32.

```
I S S S P S A U J K B K S T X C G G G P C R
D M T H W O L K P Y Y G I U W N N N I I E O
S B M A E A S O U E O B J M I I I R D H X N
C O C O I E Y T U H Q Z S V T H G E C J Q E
O D R Y B R T B U C C J O F C R P T B B D R
O Y A K B I C D A R H M I A E O E T Y L P E
P M D P M Y L H R C E L E W H R I T X A I S
S E L C U H E I A A K R O T T B O K Q N G C
T C E M I N X R Z I G P R S G S X Y D K G U
R H C T U O M S D A R O D P P L Q A I E Y E
E A A I L O I P K C T E C F U R X A E T B R
T N R I M Z G R G K S I I A I S A R T D A C
C I R D S N O A T I H U O B R T H Q S R C R
H C Y G I W R N V W S B A N A R N I F A K U
E S A L M D E O B M X K G Q D C Y E N G C T
R R L A T M R P O B C F Q L Z E K I S G A C
D U E R N P H V T O Q N Y J B O V B N S R H
P T I G M S H O U L D E R D R A G I O G R E
P H I I S H O R T B A C K B O A R D C A Y C
S L F I R E F I G H T E R D R A G Y K E R Z
A U E E F D I R E C T G R O U N D L I F T D
S Q E Y B P O R T A B L E S T R E T C H E R
```

1. _____	12. _____	23. _____
2. _____	13. _____	24. _____
3. _____	14. _____	25. _____
4. _____	15. _____	26. _____
5. _____	16. _____	27. _____
6. _____	17. _____	28. _____
7. _____	18. _____	29. _____
8. _____	19. _____	30. _____
9. _____	20. _____	31. _____
10. _____	21. _____	32. _____
11. _____	22. _____	

The Call: To Move or Not to Move

Read the scenario and answer the questions that follow. Focus on when you may need to move patients.

Your unit has been staged at the local high school during a football game. It is almost the end of the first half when spectators start screaming. A section of the old bleachers has collapsed, trapping five people.

1. Describe at least two of your initial responsibilities as a First Responder.

2. Along with school authorities, you are able to move the crowd of spectators away from the collapsed structure, leaving only those trapped at the scene. For those trapped patients, what would you need to consider to perform an emergency move?

3. Decide if you would immediately move each patient described below. Write the reason for your answer.
   a. Patient #1 is sitting at the edge of the collapsed structure with a board over her legs. She is complaining only of knee pain and reports that she fell straight down about two feet onto her buttocks.

   b. Patients #2 and #3 are on top of patient #4. Patients #2 and #3 are awake and complaining of leg and arm pain. They are scared because they cannot wake up patient #4 and cannot feel her breathing.

   c. Patient #5 is trapped in some metal debris. He says that he cannot move his legs and that his neck hurts. There are no other dangers around him.

Active Learning

NOTE: The following activities involve actual lifting and moving another person. Use good judgment and proper body mechanics before attempting any move. If you have any questions, ask your instructor before attempting this!

A key concept in lifting and moving is safety—yours and your patient's. The following activities will help you practice for situations you may encounter in the field. For these experiences, you will need common sense and some basic equipment (available where you learn, work, or volunteer). First Responder students should take part in being the rescuers as well as the patients being lifted. It will give the students perspective on how the patients experience any lifting move.

1. You respond to a residence and find a patient sitting in a chair not breathing. You must move him to the floor to care for him. Simulate this patient situation by having a fellow student sit in a classroom chair and act "limp." With the assistance of another student, lift the patient from the chair and gently place him or her on the floor.

2. Take turns with your fellow students strapping each other in patient carrying devices (such as stair chairs and portable stretchers) and moving the "patient" in the device through the classroom or station. When you are the patient, pay careful attention and try to imagine how an injured patient would feel in the device.

3. Check the websites of stretcher manufacturers (such as www.ferno.com or www.med.strykercorp. com/products/ems) and determine the weight rating of common devices such as stretchers and stair chairs. Then decide what you would do if you had a patient who exceeded the weight rating of a device you wanted to use.

6 | Breathing and Ventilation

Key Ideas

This chapter discusses the anatomy and physiology of the respiratory system and airway management. Key ideas include the following:

- The major structures of the airway include the mouth, nose, pharynx, epiglottis, larynx, trachea, and the bronchi, lungs and diaphragm.

- Oxygen is brought into the lungs during inhalation. The oxygen passes into the capillaries of the alveoli and carbon dioxide exits these same capillaries into the lungs to be exhaled as waste products.

- When managing the airway of a children or infants, remember that their airway structures are smaller and more easily obstructed than an adult's airway.

- The first priority in any emergency is to establish and maintain a patient's airway. Without an open airway and adequate breathing, a patient will die within minutes.

- An accurate and efficient assessment will provide you with the information you need to determine whether or not your patient requires airway or breathing assistance.

- A patient's airway may need to be opened using either the head-tilt/chin-lift or the jaw-thrust maneuver.

- A patient's airway may need to be cleared of secretions. This can be accomplished by placing the patient in the recovery position, using a finger sweep, or by suctioning the airway.

- Patients who are breathing, but not breathing adequately, will require you to assist ventilations. That means that you will use a pocket face mask or other device to provide artificial ventilation when the patient's rate and/or depth of breathing are inadequate.

Exam Warm-up

1. Circle the letter next to the item(s) that describes what happens during INHALATION.
    a. The patient's rib muscles contract.
    b. Air pressure inside the lungs decreases.
    c. The patient's diaphragm falls and flattens.
    d. Air pressure inside the lungs is increased.

2. Circle the letter next to the item(s) that describes what happens during EXHALATION.
    a. The patient's diaphragm rises.
    b. The patient's chest muscles relax.
    c. Air pressure inside the lungs decreases.
    d. Air pressure inside the lungs increases.

3. The chest wall is softer in infants than in adults. Therefore, _____ can alert you to respiratory distress in an infant.
    a. a proportionately larger tongue
    b. excessive movement of the chest
    c. the narrower trachea
    d. the epiglottis

4. Why can tipping an infant's head back or allowing the head to fall forward be a problem?
    a. It will make breathing effortless.
    b. The positions can close the trachea.
    c. The diaphragm will fall and flatten.
    d. Because the chest wall is softer in infants.

5. The tongue of an infant or child takes up more space than in an adult. It therefore can
    a. use a back slap immediately.
    b. block the airway more easily.
    c. keep the trachea open more often.
    d. loosen the cricoid cartilage quickly.

6. When you perform a head-tilt/chin-lift on an infant or child, you should
    a. hyperextend only the head.
    b. hyperextend the head and neck.
    c. tilt the head back only slightly.
    d. tilt the head back as far as possible.

7. The head-tilt/chin-lift and jaw-thrust maneuvers
    a. align the nasal passages with the throat.
    b. align the pharynx with the epiglottis.
    c. lift the tongue away from the throat.
    d. flex the windpipe at a 90° angle.

8. Your patient fell six feet onto concrete from a ladder. Which one of the following methods would you use to open her airway?
    a. recovery position
    b. jaw-thrust maneuver
    c. head-neck/in-line move
    d. head-tilt/chin-lift maneuver

9. You are at the scene of a patient who was found unresponsive in his bed. His roommate insists that there has been no recent fall or other injury. To open the patient's airway, use a
   a. recovery position.
   b. jaw-thrust maneuver.
   c. head-neck/in-line move.
   d. head-tilt/chin-lift maneuver.

10. _____ occurs when blood, vomit, mucus, or another liquid is in the airway.
    a. Snoring
    b. Crowing
    c. Gurgling
    d. Stridor

11. A suspected trauma patient should be placed in the recovery position.

    _____ a. True

    _____ b. False

12. A patient with an obstructed airway will NEVER exhibit chest rise and fall.

    _____ a. True

    _____ b. False

13. All of the following are signs of inadequate breathing EXCEPT
    a. cyanosis
    b. equal chest rise
    c. altered mental status
    d. grunting

14. _____ of air will remain in the dead space between the pharynx and the bronchioles during each breath.
    a. 250 ml
    b. 350 ml
    c. 150 ml
    d. 200 ml

15. Signs of adequate artificial ventilation include all of the following EXCEPT
    a. ventilating an adult once every 10 seconds.
    b. chest rise.
    c. patient's heart rate returns to normal.
    d. patient's color improves.

16. The narrow end of a pocket face mask should be placed
    a. in the cleft of the patient's chin.
    b. on the bridge of the patient's nose.
    c. just above the bridge of the patient's nose.
    d. just below the patient's lower lip.

17. All of the following are methods of performing artificial ventilation for a First Responder EXCEPT
    a. mouth-to-mask.
    b. mouth-to-mouth.
    c. mouth-to-bag valve device.
    d. mouth-to-barrier device.

18. Mouth-to-mask ventilation is very effective because_____.
    a. both hands are used to create a seal around the mask.
    b. oxygen may be utilized.
    c. it protects the caregiver with a one-way valve.
    d. it is easy to determine if ventilations are adequate.

19. Circle the letters next to the signs and symptoms of INADEQUATE breathing.
    a. drowsiness, confusion
    b. flaring of the nostrils
    c. increased effort to breathe
    d. inadequate chest wall motion
    e. seesaw motion of abdomen and chest
    f. 18 breaths per minute in an infant
    g. 15 breaths per minute in a child
    h. 12 breaths per minute in an adult
    i. gasping and grunting sounds with breathing
    j. unequal rise and fall of the sides of the chest
    k. slow heart rate accompanied by slow breathing rate
    l. retractions between the ribs or above the collarbone
    m. bluish discoloration of the skin or mucous membranes

20. Mouth-to-mask ventilation is preferred over the mouth-to-mouth and mouth-to-barrier device techniques. Circle the letters beside all the reasons why this statement is TRUE.
    a. It frees your hands for other emergency care needs.
    b. It eliminates exposure to the patient's exhaled air.
    c. It allows you to deliver ventilations of adequate force.
    d. It prevents direct contact with a patient's body fluids.

21. You must maintain a jaw-thrust maneuver during artificial ventilation of a patient with suspected spine injury.

    _____ True

    _____ False

22. You attempt to perform artificial ventilation on an unresponsive patient for the first time and find that you are unable to force air into the lungs. Your next step should be to
    a. check for a foreign body airway obstruction.
    b. reposition the patient's head and try again.
    c. suction the patient's airway for 15 seconds.
    d. insert a nasopharyngeal airway and try again.

23. A patient who has had all or part of the larynx surgically removed has had a
    a. thoracostomy.
    b. tracheostomy.
    c. tonsillectomy.
    d. laryngectomy.

24. A _____ is a permanent opening that connects the trachea directly to the front of the neck.
    a. stoma
    b. larynx
    c. stamen
    d. stollen

25. Which one of the following is NOT a recommended method for reducing gastric distention in an infant or child?
    a. Gently press down on the patient's abdomen.
    b. Breathe slowly when providing artificial ventilation to the patient.
    c. Avoid providing artificial ventilation to the patient too forcefully.
    d. Allow the patient to fully exhale between artificial ventilations.

26. Why should securely placed dentures be left in the mouth?
    a. They assist in maintaining a head-tilt/chin-lift maneuver.
    b. They assist in maintaining an airtight mask seal.
    c. They help maintain the tongue in the proper position.
    d. So they are not misplaced.

27. An oxygen delivery device that provides up to 100% oxygen and is made up of a self-inflating bag, one-way valve, face mask, and oxygen reservoir is a(n)
    a. nasal cannula.
    b. bag-valve mask.
    c. barrier device.
    d. nonrebreather mask.

28. An adult sized BVM device has a volume of approximately _____ml.
    a. 1200.
    b. 1400.
    c. 1600.
    d. 1800.

Short-Answer Review

29. Trace the flow of air through the respiratory tract during inhalation. Number the following items 1–5 in the correct sequence.

_____ **a.** alveoli

_____ **b.** pharynx

_____ **c.** mouth and nose

_____ **d.** trachea and larynx

_____ **e.** bronchial tubes

30. Fill in the information missing from the table below.

	Normal Breathing Rates
Adult	_____ to _____ breaths per minute.
Child	_____ to _____ breaths per minute.
Infant	_____ to _____ breaths per minute.

31. Describe how to perform a head-tilt/chin-lift maneuver on an adult patient.

32. Briefly describe in three steps how you can determine the presence of breathing in your patient.

a.

b.

c.

33. An ominous sign of INADEQUATE breathing is a slower than normal breathing rate. Fill in the table below.

	Inadequate Breathing
Adult	Less than _____ respirations per minute.
Child	Less than _____ respirations per minute.
Infant	Less than _____ respirations per minute.

34. Briefly describe four indications of ADEQUATE artificial ventilations.

a.

b.

c.

d.

35. Briefly describe three indications of INADEQUATE artificial ventilations.

a.

b.

c.

36. List the basic steps of mouth-to-mask ventilation.

37. Fill in the information missing from the table below.

	Artificial Ventilation Rates	
Adult	_____ breaths per minute at _____ seconds each.	
Child	_____ breaths per minute at _____ seconds each.	
Infant	_____ breaths per minute at _____ seconds each.	
Newborn	_____ breaths per minute at _____ second each.	

38. You are at the scene of a near-drowning of a 10-month-old baby. The patient has a pulse but is not breathing. There are no paramedics on scene yet to place an advanced airway. Your crew members are inexperienced at managing such a young patient, and they need your help. Respond to their concerns.

    a. "How should we open this airway? Same as an adult's?"

    b. "I'm having a really hard time fitting my mouth around the baby's mouth. It's so small. What should I do?"

    c. "How often should I breathe for this baby?"

39. To provide artificial ventilation by way of a bag-valve-mask device, one rescuer should

_____

while the other rescuer squeezes the bag.

The Call: A Drowning Victim

Read this scenario and answer the questions that follow. Focus on correctly assessing the patient's airway and breathing status and arriving at the appropriate airway and ventilation interventions. Watch the patient for status changes.

It is early afternoon on a hot summer day, and you are dispatched to the call that you have always dreaded: a pediatric drowning. You arrive on scene—a suburban residence, gather your equipment, and run around to the backyard pool. There you find three adults. They are crowded around the limp body of a two-year-old, who is lying by the side of the pool. They are screaming and crying and frantically yelling at you to hurry. As you approach the child, whose name is Gracie, you learn that she fell into the pool without striking her head, neck, or back. She lay submerged for one or two minutes before being pulled out of the water by her mother.

You move to Gracie's side and rapidly determine that she is unresponsive and not breathing but still has a weak carotid pulse. Gracie's mother is nearly sitting on top of you as she screams and cries. Your partner, John, shouts something to you as he approaches, but you are unable to hear him over the noise.

1. What should be your first action in this situation?

2. One of the adults yells at you, "Do something! You need to breathe for her! She's not breathing!" Do you agree that this should be your first step? Explain your answer.

3. After opening the airway, you determine that you need to breathe for Gracie. Number the following actions 1–3 to place the steps in the correct order.

   _____ **a.** Continue artificial ventilation at a rate of 20 breaths per minute.

   _____ **b.** Deliver two slow initial breaths.

   _____ **c.** Determine if the ventilations are adequate.

4. Gracie's stomach appears to have gotten slightly distended. What steps can you take to stop this problem from continuing?

5. After providing artificial ventilation to Gracie for two to three minutes, you notice that her color is improving dramatically. She begins moving her limbs, and her eyelids begin to flutter and twitch. Your next step should be to

Active Learning

One of the most important decisions you will make while providing artificial ventilations is the proper mask size. Selecting the proper size mask allows for an airtight seal, which creates more effective ventilations.

Find several volunteers with different size faces. Utilized different size masks for a bag-valve mask to see which gives the best fit. If you can find children that will tolerate a mask against their face all the better. Have the child assist you in placing the mask against their face. Practice effective face mask seals (one handed and two handed) on mannequins.... do you feel any air leakage as the mannequin is ventilated? Which method is more effective? One-handed or two-handed?

7 | Airway Care and Maintenance

Key Ideas

A First Responder must first open the patient's airway and assess the adequacy of his or her breathing. Once this is accomplished the First Responder will then utilize the devices in this chapter to perform airway care and maintenance. These devices include oropharyngeal airways, nasopharyngeal airways, and suction units. A First Responder may also be able to administer supplemental oxygen to a patient in respiratory distress. This oxygen is supplied either via a nasal cannula or a nonrebreather mask. As a First Responder you must also clear any foreign body airway obstruction before the patient can breathe or artificial ventilation can be administered. Key ideas include the following:

- An oropharyngeal airway holds the tongue off the back of the throat at the level of the pharynx. It is used to maintain an airway in an unconscious patient with no gag reflex.

- A nasopharyngeal airway helps keep the tongue from blocking the airway of a semi-responsive patient who may still have a gag reflex.

- Both oral and nasal airways must be properly measured and inserted correctly.

- A snoring sound during airway assessment indicates that the tongue is blocking the airway.

- A gurgling sound during airway assessment indicates that suctioning is needed.

- Poor skin color, unresponsiveness, cool skin, difficulty breathing, blood loss, chest pain, and trauma are all emergencies that require supplemental oxygen be administered to the patient, if permitted by local protocol.

- Handling of oxygen cylinders requires that safety precautions be observed.

- Low-flow oxygen is delivered through a nasal cannula. High-flow oxygen is delivered by nonrebreather mask.

- Foreign body airway obstructions are life-threatening emergencies. They may either be a mild (partial) blockage or a severe (complete) blockage.

- The procedure for clearing a FBAO is determined by the age of the patient and the level of responsiveness.

Exam Warm-up

1. The oropharyngeal airway is used to maintain the airway of an UNRESPONSIVE patient that has no gag reflex.

   _____ a. True

   _____ b. False

2. To determine the proper size oropharyngeal airway for your patient, measure it from the
   a. lips to the base of the tongue.
   b. corner of the nose to the top of the ear.
   c. tip of the nose to the tip of the earlobe.
   d. corner of the lip to the angle of the jaw.

3. To use an oropharyngeal airway in an infant or child, insert it
   a. with the outside edge of the curve of the device facing up.
   b. with the outside edge of the curve of the device facing down.
   c. flange side first.
   d. the same way as you would for an adult.

4. The nasopharyngeal airway is used to maintain the airway of a patient who has a gag reflex.

   _____ a. True

   _____ b. False

5. To determine the proper size nasopharyngeal for your patient, measure it from the
   a. lips to base of the tongue.
   b. corner of the nose to the top of the ear.
   c. tip of the nose to the tip of the earlobe.
   d. corner of the lip to the angle of the jaw.

6. If during insertion of a nasopharyngeal airway, you meet resistance, you should try
   a. finger sweeps and suctioning.
   b. an oropharyngeal airway instead.
   c. inserting it from the other end.
   d. inserting it into the other nostril.

7. Use suction for up to _____ seconds in an infant, _____seconds for a child, and ___seconds for an adult.
   a. 2,2,2
   b. 3,6,9
   c. 5,10,15
   d. 7,13,21

8. The most common cause of an airway obstruction in an UNRESPONSIVE adult is
   a. food.
   b. dentures.
   c. the tongue.
   d. aspirated vomit.

9. The treatment for a mild (partial) airway obstruction in an adult with good air exchange includes
   a. encouraging the patient to cough up the foreign body.
   b. delivering five back slaps after abdominal thrust.
   c. having the patient get into a supine position.
   d. dislodging the object with finger sweeps.

10. When relieving a severe (complete) airway obstruction in a RESPONSIVE adult patient, you should alternate back slaps with abdominal thrusts.

   _____ True

   _____ False

11. You are managing a conscious 17-year-old patient with an airway obstruction. After you apply several abdominal thrusts, the patient falls to the ground unconscious. What should you do next?
   a. Perform five more abdominal thrusts.
   b. Attempt chest thrusts as you would for CPR.
   c. Place the patient in the recovery position.
   d. After looking inside the mouth, attempt to ventilate the patient.

12. All of the following patients have a foreign body airway obstruction. Which one(s) should receive treatment identified under the "adult" category according to their ages?
   a. one-year-old
   b. three-year-old
   c. five-year-old
   d. seven-year-old
   e. nine-year-old
   f. eleven-year-old
   g. thirteen-year-old

13. Suspect an infection in an infant who has sudden onset of respiratory distress with coughing, gagging, stridor, or wheezing, especially when food or small items are found near the patient.

   _____ True

   _____ False

14. An eight-month-old baby has a mild foreign body airway obstruction with good air exchange. You may attempt to relieve the obstruction with back slaps and chest thrusts.

   _____ True

   _____ False

15. If you are alone, and you are unable to open the airway of an infant who is found UNRESPONSIVE, you must activate the EMS system within
   a. 15 seconds.
   b. 30 seconds.
   c. 1 minute.
   d. 3 minutes.

Short Answer

16. List three signs or symptoms that indicate the need for oxygen.

a.

b.

c.

17. Describe how to administer oxygen to a patient. Number the following steps 1–9 in the correct sequence.
a. Remove the protective seal.
b. Identify the cylinder as oxygen.
c. Position the regulator and align the pins.
d. Hand-tighten the T-screw on the regulator.
e. Adjust the flow meter to the proper liter flow.
f. Apply the oxygen delivery device to the patient.
g. Crack the main cylinder to remove dust and debris.
h. Attach the oxygen delivery device to the regulator.
i. Open the main cylinder valve and check the pressure.

18. Describe the four basic steps for clearing a severe foreign body airway obstruction in a RESPONSIVE adult.

a.

b.

c.

d.

19. After you determine that you must relieve a severe foreign body airway obstruction in a RESPONSIVE infant, you should proceed as follows. (Write the numerals 1–5 to show the correct sequence of steps.)
a. Deliver five back slaps.
b. Deliver five chest thrusts.
c. Position the infant face up over one of your forearms, with the head lower than the body.
d. Position the infant face down over one of your forearms with the head lower than the body.
e. Alternate set of slaps and thrusts until object is expelled.

20. Your patient is an UNRESPONSIVE infant found with a severe foreign body airway obstruction. Write the numerals 1–5 to describe the correct sequence of steps you should take as a lone rescuer.
a. Open the airway and attempt to ventilate.
b. Deliver two ventilations.
c. Open the mouth and inspect for the foreign body.
d. Repeat the cycle until the obstruction is relieved.
e. Deliver 30 chest compressions.

Vocabulary Practice

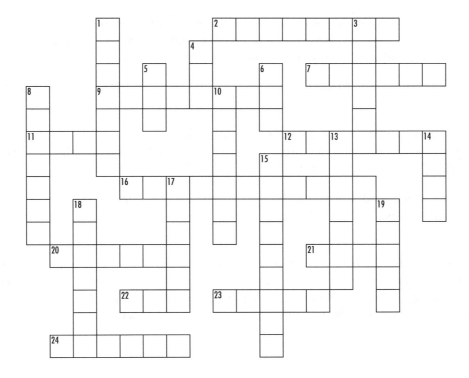

Across

2. Inhale material into the lungs.
7. Voice box.
9. One sign that body tissues are not receiving enough oxygen.
11. Air enters the body through this.
12. Type of distention.
16. Primary cause of cardiac arrest in infants is a _____ problem.
20. A clear and open airway is this.
21. An infant's trachea is _____ flexible than an adult's.
22. Short for bag-valve-mask device.
23. An infant with an FBAO will require chest thrusts and back _____ .
24. Gas essential for life.

Down

1. Windpipe.
3. Abdominal _____ , or Heimlich maneuver.
4. The lower end of the trachea is divided into how many bronchi?
5. Use a _____ -thrust maneuver to open an injured patient's airway.
6. Short for pounds per square inch.
8. An oxygen delivery device.
10. Negative pressure, or do this to keep an airway clear.
13. Harsh, high-pitched sound made during inhalation.
14. Short for chronic obstruction pulmonary disease.
15. Deliver these to relieve a complete FBAO in an infant, but not in an adult.
17. Wall dividing the two nostrils.
18. Area posterior to the mouth and nose.
19. Use a finger _____ to remove a visible object from the mouth.

Active Learning

Airway skills are among the most important you will learn. Your assessment of airway and breathing and correcting the problems you find will be critical for your patient to live. The following exercises will help your understanding of airway issues and enhance your decision-making skills.

1. Suctioning an adult should only be performed for 15 seconds. Why? While looking at the clock, hold your breath for 15 seconds. How does it feel?

2. You are suctioning a patient who is continuously vomiting copious amounts of thick vomitus. You suction for 15 seconds, then move to ventilate the patient, and find the airway once again full of vomit. What should you do?

3. In class, experiment with electric- or battery-powered and manually (hand) powered suction devices. List three pros and cons of each. Present your answers to your instructor and/or your class.

4. Bring a can of vegetable soup into class. Try suctioning the soup (broth and vegetables) with a soft suction catheter. Then try a rigid (Yankauer or tonsil-tip) and look for any differences. Will the vegetables pass through the catheter? What if the catheter clogs? By the time you are done, you will have received excellent practice cleaning a suction device.

8 | Circulation

Key Ideas

Heart disease kills many people each year. Patients who are in cardiac arrest require immediate CPR and early advanced care if they are to have any chance of surviving. This chapter focuses on recognizing patients in cardiac arrest and correctly applying CPR. Key ideas include the following:

- Patients in cardiac arrest need immediate immediate CPR and defibrillation followed by advanced medical care within 8 to 10 minutes.

- CPR helps to oxygenate and circulate the blood until defibrillation can be performed. Each minute of delay reduces the patient's chances of survival by 10%.

- Before providing CPR to your patient, you must first establish unresponsiveness, breathlessness, and pulselessness.

- The EMS system should be activated as soon as you determine an adult patient is unresponsive. For infants and children, activate EMS after two minutes of basic life support.

- CPR may be performed by either one or two rescuers.

- You may stop CPR only if you are exhausted and unable to continue, if you have turned your patient over to another trained rescuer or the hospital staff, if the patient is resuscitated, or if the patient has been declared dead by a proper authority.

Exam Warm-up

1. More than one of the following statements about the heart are TRUE. Which are they?
   a. The left side receives oxygenated blood from the lungs.
   b. The right side receives oxygenated blood from the lungs.
   c. The left side pumps blood to the lungs to be oxygenated.
   d. The right side pumps blood to the lungs to be oxygenated.

2. More than one of the following statements about an adult patient's pulse are TRUE. Which are they?
   a. It is a sign of the pressure exerted by each contraction of the heart.
   b. The waves of blood the heart sends to the body are felt as the pulse.
   c. It is felt where a large artery lies over a bone close to the skin.
   d. At rest an adult's should be between 60 and 80 beats per minute.

3. More than one of the following statements about clinical death are TRUE. Which are they?
   a. After 4 to 6 minutes brain cells begin to die.
   b. Immediate CPR and advanced care cannot reverse it.
   c. It occurs when a patient is breathless and pulseless.
   d. After 8 to 10 minutes irreversible damage occurs to the brain.

4. The letters "CPR" stand for
   a. cardiac pain relaxation.
   b. cardiographic radiation.
   c. cardiopulmonary resuscitation.
   d. cardiocompression ratification.

5. To determine pulselessness in an adult patient, assess the _____ pulse point.
   a. pedis
   b. radial
   c. brachial
   d. carotid

6. For you to properly perform CPR, the patient must be in a _____ position.
   a. prone
   b. supine
   c. recovery
   d. semi-sitting

7. To properly perform CPR, the patient must be on a _____ surface.
   a. hard flat
   b. soft flat
   c. soft tilted
   d. hard tilted

8. To determine pulselessness in an infant, assess the _____ pulse point.
   a. pedis
   b. radial
   c. brachial
   d. carotid

9. To determine pulselessness in a child, assess the _____ pulse point.
   a. pedis
   b. radial
   c. brachial
   d. carotid

10. According to AHA guidelines, if you are alone, you must attempt to resuscitate an infant or child for three minutes before activating the EMS system.

   _____ True

   _____ False

11. The correct compression site for an infant is _____ an imaginary line between the nipples.
   a. one finger-width above
   b. one finger-width below
   c. two finger-widths above
   d. two finger-widths below

Short-Answer Review

12. The "chain of survival" includes four links. List them.

   a.

   b.

   c.

   d.

13. List the four conditions under which CPR may be discontinued.

   a.

   b.

   c.

   d.

14. The following list should describe the steps preceding CPR of an adult patient. Fill in the steps that are missing.

   Step 1: Determine unresponsiveness.

   Step 2:

   Step 3: Position the patient on a firm, flat surface.

   Step 4:

   Step 5:

   Step 6: Perform artificial ventilation.

   Step 7:

   Step 8: Begin CPR.

15. Before you begin chest compressions, you must determine that your patient is

   a.

   b.

   c.

16. You will perform one-rescuer CPR on the following patients. Fill in the compression-to-breath ratio for each one.

   a. 10-year-old:

   b. 18-year-old:

   c. 3-month-old:

   d. 4-year-old:

17. You will perform one-rescuer CPR on the following patients. For each one, write in the correct hand description and position from the list.

heel of one or two hands   on lower half of sternum
heel of two hands   on top third of sternum
two or three fingers   on top half of sternum

a. 5-month-old: _____

b. 7-year-old: _____

c. 71-year-old: _____

d. 36-year-old: _____

18. Fill in the chart below with the correct compression rate and depth for each patient.

	Infant	Child	Adult
Compression Rate	_____ per minute	_____ per minute	_____ per minute
Compression Depth	_____ inch(es)	_____ inch(es)	_____ inch(es)

19. Number the following actions 1–7 to correctly order the sequence of steps for adult CPR.

_____ a. Uncover your patient's chest.

_____ b. Get in position beside the patient.

_____ c. Thrust down and depress the sternum.

_____ d. Position your hands and your shoulders.

_____ e. Position the patient on a firm flat surface.

_____ f. Locate the compression site.

_____ g. Completely release pressure to allow blood to flow back into the heart.

20. You are observing another student practice adult CPR. You notice that he is determining his hand position by placing the heel of one hand directly over the xiphoid process. He then places his other hand on top of the first and begins compressions. Do you agree with this hand placement? Disagree? Explain your answer.

21. You observe another student using jerky, jabbing movements while performing chest compressions. You advise her that she needs to perform compressions more smoothly. She asks, "Why?" What is your answer?

22. Your class is reviewing the time rule for interrupting CPR. One of the students states, "CPR should only be stopped for 10 seconds." Is this always possible? Give your student an example of a situation in which he or she may need to stop CPR for more than 10 seconds.

23. List three injuries that can occur when CPR is performed.

a.

b.

c.

24. You have found Mr. Smith, a 65-year-old man, to be pulseless and breathless. When you begin compressions, you hear and feel a crunch. What should you do next? Why?

Vocabulary Practice

1. Check your understanding of the heart by reading the clues and unscrambling the words.

    a. The heart lies in the chest between the ___.   GULNS

    b. It is protected in front by the ribs and ___.   MUNRETS

    c. It is like a ___-___ pump.   DISWETOD

    d. The ___ side receives oxygenated blood.   FELT

    e. The ___ side receives blood from the body.   THIRG

    f. Blood is kept under ___ by its pumping action.   SERRUPES

    g. The ___ is a sign of the pressure exerted with each contraction.   SPLEU

2. Read the clues about the pulse and unscramble the words.

    a. The pulse is felt where an ___ lies over a bone close to the skin.   ERRATY

    b. In an adult, it is felt most easily at the ___ artery.   DOARICT

    c. The ___ pulse can be felt in the underside of the upper arm.   AAIRCLBH

    d. Palpate the ___ pulse first when the patient is responsive.   AAILRD

The Call: Performing CPR

Read this scenario and answer the questions that follow. Focus on the steps necessary to assess a patient and to provide CPR. Note that defibrillation is a critical part of First Responder care for cardiac arrest and is taught in Chapter 9.

You and your partner are responding in the rescue unit to an "unknown medical." The dispatcher updates you with the information that a trained bystander is on scene and CPR has been started. You arrive at one of the local supermarkets and are led to a food aisle where the 70-year-old male patient has collapsed from an apparent heart attack. You find the bystander administering CPR amidst a pile of overturned canned goods, the patient's up-ended cart, and a pressing mass of onlookers.

1. After ensuring scene safety, what should your first action be?

2. If the person providing CPR needs to be relieved, what must you do?

3. But this person does not want to be relieved right away. You observe that his hands are placed on the patient's sternum in line with the patient's nipples. He is depressing the patient's chest about one inch at a rate of 60 compressions per minute. Critique his CPR method and offer suggestions, if necessary.

Active Learning

There is a physical component of CPR that involves providing ventilation and compressions. There also is an emotional component, which you cannot experience fully until you have provided CPR to a real patient. To get a better understanding of that component, ask rescuers you know the following questions:

1. Have you ever performed CPR?

2. How did it feel to provide artificial ventilation?

3. How did it feel to compress a patient's chest?

4. What happened to your patient(s)?

5. How did the patient outcome make you feel (a patient's death or a "save")?

6. In your experience, what percent of all your CPR patients live?

7. What could be done to help more patients live?

9 | Automated External Defibrillation

Key Ideas

Early defibrillation is necessary to the cardiac-arrest patient's survival. In order to get it to the patient early enough, as many people as possible must be able to perform this life-saving skill. This chapter provides an overview. Key ideas include the following:

- Automated external defibrillation by First Responders is indicated for children and adults who are unresponsive, breathless, and pulseless.

- Defibrillation is the definitive treatment for certain heart rhythms. CPR maintains a patient until the defibrillator can be applied.

- The operator of an automated external defibrillator (AED) must follow safety guidelines.

- Always treat the patient, not the AED. This means assessing the patient properly and reassessing after each intervention, such as a shock or movement.

- Post-resuscitation care is needed to monitor return of pulses, to make sure the patient is breathing, and to note any changes in the patient's condition.

Exam Warm-up

1. The letters "AED" stand for _____ defibrillator.
   a. automated external
   b. anatomical external
   c. automated electrical
   d. automatic electronic

2. You are called to a cardiac-arrest patient with CPR in progress. When you arrive on scene with your AED ready to go, you find the adult patient is still unresponsive, breathless, and pulseless. Your next task regarding AED operation is to
   a. turn on the AED power.
   b. deliver a shock from the AED.
   c. apply the AED's adhesive pads to the patient.
   d. stop CPR and instruct everyone to clear the patient.

3. Which one of the following statements is CORRECT?
   a. AEDs need to be checked once a year.
   b. AEDs only work after special drugs are given.
   c. A non-working AED could be cause for legal action.
   d. AEDs are simple devices and require no special care.

Short-Answer Review

4. What is defibrillation?

5. You arrive on scene of a seven-year-old in cardiac arrest. You have determined that she is unresponsive, breathless, and pulseless. The paramedics will arrive in approximately two minutes and her "down time" prior to your arrival was 7–8 minutes. Should you start CPR or apply the AED first? Why?

6. As your partner applies AED pads to the chest of an elderly woman, she tells him she is very afraid of the machine. He reassures her and tells her that her pulse is very weak and the AED will help her. He prevents everyone from touching the patient and presses the AED's "analyze" button. The machine advises a shock. Should the AED have been applied to this patient? Why or why not? Should this patient be shocked? Why or why not?

7. Should you use an AED on the following patients? Write "yes" or "no" beside each one.

_____ **a.** 3-year-old girl who weighs 65 pounds

_____ **b.** 7-year-old boy who weighs 56 pounds

_____ **c.** 32-year-old man who weighs 265 pounds

_____ **d.** 14-year-old girl who weighs 112 pounds

8. Explain when AED application and defibrillation should be attempted prior to CPR and when it should be withheld until after CPR has been initiated.

9. What should you do when the AED advises a shock? Number the following steps 1–6 to correctly order the steps.

_____ **a.** Deliver the first shock.

_____ **b.** Check the patient's pulse.

_____ **c.** If you are advised, deliver a second shock.

_____ **d.** Make sure everyone is clear of the patient.

_____ **e.** Wait until the AED reanalyzes the heart rhythm.

_____ **f.** Perform 2 minutes of CPR.

Vocabulary Practice

Across

1. AEDs correct _____ rhythms.
3. Short for a rhythm that does not require an AED shock.
6. A _____ improvement program should monitor AED use in the field.
8. Early _____, one of the links in the chain of survival.
9. Short for public access defibrillation.
10. Some AEDs have an _____, which shows the heart's electrical activity on a screen.
11. The AED _____ the heart rhythm before suggesting "shock" or "no shock."
12. These connect the adhesive pads to the AED.
15. Early _____, one of the links in the chain of survival.
16. White to _____, red to ribs (a memory aid for proper pad placement).
17. An AED shock can correct a lethal heart _____.
18. Post-resuscitation care includes _____ assessment of the patient.
19. You can soon expect to find AEDS at every shopping _____.

Down

2. A call _____ is necessary for quality improvement.
3. Remove any nitroglycerin _____ before applying the AED pads.
4. Apply this during post-resuscitation care.
5. Even after the pulse has returned, many patients will still need care to do this.
7. Short for automated external defibrillation.
9. After 2 minutes of CPR, check this.
11. Patients in cardiac _____ may require prompt defibrillation.
13. A heart rhythm that does not require defibrillation.
14. This is delivered by an AED.
16. Carry a disposable one to shave areas where pads are to be placed.

The Call: Using an AED

Read this scenario and answer the questions that follow. Focus on how to use an AED properly.

You and your partner have been called to the corner store, where a middle-aged man is reported to have clutched his chest and slumped over in the seat of his car. Bystanders removed him from the car and onto the ground. Upon your arrival 6 minutes later, you find them performing good CPR. While you set up the AED, your partner assesses the patient, who continues to be unresponsive, breathless, and pulseless.

1. When you open the patient's shirt, you find a nitroglycerin patch on the right upper chest wall. What should you do next?

2. You have attached the AED's adhesive pads to the patient's chest. The AED indicates that the patient should be shocked. What safety precaution should you take before pressing the "shock" button?

3. After delivering the shock, you resume CPR for 2 minutes and then pause to check for a pulse. Upon doing so, you find a weak carotid pulse, but the patient is still breathless. What should you do now?

4. After three minutes of rescue breathing, your patient is breathing on his own at a rate of 20 breaths per minute. He has adequate chest rise, but he remains unresponsive without a gag reflex. At this point, what three things should you do?

   a.

   b.

   c.

Active Learning

How long do you think it would take to administer an initial shock with an AED once cardiac arrest is identified? Timing is critical—since the patient's heart is not beating. But accuracy and efficiency are also crucial.

   Using a partner in lab, time the sequence from recognizing that the patient is in cardiac arrest to the completion of the initial shock. Remember that the purpose is not to race, but to see how long it takes to do efficient, accurate, and safe defibrillation.

10 | Scene Size-up

Key Ideas

This chapter focuses on safety, identifying the mechanism of injury or nature of illness, and determining the necessary additional resources. Key ideas include the following:

- First Responders must ensure their own safety first. This involves planning, continued observation, and an appropriate reaction to danger.

- Before entering the scene of an emergency, the First Responder must size the scene up for hazards and clues to the sequence of events.

- First Responders must use personal protective equipment appropriate for each call.

- First Responder care of a trauma patient depends on the pattern and extent of injury. The mechanism of injury can suggest what types of injuries occurred to the patient.

- It is part of scene size-up to determine and call for the appropriate resources needed on scene. Do this before you begin patient care.

Exam Warm-up

1. A "medical patient" is a patient who is
   a. hospitalized.
   b. critical.
   c. injured.
   d. ill.

2. A "trauma patient" is a patient who is
   a. hospitalized.
   b. critical.
   c. injured.
   d. ill.

3. The term "mechanism of injury" refers to the
   a. patient's chief complaint.
   b. forces that caused an injury.
   c. mechanical advantage of the body.
   d. chronic condition the patient may have.

4. The mechanism of injury can NOT tell you
   a. what injuries the patient may have.
   b. if the patient was ill before injury.
   c. how serious the patient's injuries may be.
   d. what patterns of injury you should suspect.

5. Kinetic energy is the total amount of energy
   a. stored in an object at rest.
   b. in the velocity of an object.
   c. contained by an object in motion.
   d. contained in the mass of an object.

6. The more kinetic energy an object contains, the greater the damage it can cause when it impacts the body.

   _____ True

   _____ False

7. The higher the speed of an object, the more kinetic energy it has.

   _____ True

   _____ False

8. The amount of kinetic energy that is absorbed on impact depends on how much has been absorbed by other things first.

   _____ True

   _____ False

9. A person who falls on freshly plowed soil will be injured as severely as the person who falls the same distance onto cement pavement.

   _____ True

   _____ False

10. Down-and-under and up-and-over pathways of motion are associated with _____ collisions.
    a. head-on
    b. rollover
    c. rear-impact
    d. side-impact

11. You arrive at the scene of a two-car collision. You should suspect more than one of the injuries listed below for the driver whose car was broadsided. Which are they?
    a. head and neck injuries
    b. chest injuries
    c. injury to the pelvis
    d. injury to the femur

12. The driver of a car that was rear-ended by another vehicle does NOT have his headrest up. Immediately suspect injury to his
    a. clavicles.
    b. both carpals.
    c. cervical spine.
    d. tibia and fibula.

13. You find your patient unresponsive a few feet from his motorcycle. One side of the bike has large gashes in it, and the handlebar on that side has been snapped off. You find severe scrapes and cuts all along the patient's left side, and he has a swollen, deformed left lower leg. You suspect the mechanism of injury to be
    a. ejection.
    b. head-on impact.
    c. angular impact.
    d. laying the bike down.

14. You respond to a six-year-old who has fallen 10 feet from a tree. Her fall was broken by several branches. Which one of the following would NOT help you to determine the severity of her injuries?
    a. distance of the fall
    b. body part that impacted first
    c. type of clothing she was wearing
    d. anything that interrupted the fall
    e. surface on which the patient landed

15. Your patient has been stabbed. You should suspect a low-velocity injury that is at a site far from impact.

    _____ True

    _____ False

16. Your patient has been shot by a bullet from a handgun. You should suspect a high-velocity injury that affects tissues at the impact site only.

    _____ True

    _____ False

17. During the primary phase of a blast, _____ typically causes injury.
    a. the fall onto a hard surface
    b. penetrating projectiles
    c. the pressure wave
    d. flying debris

Short-Answer Review

18. Give two examples of how you can plan ahead to stay safe at an emergency scene.

    a.

    b.

19. Decide whether or not each of the following is a sign of danger at an emergency scene. If it is, give a reason why.

    a. You witness two people arguing.

    b. There is evidence of alcohol use.

    c. There is absolute silence.

20. When you find danger at an emergency scene, there are three actions you should take. They are

    a.

    b.

    c.

21. There are three basic types of impacts that occur when a car crashes into a tree. They are

    a.

    b.

    c.

22. Compare the patterns of injuries associated with the pathways of motion listed below.

Up-and-over:

Down-and-under:

23. Two cars involved in a head-on collision were traveling about 40 mph. The driver of the late-model sedan was wearing a lap and shoulder belt, and the car's air bag deployed on impact. His headrest was up. The driver of the old pickup truck was wearing only a lap belt. The seats of the truck have no headrests. As you approach the vehicles, you note major front-end damage to both. List the injuries you suspect each driver may suffer.

Driver of the sedan:

Driver of the pickup:

24. You arrive on scene to learn that your patient fell approximately 12 to 14 feet onto hard-packed dirt, landing face down with initial contact to his abdomen and chest. Would you consider this a severe mechanism of injury? Why or why not?

Vocabulary Practice

Read the clues and fill in the blanks that follow. Then write the boxed letters as you find them on the "Scrambled Letters" line near the bottom of the page. Finally, unscramble the letters to find out what safety devices are absolutely necessary for you and the general public.

1. A headrest will prevent the head from whipping backward after this type of impact.

___ ___ [ ] ___

2. This minimizes injuries to a baby or young child involved in an auto collision.

___ ___ ___ [ ] ___ ___ ___

3. Air bags help to protect motorists from serious injury in this type of collision.

___ [ ] ___ ___ ___ ___ ___

4. This term refers to the rate at which an object changes speed.

___ ___ ___ [ ] [ ] ___ ___ ___ ___ ___ ___ ___

5. During a vehicle rollover, this can happen to an occupant who is not wearing a seat belt.

___ ___ ___ [ ] ___ ___ ___

6. This is often called a "broadside" or "T-bone" collision.

[ ] ___ ___ ___ ___ ___ ___ ___ ___ ___ ___

7. This bone can be broken when the chest strikes the steering wheel.

___ [ ] ___ ___ ___ ___ ___ ___

8. This explosive event can result in three phases, each with a typical pattern of injury.

[ ] ___ ___ ___ ___

Scrambled Letters: ___ ___ ___ ___ ___ ___ ___ ___ ___

Unscrambled Letters: ___ ___ ___ ___   ___ ___ ___ ___ ___

The Call: Motor-Vehicle Collision

Read the following scenario and answer the questions that follow. Focus on the way in which the mechanisms of injury fit into the total picture.

You are responding to a vehicle collision in your rescue unit. When you arrive on scene you can see that four cars are involved. As you begin to unload equipment, a police officer tells you the story.

A small pickup truck broke down in the middle of the roadway just over a rise. A station wagon coming over the rise at high speed rear-ended the truck. A pile-up ensued when a large sedan came upon the crash, locked its brakes, went into a sideways skid, and rolled three times. The sedan ended up over an embankment, the driver ejected. A fourth car, a foreign compact, managed to avoid the crash but slid sideways into a concrete barrier, striking the driver's side with no intrusion into the passenger space. Each car had one occupant. Each driver had taken safety precautions as follows:

- Pickup-truck driver wore a lap and shoulder belt, his headrest was up, and he had an air bag.

- Station-wagon driver wore a lap belt only and her headrest was up.

- Sedan driver had on no restraints of any kind and his headrest was down.

- Compact-car driver wore a lap and shoulder belt, her headrest was up, and she had an air bag.

1. You expect the driver of the station wagon to have taken either one of two pathways of motion. What are they?

2. Would the air bag have helped the driver of the compact car to avoid injury? Explain your answer.

3. Based on the mechanism of injury for each driver and the safety precautions each has taken, rank the four patients from most (1) to least injured (4).

   _____ Pickup-truck driver

   _____ Station-wagon driver

   _____ Sedan driver

   _____ Compact-car driver

4. What injuries should you suspect in each of the drivers in the scenario? Match the following injury patterns to the drivers.

    a. Suspect injuries to the left shoulder, left rib cage, and pelvis in the driver of the

    _____.

    b. Suspect minor neck strain and a possible broken left clavicle in the driver of the

    _____.

    c. Suspect lethal head and chest injuries in the driver of the

    _____.

    d. Suspect major facial injuries, a broken sternum, and broken ribs in the driver of the

    _____.

Active Learning

Scene size-up sets the stage for a safe and successful call. The following exercises will help hone your observation skills.

1. Look at cars you pass on the road, and note any collision damage. How do you suspect it occurred (head-on, T-bone, rear-end)?

2. Do you think that the level of damage you see could cause injury? How serious or extensive? To which parts of the body?

3. Interview people you know who have been involved in a motor-vehicle collision. Ask them:
   a. Were they injured?
   b. When did they realize they were injured?
   c. Do they feel their injuries were more or less severe than expected? Why or why not?

11 | Introduction to Patient Assessment and Vital Signs

Key Ideas

This chapter focuses on gathering accurate information about the patient's condition in order to provide the appropriate care. Key ideas include the following:

- The patient assessment process consists of observing, listening, touching, and smelling, and using those findings to make appropriate decisions about patient care.

- The First Responder's patient assessment plan consists of scene size-up, initial assessment, physical examination, patient history, ongoing assessment, and patient hand-off.

- First Responders must assess a patient's condition quickly and accurately. The patient assessment plan helps to focus on important concerns and establish patient care priorities. It also helps to maintain self-control in stressful situations.

- For First Responders, a medical patient is a patient who is ill. A trauma patient is a patient who is injured.

- A patient's vital signs consist of respiration, pulse, skin, pupils, and blood pressure.

- More important than any one vital sign is change in vital signs over time.

Exam Warm-up

1. More important than any one vital sign is change in vital signs over time.

   _____ True

   _____ False

2. A respiration consists of _____ inhalation(s) and _____ exhalation(s).
   a. one-half, one-half
   b. only one, no
   c. one, one
   d. two, two

3. A normal adult respiratory rate is _____ breaths per minute.
   a. 8–16
   b. 12–20
   c. 14–26
   d. 15–30
   e. 25–50

4. A normal respiratory rate for a child is _____ breaths per minute.
   a. 8–16
   b. 12–20
   c. 14–26
   d. 15–30
   e. 25–50

5. A normal respiratory rate for an infant is _____ breaths per minute.
   a. 8–16
   b. 12–20
   c. 14–26
   d. 15–30
   e. 25–50

6. To assess breathing properly, you should count the patient's respirations for _____ seconds and then multiply by _____ to get the respiratory rate.
   a. 40, 1
   b. 30, 2
   c. 15, 3
   d. 10, 4

7. A normal pulse rate for an adult is _____ per minute.
   a. 12–20
   b. 60–80
   c. 80–150
   d. 120–150

8. A normal pulse rate for a child is _____ per minute.
   a. 12–20
   b. 60–80
   c. 80–150
   d. 120–150

9. A normal pulse rate for an infant is _____ per minute.
   a. 12–20
   b. 60–80
   c. 80–150
   d. 120–150

10. If a patient's pulse rate is irregular or slow, count the beats for _____ seconds and then multiply by _____ to get an accurate reading.
    a. 40, 1
    b. 30, 2
    c. 15, 3
    d. 10, 4

11. A blood pressure obtained while feeling for a radial pulse as the blood pressure cuff deflates is called the
    a. radial blood pressure.
    b. diastolic blood pressure.
    c. blood pressure by palpation.
    d. blood pressure by auscultation.

12. In a blood pressure reading, the top number is called the _____ and the bottom number is called the _____.
    a. radial/femoral
    b. diastolic/systolic
    c. systolic/diastolic
    d. perfusion/circulation

Short-Answer Review

13. What are the six steps of the First Responder's patient assessment plan?

    a.

    b.

    c.

    d.

    e.

    f.

14. Vital signs include the patient's

    a.

    b.

    c.

    d.

    e.

15. Write what the following skin signs tell you about a patient's condition.

    a. Cool skin:

    b. Hot skin:

    c. Pale skin:

    d. Blueness:

    e. Black-and-blue mottling:

Vocabulary Practice

Across

2. Sphygmomanometer, or BP _____.
5. Short for blood pressure.
6. Pulse point at the wrist.
9. A bounding pulse is a _____ pulse.
10. Patient for whom normal respiration is 15–30 per minute.
11. Patient for whom normal respiration is 12–20 per minute.
12. Pupils that get smaller are said to do this.
15. Capillary _____ is an assessment of circulation in children under 6.
18. Abnormal finding for the pupils.
19. Pupils that get larger are said to do this.
20. Pulse point under the left breast.
21. A patient with an _____ is called a trauma patient.

Down

1. Use a pen light to assess these.
3. Pulse point in the groin.
4. The 80 in BP 120/80.
5. Pulse point in the upper arm.
7. Patient for whom normal respiration is 25–50 per minute.
8. Where to find the antecubital space.
12. Pulse point in the neck.
13. A medical patient is this.
14. The 120 in BP 120/80.
15. A normal pulse has _____ spaces between each beat.
16. Skin sign that may be caused by a liver disease.
17. A thready pulse is _____ and rapid.

The Call: Pedestrian–Auto Collision

Read this scenario and answer the questions that follow. Focus on the First Responder patient assessment plan.

You are called to the scene of a patient who was struck by an automobile that was traveling at about 35 miles per hour. You observe that the patient is a male in his 20s. He was thrown about 20 feet and was found lying in the road face up. You do not see any hazards, such as leaking gasoline or downed wires. When you approach the patient, you call out but do not get a response. Your crew from the engine company helps out by stabilizing the patient's spine, opening the airway with a jaw thrust maneuver and suctioning. The patient is breathing at 16 breaths per minute with adequate chest rise. An oral airway is inserted and oxygen is applied by nonrebreather mask. You do not observe any obvious bleeding. The patient is still unresponsive. You radio the incoming ambulance to advise them that the patient is seriously injured and recommend calling a helicopter for transport.

  You make sure the patient's airway and breathing are still adequate and begin to examine the patient from head to toe, looking for injuries while a crew member obtains vital signs. You find a bruise on the chest and a deformity to the right hip and femur. The ambulance arrives, and you tell them about your patient. The ambulance EMTs take over patient care. Before long, a helicopter arrives to transport the seriously injured patient to the trauma center.

1. Match the activity of the on-scene First Responders to the part of the patient assessment process in which it would most likely occur. Write your answers on the lines provided.

   scene size-up • initial assessment • physical examination
   patient history • ongoing assessment • patient hand-off

   _____ a. You determine the patient was thrown approximately 20 feet.

   _____ b. You do not see any hazards on scene.

   _____ c. You insert an airway adjunct into the patient's airway to help keep it open and clear.

   _____ d. You question witnesses to the crash about what happened.

   _____ e. You check for life-threatening bleeding.

   _____ f. You check the patient's body for injuries from head to toe.

   _____ g. You tell the ambulance crew all your findings about the patient's condition.

2. In an unresponsive patient such as this one, how might you obtain a medical history?

3. The patient is found on the road in a face-up position. What term is used to describe that position?

4. Write what you would say to the arriving ambulance crew to describe the patient's condition before they take over care.

Active Learning

You must measure and record your patient's vital signs accurately. You also must interpret what they mean to your patient. This is important in determining your patient's priority for emergency care and transport, as well as in situations where you must care for a patient over time. The following exercises will help you learn to take and interpret vital signs.

1. Take your pulse while you are at rest. Then walk briskly for two to three minutes. When you stop, immediately take your pulse again.
   a. How are they different?
   b. Was one easier to locate and count than the other?

2. Take your own pulse, and then take the pulse of two friends or family members. Record the results.
   a. Are the pulse rates the same?
   b. Was one easier to find than another?

3. Count your own respirations, and then count the respirations of two friends or family members. Record the results.
   a. Are the respiration rates the same?
   b. Was one easier to assess than another?

4. Measure your own capillary refill rate. Then put your hand in ice or the freezer for a minute or two and measure it again. (Do not expose yourself to prolonged cold.)
   a. Are the rates the same?
   b. Was one easier to obtain than the other?

12 | Patient Assessment

Key Ideas

This chapter focuses on gathering accurate information about the patient's condition in order to provide the appropriate care. Key ideas include the following:

- The First Responder's patient assessment plan consists of a scene size-up, initial assessment, physical exam, patient history, ongoing assessment, and patient hand-off.

- A proper patient assessment and history will help you to determine the severity of the patient's condition and to provide quality patient care.

- There may be instances when you are unable to complete every aspect of the patient assessment plan because of priorities, such as establishing an airway or ventilating the patient. There will also be instances where you will be able to combine steps (for example, noting a patient's level of responsiveness as you assess his or her pulse).

- Whenever possible, use memory aids such as "AVPU" (levels of responsiveness), "DOTS" (what to look for during a physical exam), and "SAMPLE" (information in the patient history) to help you remember important assessment steps.

Exam Warm-up

1. The initial assessment is the most important part of the patient assessment plan because it identifies
   a. life-threatening problems.
   b. the patient's medical history.
   c. potential long-term disabilities.
   d. painful, swollen, or deformed limbs.

2. Identify the items that are included in the initial assessment.
   a. examining the pupils
   b. measuring blood pressure
   c. assessing the patient's ABCs
   d. forming a general impression
   e. conducting a head-to-toe exam
   f. assessing level of responsiveness
   g. updating incoming EMS units
   h. the patient's chief complaint
   i. taking spinal precautions

3. You are managing a 62-year-old woman who collapsed at her office. Her airway is clear, and her respirations are 4–6 per minute and shallow. Her carotid pulse is slow and weak. Which one of the following actions should you take?
   a. Do nothing, because the patient's ABCs are fine.
   b. Reassess the patient every three to five minutes.
   c. Respirations are too slow. Begin artificial ventilation.
   d. Begin CPR in order to support this patient's breathing.

4. The patient's _____ is the response to the question, "Can you tell me why you called EMS today?"
   a. chief complaint
   b. mechanism of injury
   c. level of responsiveness
   d. airway and breathing status

5. You are assessing a patient's mental status. The patient answers all your questions but does not offer any elaboration of his own. He appears to be distracted and in distress. Using the AVPU scale, how would you describe his level of responsiveness?
   a. alert
   b. verbal
   c. painful
   d. unresponsive

6. Several ice skaters collided and fell. Your patient was underneath several other skaters. He is responsive and, in fact, appears to be quite normal until you ask him, "What happened?" His response is: "What do you mean?" Upon further questioning, you confirm that he does not recall the incident. Using the AVPU scale, what is this patient's level of responsiveness?
   a. alert
   b. verbal
   c. painful
   d. unresponsive

7. You are managing a critically injured patient who has copious amounts of blood and broken teeth blocking her airway. You should
   a. assess the airway and then move on to assess circulation.
   b. continue to try to clear the airway until you succeed.
   c. use forceful ventilations to try to clear the airway.
   d. reassess the airway every five minutes.

8. To determine INADEQUATE breathing, look for all of the following EXCEPT
   a. cyanosis.
   b. hemorrhaging.
   c. minimal chest rise.
   d. mental status changes.
   e. little or no air exhaled.
   f. extremely slow respirations.

9. If you determine that your patient's breathing is INADEQUATE, you should
   a. perform a head-to-toe exam.
   b. begin ventilating immediately.
   c. place him in a recovery position.
   d. ask bystanders if the patient was injured.

10. Generally, if your patient is a verbally RESPONSIVE adult, use the _____ pulse to assess circulation.
    a. radial
    b. femoral
    c. carotid
    d. brachial

11. During the initial assessment of an UNRESPONSIVE adult, use the _____ pulse to assess circulation.
    a. radial
    b. femoral
    c. carotid
    d. brachial

12. During the initial assessment, the pulse check for all infants is done at the _____ artery.
    a. radial
    b. femoral
    c. carotid
    d. brachial

13. If you find your patient is bleeding significantly during the initial assessment, you should
    a. phone or radio for help.
    b. control the blood flow immediately.
    c. provide CPR for two minutes and then update EMS.
    d. reassess level of responsiveness, airway, and breathing.

14. For which one of the following findings should you stop a head-to-toe exam to administer immediate care?
    a. neck pain
    b. tenderness to the groin
    c. fracture to the lower arm
    d. open wound to the leg with minimal bleeding

15. If you were to find an open wound of the chest in your patient, you should _____ immediately.
   a. manually stabilize her head and neck
   b. apply an occlusive (airtight) dressing
   c. observe for deformities and tenderness
   d. palpate the area around it for swelling

16. To assess circulation in the lower extremities, you should palpate the _____ or the _____ pulse point.
   a. dorsalis pedis, posterior tibial
   b. brachial, dorsalis tibial
   c. femoral, posterior pedis
   d. brachial, femoral

17. Repeat the ongoing assessment every _____ minutes for an UNSTABLE patient and every _____ minutes for a STABLE one.
   a. 1, 10
   b. 5, 15
   c. 10, 20
   d. 15, 25

Short-Answer Review

18. What are the six steps of the First Responder's patient assessment plan?

   a.

   b.

   c.

   d.

   e.

   f.

19. You have responded to a patient who was struck by a car, and you are about to begin patient assessment. Number the following steps 1–8 to show the order in which they should be performed.

_____ a. Assess level of responsiveness.

_____ b. Update EMS and ask for the ETA of incoming units.

_____ c. Assess the patient's pulse.

_____ d. Check for serious external bleeding.

_____ e. Manually stabilize the patient's head and neck.

_____ f. Introduce yourself and ask: "What happened? Where do you hurt?"

_____ g. Assess the airway.

_____ h. Assess for adequate breathing.

20. The memory aid AVPU is helpful in describing a patient's level of responsiveness. Write what each letter stands for.

A:

V:

P:

U:

21. How would you assess the level of responsiveness in an adult whose mental status is normally altered?

22. How could you determine a two-year-old's level of responsiveness?

23. List three signs of ADEQUATE breathing:

a.

b.

c.

24. After the initial assessment of your patient, what information should you include in your update to EMS?

25. Write the numbers 1–6 to show the order in which you should perform the head-to-toe exam on an adult.

_____ **a.** extremities

_____ **b.** chest

_____ **c.** head

_____ **d.** pelvis

_____ **e.** abdomen

_____ **f.** neck

26. Read each scenario below. Then write either "yes" or "no" to indicate whether or not you should perform a complete head-to-toe exam on the patient.

_____ **a.** Your patient has fallen 15 feet onto a concrete sidewalk.

_____ **b.** A 36-year-old man has accidentally cut his lower arm with a broken piece of glass.

_____ **c.** Your unresponsive patient has been found lying on a bench in the park.

27. There are three methods you should use to perform a physical exam. They are:

a.

b.

c.

28. The memory aid DOTS can help you remember the signs of injury you are looking for during a physical exam. Write what each letter stands for.

D:

O:

T:

S:

29. Use the memory aid SAMPLE to help you to remember important areas of questioning regarding patient history. Write what each letter stands for.

S:

A:

M:

P:

L:

E:

30. You are with an 81-year-old patient who is complaining of nausea, aching joints, weakness, and occasional dizziness. Are the patient's complaints signs or symptoms? Explain your answer.

31. You are with a 29-year-old medical patient who says he is "not feeling very well." Write two questions you might ask for the "S" part of a SAMPLE history.

32. You are waiting for the EMTs to arrive for an adult who is having trouble breathing. After you perform an initial assessment, the patient's problem appears to have eased considerably. Write two questions you might ask for the "A" part of a SAMPLE history.

33. Your patient is elderly, confused, and frightened. A shop owner found her wandering in his store. She knows who she is and where she lives, but cannot remember why she is in the store. What might you ask for the "M" part of a SAMPLE history?

34. You are with a 50-year-old patient who is having chest pain. What might you ask for the "P" part of a SAMPLE history?

35. List the major elements of the patient hand-off report.

a.

b.

c.

d.

e.

f.

g.

h.

i.

36. Joanne's patient hand-off report includes the following: "The patient's name is Pat O'Brien. He is 32 years old, and he has a painful and swollen right leg. Pat is alert with normal airway, breathing, and circulation. I've kept his leg manually stabilized in the position in which it was found for the last 10 minutes. Pat says his pain has been somewhat relieved." What information did Joanne omit from her report?

Vocabulary Practice

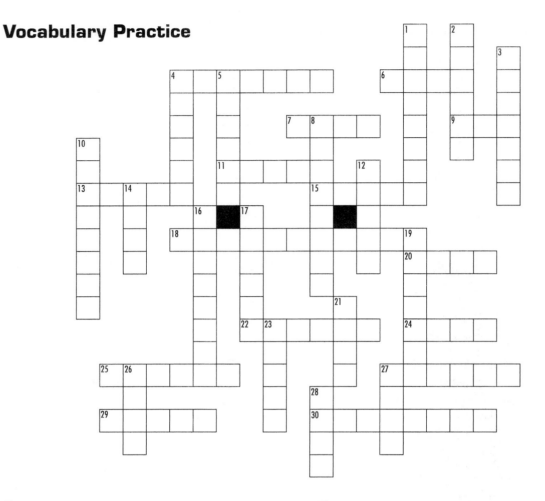

Across

4. This can be observed only by the patient.
6. A memory aid for the head-to-toe exam.
7. HEAD: check the skull, _____, and jaw.
9. Short for airway, breathing, and circulation.
11. The "A" in AVPU.
13. EXTREMITIES: check for _____, movement, and sensation.
15. CHEST: check that the sound of air entering the lungs is _____ on both sides.
18. Term meaning near the surface.
20. Use the _____ scale to assess level of responsiveness.
22. Auscultate.
24. CHEST: check the _____ for signs of deformity.
25. EXTREMITIES: check all bones and _____.
27. ABDOMEN: check the _____ (lateral sides of hips and buttocks).
29. HEAD: check for loose _____.
30. Term meaning inside.

Down

1. Term meaning near a point of reference.
2. Term meaning far from a point of reference.
3. NECK: check that the _____ is not deformed or shifted.
4. A memory aid for the patient history.
5. Term meaning toward the midline.
8. Term meaning toward the front.
10. Term meaning toward the head.
12. PELVIS: check the _____ (groin).
14. Inspect.
16. ABDOMEN: check the painful _____ last.
17. The "V" in AVPU.
19. Term meaning to the left or right of the midline.
21. Term meaning far from the surface.
23. PELVIS: check the _____ and ischium.
26. NECK or CHEST: check for _____ injuries to bandage immediately.
27. Palpate.
28. You can observe this in a patient.

The Call: A Car Crash

Read the scenario and answer the questions that follow. Focus specifically on the priorities of each of the major areas of patient assessment, from scene size-up through the patient hand-off report. Keep in mind that patient assessment answers the questions "What's going on with my patient? How can I help?" Continually ask yourself if the information you are gathering will help with the care of your patient's condition.

You are pulling a volunteer shift at the local firehouse late one night when you and one other First Responder are dispatched to a vehicle collision. You respond in the rescue truck and soon arrive at the scene of a single car rollover on a two-lane country road. There are no bystanders on scene. Your patient, a male in his 40s, has been ejected from the car and lies in the roadway face up. As your partner quickly sets out flares to protect the scene, you confirm that there are no immediate scene dangers. Then you grab your jump kit and move to the patient's side. Your partner joins you and stabilizes the patient's head and neck.

1. Your first task is to
   a. assess airway, breathing, and circulation.
   b. inspect and palpate for any major injuries.
   c. determine if the patient has a chief complaint.
   d. find out from your dispatch the ETA of the ambulance.

2. As you kneel down beside the patient, you note that he has snoring respirations and his tongue seems to be blocking his airway. The correct way to open his airway is to
   a. perform a jaw-thrust maneuver.
   b. perform a head-tilt/chin-lift maneuver.
   c. hold his head in a neutral, in-line position.
   d. use the recovery position so blood and vomit can drain more easily.

3. As you continue to assess the patient, you talk to him. He responds by calling out, speaking incoherently, and moaning. Based on this information, use the AVPU scale to describe the patient's level of responsiveness.

4. As you begin your head-to-toe exam, your patient, who had been moaning and shouting, now becomes very quiet. What should your first action be?

If you have time before the EMTs arrive, how will you perform a head-to-toe exam on this patient? Beside each area of the body, write what you would do.

5. Head:

   D:

   O:

   T:

   S:

6. Neck:

   D:

   O:

   T:

   S:

7. Chest:

   D:

   O:

   T:

   S:

8. Abdomen:

   D:

   O:

   T:

   S:

9. Back (posterior):

   D:

   O:

   T:

   S:

10. Pelvis:

    D:

    O:

    T:

    S:

11. Extremities:

    D:

    O:

    T:

    S:

Active Learning

Apply the material you have learned to a real situation. Using a fellow student, friend, or family member, complete the following exercises. Then compare your answers to the answers of other students. Talk with your instructor about your findings.

1. Listen to lung sounds in a healthy person. If someone in your family has a lung disease, listen to his or her lungs. Are there differences?

2. Find a person who has received help from the EMS system in the past. Ask his or her what happened and how the EMS personnel assessed the complaint. Ask how the patient felt while the EMS personnel examined him or her and asked questions.

3. Look at the EMS equipment you would carry into a scene where you work or volunteer (or look at the practice equipment you use in class). Describe each piece of equipment and how it is used for patient assessment.

13 | Communication and Documentation

Key Ideas

This chapter provides additional information on the types of communication and documentation expected of a First Responder. Key ideas include the following:

- First Responders have opportunities to communicate with other EMS personnel on the radio or phone as well as in person. These communications must be accurate, complete, brief, and to the point.

- First Responders must report to dispatch when en route to a call, upon arrival on scene, when additional assistance is needed, and when they return to service.

- Good communication skills can help First Responders obtain the information they need to provide proper emergency care to their patients.

- A prehospital care report is used to transfer patient information from one person to another, to provide legal documentation, and to improve the EMS system.

- Special incident reports may be required for infectious disease exposure, injury to EMS personnel, conflicts between agencies, and multiple-casualty incidents.

Exam Warm-up

1. Which of the choices below describe what a First Responder is expected to do?
   a. Update incoming EMS units.
   b. Request help from EMS dispatch.
   c. Reassure and comfort the patient.
   d. Ask medical direction for advice.
   e. Provide a hand-off report to EMTs.
   f. Obtain the patient's medical history.
   g. Determine the patient's chief complaint.

2. You are in the rescue unit and have just pulled out of the station to respond to a "man down" at a public park. You pick up your radio mike and report you are
   a. on scene.
   b. en route to the scene.
   c. available for the next call.
   d. in need of additional assistance.

3. When using a radio microphone, you should talk with your mouth _____ from the mike.
   a. 1/8 to 1/4 inch
   b. two to three inches
   c. as far away as possible
   d. about an arm-length away

4. Which of the situations listed below require special documentation?
   a. interagency conflict
   b. motorcycle collision
   c. child who choked on a hot dog
   d. exposure to blood or body fluids
   e. train derailment with 25 passengers

Short-Answer Review

5. Write five "rules" a First Responder should follow while talking on the radio.

   a.

   b.

   c.

   d.

   e.

6. You observe a fellow rescuer call for medical direction. He introduces himself by identifying his unit and the fact that he is a First Responder. He briefly outlines the reason he is calling. He then provides a brief pertinent history of the patient including the results of his assessment, the treatment he provided, and the patient's reaction to that treatment. What did he leave out?

7. The effectiveness of communication with a patient can depend on your tone of voice, body language, and approach. Four possible approaches are listed below. Write the approach taken for each of the quotes that follow.

"Teacher"—You provide information and explain things.

"Friend"—You comfort, sympathize, and empathize.

"Authority"—You take control and dictate how the call will progress.

"Advisor"—You give advice and persuade or convince the patient.

_____ **a.** From what I can tell, this swelling and deformity could indicate that you have a broken nose.

_____ **b.** I'm so sorry that you are in pain. Is there anything I can do to ease it?

_____ **c.** If you decide not to go to the hospital, it will be necessary to get the police department involved. It is imperative that you go to the hospital.

_____ **d.** I really think you ought to go to the hospital. Look at how much your family is worried. If they are worried enough to call 9-1-1, then it seems to me that you really should be checked out.

_____ **e.** Tell you what. Let's go to the hospital and get that cut stitched up, and then you will be in a better position to make a decision about what to do with your damaged car. Won't you feel better if we get your injuries taken care of first?

_____ **f.** I can imagine that your neck hurts. I realize that lying on this backboard is uncomfortable. You will be at the hospital soon. Hopefully, a doctor can get you out of this contraption quickly.

_____ **g.** At this point, your child doesn't appear to have any serious injuries. Her vital signs appear quite stable, as well. The doctor at the emergency department may want to run some tests to make sure everything is okay.

_____ **h.** Here's the plan. The only way we can get you out of this car is if you hold still while the fire department uses a pry bar to get the door open. You need to hold still.

8. List four reasons why a prehospital care report is used by First Responders.

a.

b.

c.

d.

9. Your patient, Mr. Mendez, is refusing further care even though you feel it is necessary for him. What should you document on your run report about this?

   a.

   b.

   c.

Vocabulary Practice

Match the components of a radio system with the correct description.

base station •   • radio mounted in a vehicle

mobile radio •   • rebroadcasts radio transmissions

portable radio •   • hand-held radio

repeater •   • stationary radio located in a dispatch center or hospital

The Call: PCR

Read this scenario; then fill out the prehospital care report provided. If necessary, use an additional sheet of paper for your narrative.

You are showing your new partner the ropes of East Lydius Fire and Rescue Squad when a call comes in for a single-car motor-vehicle collision at the intersection of First and Division Streets. A passerby reports that "a guy drove his car right into a tree."

As you arrive at the scene, you can see that this is a residential street with very little traffic. Your partner says, "This could be bad. The posted speed limit is 30 mph and there are no skid marks. Luckily, there are no wires or tree limbs down."

When it is safe to approach, you see a young man of about 25, who is seated behind the wheel of the car. The car engine is off. You take the key out. The patient is wearing his seat belt and the air bag is deployed. The front end of the car has some minor damage. The windshield is intact.

Several empty beer cans are on the back floor. Your partner manually stabilizes the patient's head and neck, while you talk with the patient and check him over. You ask him if he is okay and his answer is garbled. The patient continues to answer your questions, and his speech is becoming easier to understand. He says his name is Andy Kohn and that he has a terrible headache but that nothing else hurts him. Breathing is unlabored at 18 breaths per minute with good air movement. There is no odor of food or beverage on the patient's breath. You apply oxygen via nonrebreather mask. His radial pulse is strong at a rate of 68 bpm.

The patient asks if anyone else is hurt and if his car will be okay. As you prepare to take his blood pressure, you see a Medic Alert bracelet that states your patient is under Dr. Cullen's care for a seizure disorder.

First Responder Prehospital Care Report

REMO

M	D	Y
DATE

AGENCY CODE

RUN NO.

CALL REC'D

ENROUTE

AT SCENE

IN SERVICE

NAME

ADDRESS

NEXT OF KIN

PHYSICIAN

VEH. ID.

DOB

SEX ☐ M ☐ F

Ph#

AGENCY NAME

CALL LOCATION

CHIEF COMPLAINT

CALL TYPE

PAST MEDICAL HISTORY		TIME	RESP.	PULSE	B.P.	CONS
☐ HYPERTENSION ☐ STROKE ☐ SEIZURES ☐ DIABETES ☐ COPD ☐ CARDIAC ☐ ALLERGY ☐ OTHER ☐ MEDICATION (LIST IN COMMENTS)	V I T A L S I G N S		RATE ☐ Regular ☐ Shallow ☐ Labored	☐ Regular ☐ Irregular		
			RATE ☐ Regular ☐ Shallow ☐ Labored	☐ Regular ☐ Irregular		

PHYSICAL EXAM FINDINGS

TREATMENT GIVEN

DISPOSITION (SEE LIST)

DISP. CODE

CREW

NAME

DRIVER ☐ EMT # ☐ AEMT

NAME ☐ EMT # ☐ AEMT

NAME ☐ EMT # ☐ AEMT

© Regional Emergency Medical Organization, Albany, NY

Your patient tells you that he ran out of his medicine for his convulsions and was on his way to the drug store for a refill. The patient's speech is now clear and his headache is nearly gone. The EMTs arrive and you give them a hand-off report and say "Goodbye" and "Good luck" to your patient.

Active Learning

Communication and documentation are important skills. They are just as important for First Responders to master as patient assessment and care. To practice your communication and documentation skills, complete the following exercises.

1. Blindfold yourself and have a fellow student take your vital signs and medical history. First, have your partner do it without explaining what he or she is doing. Then, try it again, this time being considerate of the visual impairment. Perform the same examination while your partner is blindfolded. Compare your thoughts and feelings on the experience.

2. Using two of the medical histories you obtained from friends and family members in the last chapter, document your findings on the sample prehospital care report forms that follow this page.

First Responder Prehospital Care Report

REMO

M	D	Y

DATE

AGENCY CODE

RUN NO.

CALL REC'D

ENROUTE

AT SCENE

IN SERVICE

NAME

ADDRESS

VEH. ID.

NEXT OF KIN

PHYSICIAN

AGENCY NAME

DOB   SEX M F   Ph#

CALL LOCATION

CHIEF COMPLAINT

CALL TYPE

PAST MEDICAL HISTORY	**TIME**	**RESP.**	**PULSE**	**B.P.**	**CONS**
☐ HYPERTENSION ☐ STROKE		RATE ☐ Regular ☐ Shallow ☐ Labored	☐ Regular ☐ Irregular		
☐ SEIZURES ☐ DIABETES					
☐ COPD ☐ CARDIAC					
☐ ALLERGY ☐ OTHER					
☐ MEDICATION (LIST IN COMMENTS)					
		RATE ☐ Regular ☐ Shallow ☐ Labored	☐ Regular ☐ Irregular		

VITAL SIGNS

PHYSICAL EXAM FINDINGS

TREATMENT GIVEN

DISPOSITION (SEE LIST)

DISP. CODE

CREW

NAME   **DRIVER**   ☐ EMT ☐ AEMT #

NAME   ☐ EMT ☐ AEMT #

NAME   ☐ EMT ☐ AEMT #

First Responder Prehospital Care Report

REMO

| M | D | Y |
| DATE |

AGENCY CODE

RUN NO.

NAME

ADDRESS

VEH. ID.

NEXT OF KIN

PHYSICIAN

DOB | SEX M | F | Ph#

AGENCY NAME

CALL LOCATION

CHIEF COMPLAINT

CALL TYPE

PAST MEDICAL HISTORY	TIME	RESP.	PULSE	B.P.	CONS
❑ HYPERTENSION ❑ STROKE ❑ SEIZURES ❑ DIABETES ❑ COPD ❑ CARDIAC ❑ ALLERGY ❑ OTHER ❑ MEDICATION (LIST IN COMMENTS)	V I T A L S I G N S	RATE ❑ Regular ❑ Shallow ❑ Labored	❑ Regular ❑ Irregular		
		RATE ❑ Regular ❑ Shallow ❑ Labored	❑ Regular ❑ Irregular		

PHYSICAL EXAM FINDINGS

TREATMENT GIVEN

DISPOSITION (SEE LIST)

DISP. CODE

CREW

NAME | NAME | NAME

DRIVER ❑ EMT # ❑ AEMT | ❑ EMT # ❑ AEMT | ❑ EMT # ❑ AEMT

© Regional Emergency Medical Organization, Albany, NY

14 | Cardiac and Respiratory Emergencies

Key Ideas

This chapter describes the signs, symptoms, and First Responder care of cardiac and respiratory emergencies. Key ideas include the following:

- Any adult with pain or discomfort to the chest, neck, shoulder, arm, or jaw should be suspected of having a heart attack.

- First Responder care for patients with chest pain focuses on supporting the patient's ABCs, comforting the patient, and activating EMS as quickly as possible.

- Specific cardiac conditions include angina pectoris and acute myocardial infarction.

- Rapid treatment is necessary when disease or injury affects the body's ability to obtain oxygen.

- Respiratory distress occurs when air cannot pass easily into the lungs or has difficulty passing out of the lungs.

- First Responder care of a patient in respiratory distress focuses on supporting the patient's airway and breathing, helping the patient find a position of comfort, and activating EMS as quickly as possible.

- Specific causes of respiratory emergencies include chronic obstructive pulmonary disease, asthma, pneumonia, acute pulmonary edema, and hyperventilation.

Exam Warm-up

1. Coronary artery disease
   a. narrows the coronary artery.
   b. is unrelated to arteriosclerosis.
   c. reduces bodily pain and discomfort.
   d. increases the oxygen that goes to the heart.

2. Using the memory aid OPQRRRST can help you to
   a. get a good description of the patient's pain.
   b. perform a thorough head-to-toe physical exam.
   c. obtain a complete and relevant patient history.
   d. examine the patient for life-threatening conditions.

3. When you are managing a patient with chest pain, you should activate the EMS system
   a. if the patient truly is having a heart attack.
   b. after gathering an accurate patient history.
   c. after completing a head-to-toe exam.
   d. as soon as a possible cardiac emergency is recognized.

4. First Responder care of angina and myocardial infarction is the same as for any patient with chest pain.

   _____ True

   _____ False

5. Identify all of the following statements about angina that are TRUE.
   a. It can appear suddenly.
   b. Stress can be the cause of it.
   c. Sometimes it has no apparent cause.
   d. It causes permanent damage to the heart.
   e. Usually it is associated with physical exertion.
   f. You can tell the difference between it and a heart attack.
   g. If left untreated, it could cause a heart attack.

6. Identify all the following statements about an acute myocardial infarction that are TRUE.
   a. It means permanent death of heart muscle.
   b. It is easily distinguishable from angina.
   c. It can occur when blood to the heart is greatly reduced.
   d. It commonly occurs as a result of coronary artery disease.

7. Identify all of the symptoms listed below that are associated with a cardiac emergency.
   a. heaviness or squeezing in the chest
   b. mild to severe crushing chest pain
   c. numbness in the chest
   d. acute indigestion

8. In a cardiac emergency, men are more likely to have the classic symptom—respiratory distress.

_____ True

_____ False

9. A patient in the "tripod" position may be described as someone who is sitting _____ and fighting to breathe.
   a. bolt upright, leaning forward
   b. bent over, head between knees
   c. with one leg forward, one leg back
   d. splinting the chest with both arms

10. Identify all the conditions listed below that can cause wheezing.
    a. asthma
    b. chronic bronchitis
    c. smoke inhalation
    d. acute congestive heart failure
    e. severe allergic reaction
    f. acute pulmonary embolism

11. Which two of the following quotes about hyperventilation are TRUE?
    a. "Oxygen should never be applied to these patients. It can make them worse."
    b. "Not everyone who is breathing rapidly or deeply is hyperventilating."
    c. "When patients hyperventilate, they exhale too much carbon dioxide."
    d. "Putting a paper bag over a hyperventilator's face will cure most cases of hyperventilation."

Short-Answer Review

12. List eight risk factors for coronary artery disease.

    a.

    b.

    c.

    d.

    e.

    f.

    g.

    h.

13. List five signs and symptoms that may indicate a patient has a cardiac problem.

    a.

    b.

    c.

    d.

    e.

14. Write the word that each letter in OPQRRRST helps you to recall.

    O:

    P:

    Q:

    R:

    R:

    R:

    S:

    T:

15. You find your neighbor sitting on a couch, stating that he's having chest pain and difficulty breathing. After you activate the EMS system, you begin to comfort and reassure the patient. You then perform the following steps. Number them 1–6 in the correct order.

    _____ **a.** Loosen tight clothing and maintain body temperature.

    _____ **b.** Ensure adequate breathing.

    _____ **c.** Place him in a position of comfort.

    _____ **d.** Have the patient cease all movement.

    _____ **e.** Administer high-flow oxygen if breathing is adequate. If breathing is not adequate, assist ventilations.

    _____ **f.** Monitor the patient carefully, and be prepared to perform CPR and to use an AED if necessary.

16. You respond in your rescue unit to an "unknown medical problem." You find a 63-year-old woman who says that she is experiencing nausea, dizziness, and slight shortness of breath. These symptoms came on suddenly while she was watching television. She has a history of "heart problems" and edema in her legs but has never had a heart attack. She says she recently got over the flu. Your partner turns to you and says, "Sounds like the flu to me. She's not having any chest pain, so I don't think she's having a cardiac problem." Agree? Disagree? Explain.

17. List seven general signs and symptoms of respiratory distress.

    a.

    b.

    c.

    d.

    e.

    f.

    g.

18. List four general guidelines for First Responder care of a patient in respiratory distress.

    a.

    b.

    c.

    d.

19. You and your partner respond to a 67-year-old male complaining of shortness of breath. He suffers from emphysema. You find your patient sitting bolt upright, speaking in three- and four-word sentences, breathing 30 times per minute, so you apply high-flow oxygen by non-rebreather mask. Your partner states: "Remember, this guy may be a hypoxic-drive breather. We need to keep his oxygen at four liters per minute by cannula. We don't want him to stop breathing." Agree? Disagree? Explain.

Vocabulary Practice

Complete the crossword puzzle. HINT: The clues in capital letters refer to the memory aid OPQRRRST and what each letter stands for.

Across

2. A patient with shortness of breath may be in respiratory _____.
7. R—DOES THE PAIN BEGIN IN ONE PLACE AND THEN MOVE?
11. P—DID ANYTHING CAUSE OR START THE PAIN?
13. Short for automated external defibrillator.
16. T—HOW LONG HAVE YOU HAD THE PAIN?
17. S—HOW BAD IS THE PAIN?
19. Q—WHAT IS THE PAIN LIKE?
21. Pain in the lower center _____ may be a sign of heart attack.
22. A feeling of impending _____ may be a sign of a cardiac emergency.

Down

1. Short for myocardial infarction.
3. Sudden onset of profuse _____ may be a sign of a cardiac emergency.
4. R—WHERE IS THE PAIN?
5. Pain here may be a sign of heart attack.
6. O—WHEN DID THE PAIN BEGIN?
8. Pain between the _____ blades may be a sign of heart attack.
9. Short for cardiopulmonary resuscitation.
10. A heart attack without pain is called this.
12. Short for chronic obstructive pulmonary disease.
14. A cardiac risk factor.
15. R—DOES ANYTHING RELIEVE THE PAIN?
18. A patient who is fighting to breathe might sit in this position.
20. Pain here may be a sign of heart attack.

The Call: Patient with a Cardiac Emergency

Read the scenario and answer the questions that follow. Remember that heart attacks and other cardiac emergencies can present with a variety of signs and symptoms.

After activation of the EMS system, you respond to the eighth hole of the local golf course where a male in his 60s has reportedly collapsed. You arrive at the green and are pulling your jump kit and AED out of the back of the golf cart when one of the patient's friends approaches you. "I kept telling George that he ought to get out of the sun and take a break, but he wouldn't listen. He's got a heart problem. They put an automatic heart shocker thing in a couple of years ago. We were just finishing this hole when he sort of grabbed his chest, stumbled, and passed out on the green."

You approach the patient, who is lying on his side on the green, concerned friends around him. "Is George awake?" you ask.

"I don't think so," answers one of his friends.

1. Your first action should be to
   a. open George's airway.
   b. check George for a pulse.
   c. confirm that George is still breathing.
   d. determine George's level of responsiveness.

2. You find that George is awake but very anxious, with a patent airway, respirations 32, pulse 32, and blood pressure 66/32. His skin is pale, cool, and moist. George should probably be placed in which one of the following positions?
   a. shock position
   b. prone position
   c. recovery position
   d. supine position

3. You attempt to place a nonrebreather mask on George. He is quite combative and tries to prevent you from placing the mask on his face. Why is George so combative?

4. After you have applied oxygen, you attempt to gather a patient history. List at least five questions to which you should get answers.

   a.

   b.

   c.

   d.

   e.

5. As you are gathering a patient history from the patient, he suddenly becomes very quiet. "George?" you call to him. There is no answer. "George!" you shout. Still there is no answer. To decide if you have to defibrillate, you must perform the following steps. Your AED is immediately available. Number them 1–7 in the correct order.

_____ Lay George flat on his back on the golf green.

_____ Give two, full breaths over one second each.

_____ Check the carotid pulse and determine pulselessness.

_____ Open the airway.

_____ Attach the defibrillator.

_____ Determine that George is not breathing.

_____ Shake George to verify unresponsiveness.

6. After the AED delivers its first shock to George's heart, you are able to feel a carotid pulse. You continue with artificial ventilation until the paramedics arrive. After they take over, you give them a report. Write your hand-off report below, being sure to include your original assessment of George, his status change, and the care you provided.

Active Learning

1. Speak to a relative (parent or grandparent, for example) or neighbor who has a respiratory problem. Ask:
   a. What does having difficulty breathing feel like?
   b. When your condition worsens or you have an attack, how do you know?
   c. What makes your breathing better when you have trouble breathing?
   d. What medications do you take?

2. Speak to a relative (parent or grandparent, for example) who has a heart problem or who has had a heart attack. Ask:
   a. What did the pain feel like when you had a heart attack or chest pain?
   b. What medications do you take?

15 | Medical Emergencies

Key Ideas

This chapter focuses on common medical complaints other than cardiac and respiratory emergencies. These complaints include general medical complaints such as "I don't feel well," an altered mental status, poisoning, and abdominal pain and distress. Key ideas include the following:

- There are many medical reasons for an altered mental status. The most common are diabetic emergencies, stroke, and seizures. Altered mental status can range from mildly disoriented to combative to unresponsive. An accurate history should include when the patient last ate, what type of medication the patient has taken, and when it was taken. This information can give the hospital staff clues to the underlying problem. First Responder care focuses on assessing and monitoring the patient's airway and breathing, and administering oxygen.

- First Responder care for both hyperglycemia and hypoglycemia focuses on supporting the patient's airway and breathing and, if permitted, the administration of sugar.

- All abdominal pain should be taken seriously. Any abdominal pain that is persistent or is significant enough for the patient or family to call for assistance should be considered an emergency. First Responder care consists of ensuring an open airway and adequate breathing, administering oxygen, and staying alert for signs of shock.

- An accurate history of a poisoning includes determining the route of the poisoning, the amount of poison that has entered the patient's body, and when the exposure occurred. Top priority in a poisoning emergency is the patient's airway. If EMS resources are delayed, call the regional poison control center or medical direction for instructions.

Exam Warm-up

1. When your patient's chief complaint is as general as "I feel weak," you should proceed with your patient assessment plan the same as you would for any patient.

   _____ True

   _____ False

2. When a patient finds it difficult to understand what you are saying, he has an altered mental status.

   _____ True

   _____ False

3. Sometimes unusual responses or unusual behaviors are normal for a patient.

   _____ True

   _____ False

4. From the list below identify possible causes of altered mental status.
   a. Decreased levels of oxygen in the blood
   b. Low blood sugar
   c. Stroke
   d. Seizures
   e. Fever
   f. Infection
   g. Poisoning
   h. Head injury
   i. Psychiatric conditions

5. Which one of the following items about First Responder care of patients with an altered mental status is TRUE?
   a. Don't frighten them by saying you called an ambulance.
   b. Avoid asking questions to get a patient history.
   c. Be gentle and empathetic, truthful and kind.
   d. Explain that everything will be okay.

6. The human body needs both oxygen and sugar to produce the energy that sustains it.

   _____ True

   _____ False

7. A condition in which a patient has too little blood sugar is called
   a. hypothermia.
   b. hypoglycemia.
   c. hyperglycemia.
   d. hyperchondria.

8. A condition in which a patient has too much blood sugar is called
   a. hypothermia.
   b. hypoglycemia.
   c. hyperglycemia.
   d. hyperchondria

9. Read the statements below. Which ones are NOT appropriate to make in front of a stroke patient?
   a. It looks like this patient had "the big one." Weird vital signs, paralysis on one side . . . Nope, Mr. Gonzalez does not look good.
   b. Mr. Gonzalez, I can see that you are having trouble speaking. I'll be able to provide you with better care if you try harder to speak more clearly.
   c. Mr. Gonzalez, I think you are having a stroke. It looks like it's pretty bad, so I'm going to get you to the hospital.
   d. Mr. Gonzalez, let's arrange for a ride over to the hospital. I know that you're concerned about not being able to speak clearly, so I'm going to have a doctor check you out.

10. Of all causes of seizure listed below, which one is the MOST common in infants and children?
    a. hypoglycemia
    b. stroke
    c. infection
    d. fever

11. Which two of the following items about status epilepticus are TRUE?
    a. Two or three seizures occur within a few hours of one another.
    b. A single seizure lasts longer than 30 minutes.
    c. A series of seizures occur in rapid progression.
    d. A single seizure lasts longer than 10 minutes

12. The post-seizure phase is characterized by
    a. unusual smell or flash of light that lasts a split second.
    b. unresponsiveness followed by extreme muscle rigidity.
    c. violent jerking of the arms and legs.
    d. deep sleep with gradual recovery.

13. Which of the following directions about proper assessment of a patient with abdominal distress are CORRECT?
    a. The initial assessment is the first priority.
    b. Gather a good patient history.
    c. Determine whether the patient is restless or quiet.
    d. Find out if movement causes pain.
    e. Check to see if the abdomen is distended.
    f. Note if the patient can relax the abdominal wall.
    g. Palpate the abdomen gently.
    h. Examine the area of pain first.
    i. Determine if the abdomen is rigid or soft.
    j. Stay alert for signs of shock.

14. Your patient is suffering from abdominal pain and is complaining of feeling nauseated. If appropriate, you should place the patient in a _____ position.
    a. supine
    b. left lateral
    c. prone
    d. shock

15. Activated charcoal may be used with syrup of ipecac in cases of severe poisoning.

    _____ True

    _____ False

16. Which one of the following statements about activated charcoal is TRUE?
    a. It is effective against all inhaled and injected poisons.
    b. It is very absorbent, which means it binds with poisons in the stomach.
    c. It may be effective five hours after poison ingestion.
    d. It should be given along with syrup of ipecac.

17. Common signs and symptoms of poisoning by absorption include all of the following EXCEPT
    a. itching or irritation.
    b. redness, rash, or blisters.
    c. abdominal pain or discomfort.
    d. liquid or powder on the skin.

18. Rescuers have responded to an attempted suicide. They are told that the patient has closed her garage and is sitting inside it in her car with the engine idling. What should the rescuers do first?
    a. Remove the patient from the garage immediately.
    b. Attempt to ventilate the garage.
    c. Put on a self-contained breathing apparatus.
    d. Apply 100% oxygen to the patient.

Short-Answer Review

19. Describe First Responder care for a patient who has a general complaint such as "I don't feel well."

20. What questions might you ask to find out if your patient has an altered mental status?

21. It's about two o'clock in the morning. You and your partner spot two young men in their 20s standing in front of a bar. One of them waves you over. "Hey, this is my friend Matt. He isn't acting right. He looks drunk, but I've been with him all night and we only had a couple of beers." When you ask the patient what's wrong, he tells you he's feeling dizzy. You observe that his speech is slurred and he is staggering. How should you proceed?

22. Why is it especially important to get an accurate history from a patient with an altered mental status?

23. You and your partner are managing a patient with an altered mental status. The patient has a history of diabetes. You move to apply oxygen to the patient, and your partner says, "Don't bother. This guy is a diabetic. He needs sugar, not oxygen." Do you agree or disagree with this statement? Explain your answer.

24. When blood sugar is too low or too high, the body reacts. The most common reaction is

25. The patients described below are suffering from either hypoglycemia or hyperglycemia. Decide which condition for each patient. Write in the spaces provided.

_____ **a.** A patient takes more than the prescribed dose of insulin.

_____ **b.** A patient exercises more strenuously than usual.

_____ **c.** A patient with diabetes injects too little insulin.

_____ **d.** A patient eats too many sugary foods.

_____ **e.** A patient skips lunch in preparation for a big dinner.

26. Write nine signs and symptoms that could indicate a patient is suffering from hypoglycemia or hyperglycemia.

a.

b.

c.

d.

e.

f.

g.

h.

i.

27. During scene size-up, what four observations might you make in the home of a patient who has diabetes?

    a.

    b.

    c.

    d.

28. You are assessing a 28-year-old man who is wearing a medallion around his neck that says he has diabetes. He was found wandering aimlessly in the street. He is now awake but slightly confused and slow to answer your questions. List five questions you could ask this patient to gather information about his emergency.

    a.

    b.

    c.

    d.

    e.

29. Describe the rule regarding the administration of sugar to patients. Is it necessary to confirm that the patient is specifically hypoglycemic or hyperglycemic before administering sugar? Explain.

30. Patients who are at risk for stroke include

    a.

    b.

    c.

31. Explain the difference between a transient ischemic attack (TIA) and a stroke.

32. List three types of signs or symptoms a patient who has had a stroke might exhibit. Give an example of each one.

    a.

    b.

    c.

33. Evaluate the following statements regarding stroke and the treatment for stroke. Write "agree" or "disagree" beneath each one. If you disagree with the statement, explain.

    a. Provide the same emergency care you would provide to any patient with an altered mental status.

    b. You need not be especially alert to the patient's airway or breathing status, because stroke usually affects only the limbs, speech, or facial muscles.

    c. If you suspect stroke in a patient, take a carotid pulse and radial pulse on both sides of the body.

    d. Do not talk to the stroke patient during emergency care, especially if the patient cannot communicate. His or her inability to respond to you will only frighten the patient further.

34. You have responded to a six-year-old with possible seizures. One of the parents tells you that the child has been having seizures "on and off for most of the day." When you inquire about what the seizures look like, he tells you: "Oh, he's probably had 10 to 20 seizures today." Your partner grows quite concerned and says, "Sounds like status epilepticus to me," and rushes off to get the airway and oxygen equipment. Does his response seem appropriate? Why or why not?

35. List at least four questions that will help you gather pertinent information about a seizure patient.

a.

b.

c.

d.

36. You have responded to a man reportedly in seizure. You arrive at the entrance to an alleyway and notice a patient lying against a building about 30 feet away, still in seizure. A witness tells you that the patient fell to the ground and struck his head when his seizure began. To manage this patient, number the following actions 1–6 in the correct order.

a. Perform a head-to-toe exam to look for any trauma, incontinence, medical identification bracelets, and so on.

b. Size up the scene. Check for hazards and any clues that might explain his seizures.

c. Protect the patient's head until the seizure stops.

d. When the seizure stops, provide manual stabilization of the patient's head and neck.

e. Attempt to gather a medical history from the patient.

f. Perform an initial assessment and provide treatment as appropriate.

37. Describe the type of approach you think would be most effective for communicating with a post-seizure patient who is still somewhat disoriented.

38. List six signs and symptoms of abdominal pain and distress.

a.

b.

c.

d.

e.

f.

39. List four major routes by which patients are poisoned, and give an example for each.

a.

b.

c.

d.

40. Your neighbor has just banged on your door, stating that her two-year-old ate a handful of mouse poison. You call 9-1-1 and run over to your neighbor's house to help. List four questions you would ask your neighbor in order to gather a good patient history about the event.

a.

b.

c.

d.

41. You have responded to a residence where it appears that a woman in her 40s has been exposed to carbon monoxide from a faulty kerosene heater. She is experiencing headaches, dizziness, and chest tightness. Since she has been removed from the house, she states that her symptoms are clearing up. Your partner says that he feels okay releasing her to follow up with her personal physician. Do you agree or disagree with this decision? Explain.

Vocabulary Practice

Circle the words or terms that are related to medical emergencies and write them on the lines below the puzzle.

```
A E P C I C H L O R I N E G A S E S M N
G B A O Y N X T J X B Q W M S K U S O S
U C S C I A S I J M K K I T O L Y I U C
A A H O T S N U P T F I I R O R T T A A
R R Y M R I O I L C T N T B U C A P B R
D B P I Q P V N D I J S M E E T C H R B
I O O N L P T A I E N E N J S I K N A O
N N G I U B N I T N R A N L N J N B I N
G M L S H O F S O E G I A Z E X G F N D
P O Y T V V Y I C N D T W E X Z Y V A I
O N C R Q Z G T S N N C D G U V O E T O
S O E O P V A U O E V I H I L K L W T X
I X M K K I B I M G R M N A A U N C A I
T I I E X M T D H V T C G G R B C U C D
I D A O O A E U W W B Z M O E C E O K E
O E P R L R U L Z V Y Q R P D S O T S K
N Y H A E C O L I C K Y P A I N T A E E
H T H T H Y P E R G L Y C E M I A I L S
K N L C E R E B R O V A S C U L A R O T
I A S T A T U S E P I L E P T I C U S N
```

1. _____	10. _____	19. _____
2. _____	11. _____	20. _____
3. _____	12. _____	21. _____
4. _____	13. _____	22. _____
5. _____	14. _____	23. _____
6. _____	15. _____	24. _____
7. _____	16. _____	25. _____
8. _____	17. _____	26. _____
9. _____	18. _____	27. _____

The Call: Altered Mental Status

Read this scenario and answer the questions that follow. Pay attention to the signs and symptoms that indicate this patient has experienced some type of significant brain problem.

It's dinnertime at the station. You and the rest of the volunteer fire squad are getting ready to sit down to finish off some meatballs and spaghetti when you are dispatched to a "male in his 60s, unknown medical problem." You arrive at a residence and are flagged down by the patient's wife. "John just collapsed in the kitchen," she states as you pull your equipment from the truck. "He's awake now, but he doesn't seem right. Nothing like this has ever happened before."

She tells you that John was washing his hands at the sink when he stumbled back against a counter and slid down to a sitting position. He "just stared off into space" for at least a minute. He then appeared to become somewhat aware of his surroundings, but was unable to speak or move his left side. You find John still sitting on the kitchen floor. He looks at you as you approach, but does not speak.

1. As you complete your assessment of John, you find he is able to move all extremities and he has begun to speak clearly. "What happened, Grace?" he asks his wife. Describe a life-threatening condition that could still occur to John based on what you know about his condition.

2. After a few minutes, you observe that John seems to be responding better. He seems to be alert and able to speak normally. List five questions that you could ask him in order to better understand his collapse and current condition.

   a.

   b.

   c.

   d.

   e.

3. After establishing that John is alert and oriented, what other signs or symptoms should you reassess?

4. When the EMT-Paramedics arrive, they take over emergency care of John. He tells them that he feels fine and does not want to wear any oxygen or go to the hospital. Do you agree with him? Explain your answer.

Active Learning

1. Have a classmate role-play a seizing patient. While the "patient" is actively seizing, consider these questions:
   a. How would you manage the airway during the seizure?
   b. How would you position the patient and protect him or her from injury?
   c. How much care would you be able to provide during the seizure?

2. Now, let your partner have a turn. Role-play the seizing patient for him or her.

16 | Environmental Emergencies

Key Ideas

This chapter focuses on recognizing the causes, signs and symptoms, and emergency care of heat and cold emergencies, as well as poisonous and nonpoisonous snake, insect, spider, and scorpion bites, insect stings, and poisoning by common marine life. Key ideas include the following:

- The human body is constantly trying to maintain its average core temperature of around 98.6°F (37°C).

- In the cold, the body holds onto its heat by constricting blood vessels near its surface. Also, hair erects, thickening the layer of warm air trapped near the skin. The body can produce more heat, if needed, by shivering and by producing certain hormones such as epinephrine.

- The body loses heat through convection, conduction, radiation, evaporation, and respiration.

- Cold-related emergencies include generalized hypothermia and local cold injuries. First Responder care focuses on supporting the patient's ABCs and rewarming as appropriate.

- Heat-related emergencies include heat cramps, heat exhaustion, and heat stroke. First Responder care for these emergencies focuses on supporting the patient's ABCs and cooling the patient as necessary.

- Poisonous snakebites are considered medical emergencies. Only about one-third of all bites manifest symptoms. When symptoms do develop, they appear quickly.

- Priorities in treating snakebites and other venomous bites and stings focus on supporting the patient's ABCs, limiting the spread of the venom, and arranging for transport without delay.

- In most cases, insect bites and stings can be treated by removing the stinger, cleaning the wound thoroughly, and applying cold to the site to reduce inflammation and pain.

- First Responder care of venomous marine animal bites and stings focuses on slowing the spread of the toxin, removing any stingers or barbs, irrigating and washing the wound, and applying heat to deactivate the toxin.

Exam Warm-up

1. Shivering is
   a. a sign of the brain being deprived of oxygen.
   b. the body's attempt to generate heat.
   c. a normal finding in hyperthermia.
   d. a life-threatening condition.

2. When the body loses more heat than it can produce, ___ may occur.
   a. hypoglycemia
   b. hyperthermia
   c. hypothermia
   d. hyperglycemia

3. Infants and children are better able to maintain body temperature than adults are.

   _____ True

   _____ False

4. When managing an unresponsive hypothermic patient, check the pulse for _____ seconds before starting CPR.
   a. 15
   b. 30
   c. 45
   d. 60

5. Identify the three items that are NOT appropriate care for a patient with generalized hypothermia.
   a. Massage cold extremities gently.
   b. Comfort, calm, and reassure the patient.
   c. Have the patient sip a hot drink or hot soup.
   d. Remove the patient from the cold environment.
   e. Administer warm, humidified oxygen if possible.
   f. Allow the patient to walk to stimulate circulation.
   g. Remove wet clothing, and cover the patient with a blanket.

6. Exposure to extreme cold for a short time or moderate cold for a long time can cause hyperthermia.

   _____ True

   _____ False

7. The patient with mild hypothermia will present with _____ and will still be alert.
   a. cold skin and shivering
   b. fixed and dilated pupils
   c. extremely slow pulse rate
   d. extremely slow breathing rate

8. It is recommended that heat packs be applied to the neck, armpits, and groin of a mildly hypothermic patient.

_____ True

_____ False

9. One sign of an early or superficial local cold injury is
   a. swelling and blistering.
   b. mottled and cyanotic skin.
   c. the skin is firm to the touch.
   d. blanching when skin is touched lightly.

10. First Responder care of a late or deep local cold injury includes all of the following EXCEPT
    a. rewarm it by soaking in 105°F water.
    b. cover it with a dry cloth or dressings.
    c. manually stabilize the injured extremity.
    d. monitor the patient for signs of hypothermia.

11. When the body cannot get rid of excess heat, _____ may occur.
    a. hypoglycemia
    b. hyperthermia
    c. hypothermia
    d. hyperglycemia

12. A patient with moist, pale, and normal-to-cool skin has the very serious and life-threatening condition known as heat stroke.

_____ True

_____ False

13. You are called to a snakebite incident. As you pull up near the residence, you spot an older man waving you down. As you prepare to exit your vehicle, what is your first priority?
    a. Ensure scene safety.
    b. Perform an initial assessment.
    c. Identify the mechanism of injury.
    d. Form a general impression of the patient.

14. A rapidly developing, life-threatening condition that results from an allergic reaction to a bite or sting is called
    a. anaphylactic shock.
    b. shortness of breath.
    c. altered mental status.
    d. automated defibrillation.

15. You should position the site of a bite or sting _____ the level of the patient's heart.
    a. slightly above
    b. slightly below
    c. to the right of
    d. to the left of

16. If at any time during First Responder care of a patient who has been bitten or stung you suspect an allergic reaction, you should _____ immediately.
    a. inform EMS dispatch
    b. apply cold compresses
    c. immobilize the extremity
    d. apply a constricting band

17. Your patient has had a venomous snakebite to her arm. The bite occurred about five minutes ago. You have performed your initial assessment, and now find the bitten area is swollen, red, and quite painful. Your patient is extremely agitated, crying, and shaking. Which one of the following should be your next action?
    a. Calm her, instruct her to lie still, and position her arm below the level of her heart.
    b. Wipe the affected area with alcohol, peroxide, or other mild antiseptic.
    c. Suction the bite using an approved suction device.
    d. Place a constricting band above the bite.

18. A constricting band should be applied no more than _____ minutes after a patient was bitten by a snake.
    a. 10
    b. 30
    c. 50
    d. 70

19. Apply a constricting band _____ inch(es) above the site of the snakebite.
    a. 0 to 1
    b. 2 to 4
    c. 6 to 8
    d. 8 to 12

20. Identify all the characteristics below that indicate a snake may be poisonous.
    a. small, sharp teeth
    b. two large, hollow fangs
    c. pits between its eyes and mouth
    d. triangular head larger than its neck
    e. shapes on a background of white skin

21. Which one of the following treatments should NOT be performed on a patient who has received a coral-snake bite?
    a. Provide mouth-to-mask ventilation with supplemental oxygen.
    b. Administer 100% oxygen by way of nonrebreather mask.
    c. Suction debris and excess fluids from the airway.
    d. Suction venom from the bite with an extractor.

22. The venom sac attached to a bee stinger can continue to secrete venom into a patient's skin for up to _____ minutes.
    a. 5
    b. 10
    c. 15
    d. 20

Short-Answer Review

23. There are five stages of hypothermia. Each one can progress to the next, more serious stage. Number the stages 1–5 to show the order of worsening hypothermia.

_____ a. apathy and decreased muscle function

_____ b. decreased level of responsiveness

_____ c. death

_____ d. decreased vital signs

_____ e. shivering

24. Your patient is a 35-year-old woman who was found stumbling along a hiker's trail. She is slightly disoriented and complaining of stiff joints and weakness. She appears to be clumsy, confused, and forgetful. Her skin is cold to the touch. Given this information, list five questions you would want to ask for a SAMPLE history.

a.

b.

c.

d.

e.

25. List three risk factors that contribute to a patient's vulnerability to generalized hypothermia.

a.

b.

c.

26. Indicate whether each sentence describes mild hypothermia or severe hypothermia. Write "mild" or "severe" beside each one.

_____ a. Patient is shivering uncontrollably.

_____ b. Patient states he is quite cold.

_____ c. Patient is awake but disoriented as to person, place, and time.

_____ d. Patient responds to questions slowly but appropriately.

_____ e. Patient has a slowed pulse rate and respiratory rate.

_____ f. Patient has an increased pulse rate and blood pressure.

_____ g. Patient's speech does not make sense.

_____ h. Patient's movements are normal but uncoordinated.

_____ i. Patient has muscular rigidity.

27. You are extricating a severely hypothermic patient from a mountainous region. As you are lifting the stretcher into the ambulance, one member of the rescue party accidentally slams the side of the stretcher. Your partner shouts, "Hey! Be more careful! What are you trying to do, kill the guy?" Why would your partner say this? Why is it so important to handle a severely hypothermic patient gently?

28. Explain briefly how each factor listed below contributes to hyperthermia.

a. Climate:

b. Exercise and activity:

c. Drugs and alcohol:

d. Age and medical condition:

29. List five signs and symptoms of a heat-related emergency.

   a.

   b.

   c.

   d.

   e.

30. You are managing a 27-year-old runner who has dropped out of a mini-marathon after becoming dizzy and nauseous. He presents with pale, cool, and extremely wet skin, headache, weakness, and a rapid pulse. Describe the steps for treating this type of emergency.

31. You are called to a bite or sting emergency. To protect your own safety and the safety of others at the scene, what questions related to safety should you consider? Write three examples.

   a.

   b.

   c.

32. Write the general signs and symptoms of bites and stings that are NOT life-threatening.

33. List the respiratory signs and symptoms of an allergic reaction to a bite or sting.

34. General guidelines for First Responder care of a patient with a bite or sting include the following steps. Write 1–7 to show the correct order in which they should be performed.

_____ **a.** Apply a cold pack to the wound site.

_____ **b.** If a stinger is present in the wound, remove it.

_____ **c.** If breathing is adequate, administer oxygen.

_____ **d.** Inspect the bite or sting site.

_____ **e.** Perform an initial assessment, and treat all life threats.

_____ **f.** Position the injured limb, and manually stabilize it.

_____ **g.** Wash the area around the bite or sting.

35. Critique the following quotes. Write "agree" or "disagree" after each one. If you disagree, write your reasons.

a. "This guy was just bitten by a rattlesnake. See if you can get some ice cubes, and we'll ice down the bite."

b. "It's been about 35 minutes or so since John was bitten by that diamondback rattler. We won't need the suction kit. Let's keep him calm, keep the limb stabilized, and get him to the hospital."

c. "The constricting band needs to be tighter. I can still feel a radial pulse at the wrist."

36. You have just returned home from a day-long hike in the woods with several of your friends. When one of them removes his shirt, you see that a tick has attached itself to his belly. To remove it you should:

37. Your eight-year-old son has just been bitten by a yellow jacket. After your initial assessment, you remove the stinger. Explain how.

Vocabulary Practice

1. Write the following terms beside their correct definitions and examples. Each term may be used more than once.

convection   conduction   radiation   evaporation

_____ a. This is the transfer of heat from the surface of one object to the surface of another object without physical contact.

_____ b. Heat loss occurs through this process when one sweats.

_____ c. Cold air that touches the skin is warmed and then replaced by other, cooler molecules of air.

_____ d. Wind chill relates to this process.

_____ e. Body heat is pulled away 240 times faster by this process when one's clothes are wet.

_____ f. Covering the head, hands, and feet will reduce heat loss through this method.

_____ g. This method of heat loss is only effective when air humidity is relatively low.

2. Write the correct term beside the statement that best describes the signs and symptoms that result from its bite or sting. Each term may be used only once.

tick   stingray   tarantula
mite   scorpion   black widow spider
bee   fire ant   brown recluse spider

_____ a. Its bite causes pain and spasm in the large muscle groups, leading to respiratory failure and death.

_____ b. Its bite causes intense itching, with the site often enlarging to form nodes lasting two or three weeks.

_____ c. Its sting is potentially fatal, usually occurs on victim's hands, and leads to drooling, poor coordination, incontinence, and seizures.

_____ d. It bites and stings downward as it pivots, producing extremely painful fluid-filled vesicles.

_____ e. Its bite can lead to a large ulceration, fever, joint pain, nausea, vomiting, and chills.

_____ **f.** Unlike the black widow, this spider's bite causes only moderate pain; other symptoms are very rare.

_____ **g.** An allergic reaction—sometimes severe—to this "garden variety" insect's sting is not uncommon.

_____ **h.** Its bite can lead to Rocky Mountain spotted fever, Lyme disease, and other serious bacterial problems.

_____ **i.** It can leave a painful spine embedded in the patient's skin that should be stabilized in place before transport.

The Call: Hyperthermia at a Structure Fire

Read the scenario and answer the questions that follow. Bear in mind that hyperthermic emergencies can happen even to healthy, fit patients.

You have responded to the scene of a structure fire. It is a hot day, and firefighters are battling a blaze that has fully engulfed a two-story home. You report to the incident commander who directs you to a firefighter who is sitting on the tailboard of one of the fire engines. He has stripped off his turnout jacket and helmet and appears somewhat dazed.

"How are you doing?" you ask the firefighter.

He stares at you blankly for a moment. "Fine. I'm just fine." He appears to be quite hot.

"How about if I just check you out. Your captain seems to think you may have gotten too hot."

"No, I'm fine, really. I just need to sit for a minute. That's all."

1. How should you respond to the firefighter at this point? Why?

2. When you examine the firefighter, you find that he is very hot to the touch, with respirations of 36, strong pulse of 120, and blood pressure at 92/76. As you complete your exam, he vomits. You continue to talk to him and observe he is becoming more confused. What do you suspect this patient is suffering from?

3. Another firefighter looks at your patient and states, "Get Frank some water. He looks like he could drink a gallon." Do you agree with this request? Disagree? Explain your answer.

4. List steps for First Responder care of this patient.

The Call: Back-Country Snakebite

Read the scenario and answer the questions that follow. Be careful to assess the patient's status when trying to decide which interventions would be most helpful. Think about early vs. late signs of pit-viper envenomation, and how these signs may progress as the patient worsens.

You are out on horseback patrolling a hiking area in a mountainous region. You carry a First Responder bag equipped with bandaging materials, manual suction, airway devices, BVM, a small oxygen tank, and a radio. You are about 15 miles from the main campground and ranger station. As you round the bend on a hiking trail, you come upon a frantic scene. Two exhausted hikers are stumbling along, carrying a third hiker who appears disoriented. They spot you and scream, "Quick! Jack's been bitten by a rattlesnake! He's bad! You've got to help us!"

You quickly dismount and help them carry Jack to a shady spot. "Jack was bouldering with us, and he was bitten by a small rattlesnake about an hour ago," explains one of Jack's friends. Jack's hand is swollen and discolored and has two puncture marks on the back. Jack appears pale and sweaty. He responds to you verbally, but seems confused and dazed.

1. Your first action should be to
   a. apply a constricting band to Jack's arm.
   b. report to dispatch and request transport for Jack.
   c. administer oxygen to Jack via nonrebreather mask.
   d. suction the wound to remove any remaining venom.

2. You further assess Jack and find that his radial pulses are very weak and rapid. He is breathing 36 times per minute. He has vomited twice, according to his friends, and has retched several times since you began emergency care. The correct position in which to place Jack is
   a. recovery position.
   b. a position of comfort.
   c. supine with legs elevated.
   d. sitting up with legs dangling.

3. Your dispatcher is checking into the availability of a helicopter. The trail to the station is wide enough for a ranger vehicle, but it is quite bumpy. If available, the advanced life support helicopter is about 20 minutes of flight time to you and another 20 minutes of flight time back to the hospital. How do you want to evacuate Jack? Set out a plan for evacuating him, taking into account contingency plans if one form of transportation fails.

4. Jack's level of responsiveness is decreasing. He is now responsive only to painful stimuli. His vital signs are pulse 136, respirations 8, BP 76/44. Describe your plan for treating Jack. Do you want to ventilate him with a BVM? Continue high-flow oxygen via nonrebreather mask? Attempt to insert a nasopharyngeal or oropharyngeal airway? Explain.

Active Learning

1. Go to weather.com on the Internet and determine the coldest and warmest days in your area. What was the wind chill on the coldest days? What was the heat index on the warmest days? How do you think each would affect patients?

2. Do you have poisonous snakes in your area? If so, which ones? What is the specific care for each type of snakebite?

17 | Psychological Emergencies and Crisis Intervention

Key Ideas

This chapter provides an overview of First Responder care for patients who are having behavioral and psychological emergencies. It includes discussion about drug and alcohol emergencies, as well as rape and sexual assault. Key ideas include the following:

- In emergencies of any kind, the people involved are susceptible to emotional injury.

- A behavioral emergency is one in which a patient exhibits "abnormal" behavior, or behavior that is unacceptable or intolerable to the patient, family, or community.

- A behavioral emergency may be the result of a physical illness or injury.

- Psychological care of patients means that you are accepting and helpful, not critical or judgmental.

- Assessing your patient for a possible behavioral emergency should be part of every scene size-up.

- Because signs and symptoms vary so widely and are so similar to many medical conditions, the most reliable indications of a drug- or alcohol-related emergency are likely to come from the scene and the patient history.

- Patients who are suffering from an alcohol or drug overdose are a high priority for transport to a hospital.

- Rape and sexual assault involve both emotional and physical trauma, as well as significant legal issues. When you care for such a patient, remember that his or her coping system has already been stressed to the limit by the attack. Supporting the patient is of critical importance.

Exam Warm-up

1. A behavioral emergency may best be defined as one in which a patient exhibits _____ behavior that is _____ to the patient, family, or community.
   a. abnormal, unacceptable
   b. normal, unacceptable
   c. unacceptable, normal
   d. acceptable, normal

2. You are dealing with a patient who is refusing care for a life-threatening problem. Which one of the following should you NOT do?
   a. Restrain the patient and provide lifesaving care.
   b. Inform the patient of the risks of refusing care.
   c. Adequately document the patient's refusal of care.
   d. Attempt to find out why the patient is refusing care.

3. Which two of the following First Responder quotes represent an effective means of managing a patient who has stated, "I just want to kill myself."
   a. "You don't really want to kill yourself. There's so much to live for. Can't you focus on all the good things in your life?"
   b. "You've obviously given up on yourself. What's happened to you? Don't you care how you affect others? Don't you understand that suicide is forever?"
   c. "I need to know. Are you really planning to kill yourself tonight?"
   d. "Have you decided how you would kill yourself?"

4. You have arrived at the home of a patient with a history of mental illness. His girlfriend meets you out front and tells you that he's inside, "he's pretty worked up," and that he may have a weapon ("a knife or club or something"). Which two of the following would be correct responses?
   a. Wait outside and call for the police.
   b. Do not allow the woman to reenter the house.
   c. Discreetly investigate to verify the status of the patient.
   d. Call out to the patient from a distance to verify his status.

5. The term "reasonable force" refers to the amount of force needed to
   a. provide lifesaving care.
   b. immobilize a threatening patient.
   c. restrain a patient with metal cuffs.
   d. keep a patient from injuring anyone.

6. The law expects the amount of force you use on a patient to be the same, whether the patient is huddling quietly in a corner or loudly threatening you.

   _____ True

   _____ False

7. One way to protect yourself against false accusations by a patient is to carefully and completely document everything that occurs during a call.

_____ True

_____ False

8. The self-administration of one or more drugs in a way that is not in accord with approved medical or social practice is called
   a. overdose.
   b. drug abuse.
   c. withdrawal.
   d. alcoholism.

9. The effects on the body that occur after a period of abstinence from the drugs or alcohol to which the body has become accustomed are called
   a. overdose.
   b. drug abuse.
   c. withdrawal.
   d. alcoholism.

10. A(n) _____ emergency is one that involves poisoning by drugs or alcohol.
   a. overdose
   b. drug abuse
   c. withdrawal
   d. alcoholism

11. Which two of the following would be appropriate actions when managing a female patient who was raped and who states that she has no major vaginal or anal injuries?
   a. Allow the patient to wash her hands, arms, and face, but not her genitals.
   b. Examine the vagina and anus to rule out significant bleeding and trauma.
   c. Perform an initial assessment and a quick head-to-toe exam to rule out major trauma.
   d. Inform the patient of the steps to be taken between now and her arrival at the hospital.

Short-Answer Review

12. List five factors that can cause a change in a patient's behavior.

   a.

   b.

   c.

   d.

   e.

13. You are managing an extremely ill four-year-old who had a seizure at home and now appears to be unresponsive. She has been running a high fever for the past three days. Her parents are very anxious. They demand that you immediately take their child to the hospital. When you tell them that you are waiting for the ambulance to arrive, they begin screaming at you, saying that you are incompetent and that if anything happens to their daughter, you will be held personally responsible.

   a. Are these parents having a behavioral emergency? Explain.

   b. Describe an effective strategy for dealing with these parents.

14. Read the following quotes. Write below each one whether you "agree" or "disagree" with the way in which the First Responder deals with a patient having a behavioral emergency. If you disagree, explain your answer.

   a. "Look, pal, I know that you're upset, but killing yourself over a bad relationship is not the answer. Buddy, there's always gonna be other opportunities out there. Keep your chin up."

   b. "Look, I realize that you don't think your neck is hurt. However, you need to let me check you out now. Your neck could be broken. Do you want to spend the rest of your life in a wheelchair? I'm here to help you. Don't you want help?"

   c. "Paul, I have to tell you that we will be taking you to the hospital for an evaluation. You tried to hurt yourself tonight and we need to make sure you stay safe. I understand that you disagree with us, but we agree with the police officers, and they've decided you need to go."

d. "Trish, my name is Scott. I'm a volunteer with the local fire department. I'm just here to make sure you're okay. Do you want to talk about what happened? Did somebody hurt you? . . . Sure, I can understand that you don't want to talk about it, Trish. Can you tell me if you are hurt anywhere?"

e. "Look, Pat, we all get mad at stuff that goes wrong in our lives. But I'm pretty sure most of us wouldn't consider busting our hand through a plate glass window just because our kids forgot to pick up cat food at the store. You need to sort of stand back and take a look at what you've done, I think."

15. The amount of force you use to restrain a patient depends on four factors. List them.

   a.

   b.

   c.

   d.

16. List four common signs and symptoms of a life-threatening drug- or alcohol-related emergency.

   a.

   b.

   c.

   d.

17. Your patient is unresponsive. You suspect this is a drug- or alcohol-related emergency. To confirm your suspicions, what should you do immediately after your initial assessment?

18. During a drug- or alcohol-related emergency, your immediate goals are to

   a.

   b.

   c.

Vocabulary Practice

Read the clues. Then unscramble the words or terms related to behavioral emergencies.

1. The way a person acts or performs.

   HIBORAVE

2. Use of a drug in a way that is not in accord with medical or social practice.

   ABDEGRSUU

3. Emergency that involves poisoning by drugs or alcohol.

   DEVOORSE

4. Occurs after abstinence from the drugs to which a body is accustomed.

   AADHILRTWW

5. Type of asphyxia to which hog-tie or hobble restraints are associated.

   NAILOOPIST

6. Factor that can change a person's behavior.

   JUNYIR

7. Irrational fear of a specific thing.

   ABHIPO

8. Kind of force needed to keep a patient from injuring himself or others.

   LEANEBORAS

The Call: An Alleyway Rape and Assault

Read this scenario and answer the questions that follow. Remember that managing a patient can mean managing the patient's emotions as well as actual physical injuries.

It is nearly midnight on a Saturday night, and you have responded to a possible assault victim in an alleyway behind a seedy motel. Dispatch informs you that it may be a stabbing and assault. You arrive to find the scene chaotic. Police officers are everywhere.

You check in with the incident commander and she tells you that your patient is a 27-year-old female who apparently met a drug dealer at the motel to purchase drugs. Instead, the dealer dragged her into the alley, raped her, and then stabbed her. He was frightened off by the motel manager, who heard the commotion in the alley and went to investigate.

You approach the patient, who sits huddled with a blanket wrapped around her shoulders. She is crying softly, and sits clutching herself.

1. As a First Responder, what would you say to this patient initially? Write out a few sentences.

2. Your patient, Rachel, tells you that she was stabbed once in the upper arm, "pushed around some," and raped. Her skin appears pale, warm, and dry. Her heart rate is 88. How would you proceed with your physical exam of this patient? Why?

3. You delegate the treatment of Rachel's arm laceration to a male First Responder. As he moves to touch the wound with some dressings, she pulls away sharply, clutching herself harder and shouting, "Don't get near me! Don't touch me!" The First Responder pulls away in alarm. How would you deal with her response? Describe at least two strategies for handling this situation.

4. Aside from the knife wound and a few minor bumps and bruises, the patient does not appear to have any significant physical injuries. Blood loss from her stab wound is minor overall. The patient states that she does not have any major vaginal bleeding. What is your treatment plan for this patient at this point? Be specific.

Active Learning

Using a partner from class, or a current EMT or First Responder, role-play an interaction between a First Responder and a victim of sexual assault. Play both roles.

18 | Bleeding and Shock

Key Ideas

This chapter focuses on how to control both external and internal bleeding and how to recognize and manage shock. Key ideas include the following:

- Treating life-threatening bleeding takes priority over all other treatments except emergency care of the patient's airway and breathing.

- First Responder care of a patient who has external bleeding includes direct pressure, elevation, and the use of pressure points.

- Internal bleeding is managed by maintaining the patient's ABCs and treating for shock.

- Shock, or hypoperfusion, is a condition that results from the inadequate delivery of oxygenated blood to the body's cells.

- Shock may progress in stages from compensatory shock to decompensated shock to irreversible shock.

- The key to effective prehospital care of the shock patient is early recognition, immediate treatment, and rapid transport to an emergency department.

Exam Warm-up

1. When managing an agitated patient with a profusely bleeding head injury, which one of the following describes adequate BSI precautions?
   a. gloves and eye protection
   b. gloves only
   c. gloves and a gown
   d. gloves, gown, and eye protection

2. Pressure should be held at a pulse point until
   a. the bleeding stops.
   b. a tourniquet can be applied.
   c. bleeding slows to an acceptable rate.
   d. other rescuers arrive to take over care.

3. Which pressure points are most commonly used to control bleeding in the arm and leg?
   a. brachial, femoral
   b. ulnar, carotid
   c. brachial, radial
   d. femoral, pedal

4. Which one of the following statements about tourniquets is NOT true?
   a. They can cause permanent disability or even loss of the limb.
   b. They can be improvised from a scarf, towel, belt, or necktie.
   c. They should be released for 1 minute every 5 minutes to prevent tissue death.
   d. They should be used only as a last resort.

5. An arterial pulse point is a place where
   a. the blood pressure drops low enough for bleeding to stop.
   b. an artery is protected on all sides by bone and muscle.
   c. an artery is close to a bone and the surface of the skin.
   d. nerve fibers and blood vessels run closely together.

6. The best position for a patient with a nosebleed is
   a. lying face up with the head tilted back.
   b. sitting up with the head tilted back.
   c. lying on the right or left side.
   d. sitting up and leaning forward.

7. Perfusion is the process by which
   a. cells receive oxygen and have wastes removed.
   b. oxygen-carrying red blood cells are created.
   c. blood begins to clot when bleeding occurs.
   d. cells break down nutrients to make food.

8. Identify all the signs of compensatory shock listed below.
   a. mottled skin
   b. unresponsiveness
   c. normal blood pressure
   d. slightly elevated pulse rates

9. Identify all the signs of decompensated shock listed below.
   a. extreme thirst
   b. very rapid heart rates
   c. normal blood pressure
   d. major changes in mental status

10. Which two of the following statements about irreversible shock are TRUE?
    a. It can be stopped with aggressive treatment.
    b. It leads to the destruction of major organs.
    c. It causes slightly narrowed pulse pressures.
    d. It shunts blood away from the liver and kidneys.

11. The body compensates for major blood loss by directing blood away from the
    a. liver and kidneys and to the pancreas and spleen.
    b. skin and extremities and to the major organs.
    c. major organs and to the skin and extremities.
    d. major organs and to the liver and kidneys.

12. Which one of the following is a late sign of shock?
    a. pale skin
    b. low blood pressure
    c. skin color changes
    d. restlessness or anxiety

13. Which one of the following would be among the earliest signs and symptoms of shock?
    a. cool, moist skin
    b. low blood pressure
    c. very rapid heart rate
    d. restlessness or anxiety

14. The _____ the time before symptoms appear in anaphylactic shock, the _____ the risk of a fatal reaction.
    a. greater, shorter
    b. shorter, shorter
    c. shorter, greater
    d. greater, greater

15. Common signs and symptoms of anaphylactic shock include
    a. fever accompanied by aches and chills.
    b. itching, swelling, and difficulty breathing.
    c. crushing chest pain with shortness of breath.
    d. paralysis of the legs and slow, bounding pulse.

16. The first treatment step in managing shock is to
    a. loosen restrictive clothing.
    b. stop all major bleeding.
    c. keep the patient warm.
    d. ensure an open airway.

The next three questions refer to a 12-year-old female named Paula, who tried to ride her bike through an intersection and was struck by a car that was traveling 30 mph. She was thrown 25 feet onto concrete pavement.

17. You find your patient on the ground in the middle of the intersection, surrounded by onlookers. She appears to be unconscious. What will be your first action at this scene?
    a. Check circulation and control bleeding.
    b. Assess the patient for major injuries.
    c. Make sure that the scene is safe.
    d. Assess the patient's ABCs.

18. As you complete your initial assessment of your patient, you notice that she has snoring respirations at a rate of six breaths per minute. You also notice that she is bleeding profusely from a large laceration just below her left groin. Your next action would be to:
    a. provide mouth-to-mask ventilation.
    b. open her airway using a jaw-thrust maneuver.
    c. open her airway using a head-tilt/chin-lift maneuver.
    d. apply direct pressure and elevation to the injured leg.

19. Which bleeding control measures would be most appropriate for this patient?
    a. direct pressure and pressure point
    b. direct pressure and tourniquet
    c. direct pressure and elevation
    d. elevation and pressure point

Short-Answer Review

20. In order of preference, list the three basic steps for controlling bleeding.

    a.

    b.

    c.

21. List five signs and symptoms of internal bleeding.

    a.

    b.

    c.

    d.

    e.

22. A First Responder has approached you looking for some advice. Here is her story:

"I just helped the EMTs transport a young man who ran his car into a telephone pole. His car was a real mess. It took us about 20 minutes to cut him out of it. He had some serious cuts and bruises from all the broken glass and metal. In fact, I helped to control bleeding to his right forearm. He also said that he had neck and back pain.

"Initially he looked pretty good. The weird thing was that by the time we got him extricated with a short backboard, he was as white as a sheet. After we immobilized him on a long backboard and loaded him in the back of the ambulance, he was breathing really fast and getting combative. The EMT was unable to get a blood pressure, and his pulse was almost too fast to count.

"As we transported him with lights and siren, we applied 100% oxygen and elevated his legs. We frantically looked for any signs of trauma, but except for the cuts and bruises and some abdominal pain, we couldn't find anything. The guy died in the emergency department. What do you think happened? Did we miss something?"

What do you think happened to this patient?

23. Your patient has been hit by a car that was traveling 20 mph. You have completed your initial assessment and have performed a quick head-to-toe exam. You find the patient responsive to pain only. She has a large bruise to her forehead, large scrapes to her left side, a serious cut to her leg, and a painful, swollen, deformed right arm. Her vitals are: respirations 6, pulse 120, BP 116/72, with pale, cool, moist skin. Which two of the above findings concern you the most? Why?

24. You responded to a call for a hit-and-run collision with a pedestrian. Pat is your patient, a 16-year-old boy who was jaywalking when he was hit. He is in serious condition. The following is a list of tasks you completed while managing him. Write whether each one was a "high" or "low" priority.

a.   Maintain Pat's airway using an appropriate airway maneuver.

b.   Ventilate him with supplemental oxygen.

c.   Try to determine his previous medical history.

d.   Cover his cuts and bruises.

e.   Determine if any on-scene bystanders witnessed the incident.

f.   Establish that the scene is safe from hazards.

g.   Reassess Pat's level of responsiveness every five minutes.

h.   Inform bystanders of Pat's condition.

i.   Determine the speed of the car that struck him.

Vocabulary Practice

Across

1. Bleeding that is dark red and flows steadily.
4. Type of BSI precaution.
7. A cause of profound fluid loss (and shock) during illness.
8. Short for body substance isolation.
11. Short for advanced life support.
12. If possible, do this to bleeding limbs.
14. The hour between injury and surgery.
16. Arterial pulse point in the arm.
19. Hypoperfusion.
20. Use the _____ of one hand to compress the femoral pulse point.
21. Common cause of anaphylactic shock.
22. In anaphylactic shock, the mouth, tongue, or throat may do this.
23. Bleeding from this can be fast and profuse.

Down

2. If allowed, administer this to trauma patients.
3. This may be a sign of internal bleeding.
5. This may signal compensatory shock.
6. Skin that is pale, _____, or bluish may be a sign of shock.
9. A _____ pulse may be a sign of shock.
10. Arterial pulse point in the leg.
13. Apply this kind of pressure to a bleeding wound.
14. Type of BSI precaution.
15. Dark tarry _____ may be a sign of internal bleeding.
17. Skin that is _____ and moist may be a sign of shock.
18. There are _____ stages of shock.
19. Apply this to an extremity that has an open wound and a bone or joint injury.

The Call: The Trouble with Bees

Read this scenario and answer the questions that follow. Focus on the early recognition of shock and the appropriate assessment and treatment of a shock patient.

It's a sunny day at the park, and you are enjoying a day off the rescue unit with your family. You have just sat down to a picnic lunch when you hear a commotion at the table next to yours. There is screaming and shouting and a voice crying out, "Dad, I've been stung by a bee!"

You trot over to investigate, and this is the scene before you: a 10-year-old girl is frantically trying to scrape the stinger of a bee from her shoulder blade, while her father is dumping the contents of the picnic basket out onto the ground. "Where's your bee-sting kit?" he yells. "I can't find it!" The girl is too busy to answer. Her father turns to you. "Please help! I can't find Annie's allergy kit, and she has terrible allergic reactions to bee stings!"

1. Your first action should be to
   a. have emergency crews dispatched.
   b. help Annie's father find her allergy kit.
   c. assist Annie with scraping off the bee stinger.
   d. assess Annie's airway, breathing, and circulation.

2. Which two body systems might be affected by Annie's allergic reaction that could cause death?

   a.

   b.

3. Annie is very agitated. She is jumping up and down, crying, and screaming, "Help me!" What should your response be?

4. Describe your initial assessment of Annie by writing the signs and symptoms of anaphylaxis that you would be watching for.

5. As you complete your assessment, Annie begins to complain that she can't breathe and that she feels dizzy. Her face and chest are quite flushed, and she is audibly wheezing. She remains conscious but is tiring rapidly. She is breathing 40 times per minute. Her pulse is rapid and weak at the wrist. The on-duty First Responder crew arrives. You call out to them from the picnic bench and turn back to find that Annie is now slumped over and unresponsive. What should your first action be?

6. Given Annie's status, what maneuver would you use to open her airway? Explain your decision.

7. As you assist Annie's airway, breathing, and circulation, her father rushes up to you and states that he has found Annie's allergy medicine. He reaches for her arm, and one of the First Responders grabs it. He states, "Hold off giving her any medicine now. The paramedics are only a few minutes away, and they carry medicine for allergy attacks." Do you agree or disagree with this decision? Explain.

Active Learning

The body can compensate for small amounts of blood loss before showing signs of shock. When a person donates blood (about a pint), there are no serious effects. Blood loss greater than this will begin to cause problems.

1. Blood loss is described in stages. To get a good idea of the quantity of blood a person must lose to reach each stage, study the list below.

   Stage 1:   500 to 750 ml (two to three cups)
   Stage 2:   750 to 1,250 ml (about one quart)
   Stage 3:   1,250 to 1,750 ml (one and one-half quarts)
   Stage 4:   More than 1,750 ml (almost two quarts)

2. Next, for each stage, pour water (this will represent blood) into a measuring container to observe how much must be lost to reach each stage.

3. Finally, correlate this information with Figure 18-2 on page 329 of your textbook. What symptoms will you see during each stage?

19 | Soft-Tissue Injuries

Key Ideas

This chapter focuses on the assessment and management of soft-tissue injuries. Key ideas include the following:

- Wounds are classified as open or closed, single or multiple. They are also classified by location.

- Closed wounds include contusions, ecchymosis, and hematoma. Open wounds include abrasions, lacerations, penetration/puncture wounds, avulsions, and amputations.

- In general, First Responder care of soft-tissue injuries includes treatment for external and internal bleeding.

- Certain open injuries need special consideration during First Responder care:

  - Care for penetrating chest injuries, large open neck wounds, and eviscerations usually involves the application of occlusive dressings.

  - An object embedded in an open wound must be stabilized in place (unless it is in the patient's cheek, and then it may be removed).

  - In an amputation, both the patient and the amputated part must be given emergency care.

  - In an avulsion, emergency care includes making sure the flap is lying flat and aligned in its normal position.

  - Open wounds caused by bites should be washed before bandaging. Report the bite incident as per local protocol.

- The basic purposes of dressings and bandages are to control bleeding, to prevent further contamination and damage to the wound, to keep the wound dry, and to immobilize the wound site.

Exam Warm-up

1. Of the following, identify all soft-tissue injuries that carry a high risk of infection.
   a. abrasion
   b. laceration
   c. puncture
   d. human bite

2. Lacerations can cause which of the following problems?
   a. infection
   b. permanent scarring
   c. cut tendons or nerves
   d. severe, uncontrolled bleeding

3. Control of bleeding from an amputation should first be attempted using
   a. a splint.
   b. a tourniquet.
   c. pressure points.
   d. direct pressure.

4. Which one of the following injury sites would most likely result in shock?
   a. radius
   b. humerus
   c. femur
   d. fibula

5. You are caring for a patient who has a one-foot steel rod impaled in his abdomen. Which one of the following would NOT be an appropriate action?
   a. Manually stabilize the steel rod.
   b. Remove clothing to expose the injury site.
   c. Cut the rod to make it easier to manage.
   d. Administer oxygen by way of a nonrebreather mask.

6. First Responder care for a patient who has a pen impaled through his cheek includes which one of the following?
   a. Stabilize the pen with bulky dressings.
   b. Cut the pen to make it a manageable size.
   c. Position the pen so it cannot occlude the airway.
   d. Remove the pen and apply bulky dressings to the wound.

7. Because significant soft-tissue injuries to the chest can allow air to flow into the chest cavity, apply a(n) _____ dressing to all open chest wounds.
   a. occlusive
   b. pressure
   c. bulky
   d. roller

8. Open soft-tissue injuries to the neck should be sealed airtight with a(n) _____ dressing.
   a. occlusive
   b. pressure
   c. bulky
   d. roller

9. On rare occasions, you may be required to manage an evisceration. How would you dress or bandage it?
   a. Replace exposed organs and cover with light, dry gauze.
   b. Replace exposed organs and cover with a thick, moist dressing.
   c. Leave exposed organs as found and cover with light, dry gauze.
   d. Leave exposed organs as found and cover with a thick, moist dressing.

10. First Responder care for a patient with an avulsion to the scalp includes which one of the following?
    a. Place the skin flap in its normal position.
    b. Fold the skin flap away from the open wound.
    c. Dress the wound exactly the way you found it.
    d. Remove the skin flap and place it on a cold pack.

11. Dog bites should include which of the following treatments?
    a. Check for tooth fragments.
    b. Wash the wound with soap and water.
    c. Apply direct pressure to control bleeding.
    d. Follow local protocols on reporting requirements.

12. One of the primary purposes of a dressing is to
    a. prevent the bandage from sticking to the wound.
    b. prevent further contamination of the wound.
    c. ensure that the wound remains sterile.
    d. hold a bandage in place.

13. Which one of the following would NOT make a good dressing?
    a. bath towel
    b. handkerchief
    c. toilet tissue
    d. sanitary napkin

14. Which one of the following is an example of an occlusive dressing?
    a. burn pad
    b. gauze pad
    c. ABD dressing
    d. petroleum gaze

15. You are caring for a patient with a three-inch laceration to his arm and minimal bleeding. This wound would best be covered with which two of the following?
    a. a burn pad
    b. a bandage compress
    c. a gauze pad
    d. petroleum gauze

16. Which two of the following statements about bandaging are TRUE?
    a. Make sure the bandage is sterile.
    b. Remove a patient's jewelry first.
    c. Bandages should allow air to reach the wound.
    d. Loosen bandaging if it proves to be too tight.

17. Self-adhering, form-fitting bandages are known as
    a. cravats.
    b. roller bandages.
    c. bandage compresses.
    d. triangular bandages.

18. The saw Ray Gonzalez was using slipped and sliced open his thigh. When he sees all the blood, he is terrified. "I'm going to die!" he says in a husky whisper. You respond:
    a. "Most people don't die from cuts like this. Just relax. It'll be okay."
    b. "You're not going to die. Now, if you had gotten cut where your femoral artery is, that would be a different story."
    c. "I'm going to help you by controlling the bleeding. You can help me by lying back down so that I can see where to put my dressings."
    d. "It looks pretty bad, but I'll do what I can to get this bleeding under control."

19. You are still with Ray Gonzalez, the patient described above. You don gloves and then place a handful of 4 × 4 gauze pads on the wound. They are quickly saturated with blood. You realize you are going to need a dressing that is really absorbent. Which one dressing or bandage should you apply to this wound next?
    a. more gauze pads
    b. an occlusive dressing
    c. a roller bandage
    d. a trauma dressing

20. After applying direct pressure to Mr. Gonzalez's wound for several minutes, it appears that the bleeding has slowed to a trickle. Which one of the following bandaging materials would make the best pressure bandage?
    a. cravats
    b. triangular bandages
    c. roller bandages
    d. elastic bandages

Short-Answer Review

21. Your patient has just been struck in the forearm by a baseball bat. Describe what the contusion might look like and how you would care for this injury.

22. Following is a quote from a First Responder describing a patient in a vehicle collision: "We knew by looking at the bent steering column that this guy could have severe blunt trauma, so we immediately treated him for internal bleeding and shock. But it was weird. He initially looked so good. Some abdominal pain, yes, but his skin was warm and pink, he had a strong radial pulse, and good mental status. During the ongoing assessment, though, we found that he had really decompensated."

    a. What does the First Responder mean when she says that the patient "really decompensated"?

    b. How would the heart rate, blood pressure, mental status, and skin signs of a "decompensated" patient change?

23. List three factors that influence the severity of a stab wound.

    a.

    b.

    c.

24. The steps below describe how to manage a patient with an amputation of the forearm. Write 1–8 to put the steps in the correct order.

    _____ **a.** Remove clothing to expose the entire injury site.

    _____ **b.** Wrap the severed part in saline-moistened, sterile gauze.

    _____ **c.** Dress and bandage the stump.

    _____ **d.** Ensure an open airway and adequate breathing.

    _____ **e.** Control bleeding with direct pressure and elevation.

    _____ **f.** Size up the scene for hazards and the mechanism of injury.

    _____ **g.** Wipe away loose particles of foreign matter from the wound.

    _____ **h.** Perform an ongoing assessment until the EMTs arrive to take over care.

25. You are at the scene of a stabbing. Another First Responder turns to you and states the following: "The patient was stabbed in the back just above the scapula. It looks like there is minimal bleeding from the wound. The police found the knife, and it only has a two-inch blade, so this guy should be okay." Agree? Disagree? Explain.

26. Describe four uses of triangular bandages:

    a.

    b.

    c.

    d.

27. Analyze the following statements made by First Responders about bandaging. Then write "agree" or "disagree" beside each one. If you disagree, explain why.

    _____ a. "My patient just told me that the bandage is too tight, but I convinced her to leave it the way it is so that the laceration won't start bleeding again."

    _____ b. "The laceration is about four inches long on the side of the patient's foot. It was bleeding pretty badly when I arrived on scene, so I went ahead and covered up the entire foot with bandages."

    _____ c. "I thought that the bandage on the forearm wound might be too tight, but the patient said it felt fine. His fingers were warm and pink, and he had a good radial pulse, so I left it."

    _____ d. "My partner had covered the wound with some gauze dressings and roller bandages, but the edges of the wound were exposed, so I removed the bandaging and added a larger trauma dressing to cover the entire area."

    _____ e. "I made a pressure bandage by applying some dressings to the wound and then folding two triangular bandages into cravats and tying them tightly around the dressings."

28. Your patient received a knife wound to his thigh. It was bleeding considerably, but you have it under control and have dressed and bandaged the wound. Your patient props himself up from his supine position and asks, "Do you think I cut off blood flow to the rest of my leg?" Describe how you would go about determining whether or not there is blood circulating to his lower leg.

Vocabulary Practice

Next to each mechanism of injury below, write the type of soft-tissue injury you would expect to see.

avulsion   amputation   puncture/penetration
laceration   bite   abrasion

_____ **1.** Patient was thrown from her bicycle and slid across the pavement.

_____ **2.** Patient's wound occurred when his arm slid along the jagged metal of the car frame.

_____ **3.** Patient suffered an injury when she stepped on a nail.

_____ **4.** Headliner of a car caught the patient's forehead as he was ejected.

_____ **5.** Toddler came screaming from the sandbox, "Fido hurt me!"

_____ **6.** A gang member said that he was cut with a razor blade.

_____ **7.** Police officers state that the assault victim was attacked with a broken whiskey bottle.

_____ **8.** Witnesses think the patient's finger was caught in the power planer.

_____ **9.** Small power sander shot a large splinter of wood at patient's arm.

The Call: Child vs. Rusty Pipe

Read the scenario and answer the questions that follow. Focus on the priorities for managing a soft-tissue injury. Remember your patient assessment plan.

You have just exited a transit bus on your way home from work when you hear screams. You decide which house they are coming from—the Johnsons—and trot over. Along the side of the house, you spot an overturned bicycle and a huge splatter of blood on the walkway. From the backyard you hear the strangled sobs of a child and the frantic voice of a woman, probably his mother.

You follow the trail of blood to the backyard. "Can I help?" you call out as the mother and child come into view.

"Please, please help! Danny is bleeding badly," answers the child's mother. She has taken the child to a garden hose and is dousing a large, jagged laceration of the child's leg with water. It is still bleeding profusely. "He cut himself on a rusty pipe at the side of the house," she explains. Her four-year-old son is frantic, sobbing, and struggling to free himself from her hold.

1. What should be your first step in getting ready to assist this child?

2. Describe your strategy for helping the child to calm down.

3. You move to turn the hose off. The mother says, "Keep the water on. He cut his leg on a rusty drain spout. I don't want him to get tetanus." What is your response?

4. You finally are able to examine the wound. It is a three-inch-long laceration, about one inch deep, on the front of his thigh. It stretches from midway down his thigh to his knee. Describe the location and extent of the wound. Use three of the following terms: proximal, distal, anterior, posterior, midway.

5. List the steps you would need to take to control the bleeding from this injury.

6. You have controlled the child's bleeding and have calmed both him and his mother. Paramedics have just arrived. Give them a hand-off report. (Information: you estimate that the child has lost perhaps 200 milliliters of blood.)

Active Learning

1. For each of the soft-tissue injuries listed below, give an example of a mechanism of injury or situation that could cause the injury.

Laceration: _____

Abrasion: _____

Puncture: _____

Impaled object: _____

Avulsion: _____

2. For each of the examples you've written above, decide:
   a. Is it a safety hazard for you?
   b. What precautions should you take before approaching the patient?

20 | Injuries to the Chest, Abdomen, and Genitalia

Key Ideas

This chapter describes different types of chest, abdominal, and genital injuries along with appropriate assessment and emergency care. Key ideas include the following:

- Chest injuries are serious emergencies that require immediate activation of the EMS system with rapid transport to a trauma center or other medical facility.

- First Responder care of chest injuries focuses on maintaining the patient's airway, breathing, and circulation. Additional treatment includes stabilizing flail chests and fractured ribs, and sealing puncture wounds with occlusive dressings.

- Injuries to the abdomen can cause bleeding and shock, infection, and internal organ damage. Surgery is usually required to repair major abdominal injuries.

- First Responder care for abdominal injuries focuses on supporting the patient's airway, breathing, and circulation.

- First Responder care for injuries to the genitalia includes treating for shock and managing the soft-tissue injuries.

Exam Warm-up

1. Which one of the following is NOT a sign of a chest injury?
   a. coughing up blood
   b. elevated blood pressure
   c. difficulty breathing
   d. signs of shock

2. The most serious threat posed by injuries to the chest is possible damage to the
   a. heart and lungs.
   b. stomach and intestinal organs.
   c. intercostal muscles and ribs.
   d. esophagus and ribs.

3. Mechanisms of blunt injury to the chest may include which one or more of the following?
   a. being thrown against a steering wheel
   b. arm crushed against the side door in a side-impact collision
   c. primary phase of a blast or explosion
   d. head-first fall of 15 feet or more

4. A flail chest occurs when two or more adjacent ribs are broken, each in two or more places.

   _____ True

   _____ False

5. A flail chest may be the result of
   a. a bruised or perforated lung.
   b. fractures of the sternum, cartilage, or ribs.
   c. a puncture wound to the chest.
   d. a severe tension pneumothorax.

6. When the patient exhales, the flail segment protrudes while the rest of the chest wall contracts. This is called
   a. a typical guarding position.
   b. a sucking chest wound.
   c. paradoxical breathing.
   d. pneumothorax.

7. Flail chest can lead to immediate life-threatening problems. Identify all those listed below.
   a. hypoxic drive
   b. abdominal evisceration
   c. severed femoral arteries
   d. puncture wounds of the lung
   e. serious bleeding into the thorax
   f. inadequate oxygenation of the heart

8. To stabilize a flail chest
   a. apply an airtight dressing.
   b. tape a small pillow over the injury site.
   c. place six or seven pounds over the flail area.
   d. lay the patient down on the side opposite the flail area.

9. Open chest injuries do NOT upset the delicate balance of pressure between the inside and outside of the chest.

   _____ True

   _____ False

10. Open injuries to the back are considered open chest injuries.

_____ True

_____ False

11. Sometimes an open wound to the chest bubbles or makes a sucking noise. Such a wound is typically called
   a. grating or crepitus.
   b. tracheal deviation.
   c. sucking chest wound.
   d. bubbling chest wound.

12. If the patient with an open chest injury develops increased respiratory distress after application of an occlusive dressing, you must
   a. add another occlusive dressing over the wound site.
   b. tape down the fourth side of the dressing.
   c. use your hand to form a tighter seal.
   d. release the seal immediately.

13. The term "pneumothorax" may be defined as collapse of the lungs caused by blood in the chest.

_____ True

_____ False

14. The term "hemothorax" may be defined as collapse of the lungs caused by air in the chest.

_____ True

_____ False

15. The most comfortable position for a patient with an abdominal injury usually is
   a. supine, with the knees flexed.
   b. left lateral recumbent.
   c. sitting up.
   d. prone.

16. First Responder care for an abdominal evisceration includes
   a. positioning the patient on his or her side.
   b. placing a moist, sterile dressing over the evisceration.
   c. gently replacing the eviscerated organs in the abdomen.
   d. covering the eviscerated organs with plastic wrap.

17. You should maintain the temperature of the area of an abdominal evisceration by covering the dressings with
   a. a heating pad.
   b. chemical hot packs.
   c. a particle-free towel.
   d. immersion in warm water.

18. First Responder care for a torn or avulsed penis includes all the following EXCEPT
    a. removing any penetrating objects.
    b. controlling bleeding with direct pressure.
    c. applying a cold pack to relieve pain and swelling.
    d. wrapping the penis in a moistened, sterile dressing.

19. Which one of the following is NOT a recommended treatment step for injuries to the female genitalia?
    a. Treat the patient for shock.
    b. Control bleeding with direct pressure.
    c. Insert sterile dressings into a bleeding vagina.
    d. Use cold packs over the dressings to relieve pain.

20. You are treating a female sexual assault victim. She has bruises to her arms and neck. She states that she has no vaginal bleeding. Which two of the following responses would NOT be appropriate for you to make?
    a. "I understand what you've told me, but I still need to check your vagina for injuries."
    b. "Tell me specifically what happened so I'll know where you might be injured."
    c. "It's best that you don't wash up until you've been checked at the hospital."
    d. "Are you hurt anywhere else?"

21. Dave, a man in his 20s, rode his motorcycle around a bend at about 40 mph, laid the bike down, and slid into a tree. There was no loss of consciousness, but he is lying on his back with his knees drawn up. He still has on a full set of riding leathers. Bystanders have removed his full-face helmet. The first step in First Responder care of Dave should be to
    a. give him high-flow oxygen.
    b. assess Dave's abdomen and pelvis.
    c. check his airway, respirations, and pulses.
    d. maintain manual stabilization of his spine.

22. Dave—the same patient described in the previous question—appears to be alert and oriented but in a lot of pain. You find that his respirations are 26, his pulse rate is 120, and his blood pressure is 134/78. His skin is pale, warm, and slightly moist. These findings suggest that Dave may be experiencing _____ shock.
    a. progressive
    b. compensatory
    c. irreversible
    d. latent

Short-Answer Review

23. Write five signs and symptoms of chest trauma.

a.

b.

c.

d.

e.

24. In general, First Responder care of a closed chest injury must include the following steps. Write 1–4 to place them in the correct order.

_____ **a.** Perform a quick physical exam.

_____ **b.** Control any signs of external bleeding.

_____ **c.** Ensure adequate ventilations.

_____ **d.** Maintain an open airway.

25. Why is the immediate activation of the EMS system an important step in caring for a chest-injured patient?

26. First Responder care for both an open chest injury and a closed one are basically the same with one very important exception. What is it?

27. Describe how you should apply an occlusive dressing over a sucking chest wound.

28. List eight signs and symptoms that would indicate a patient has an abdominal injury.

a.

b.

c.

d.

e.

f.

g.

h.

29. Very briefly describe First Responder care of a patient with a closed abdominal injury.

30. Read the following statement: "Our patient was struck in the stomach with a shovel. He has some moderate abdominal pain. All I can see is a small laceration to his abdomen with minimal bleeding, so I don't think he's hurt too badly." Do you agree with this rescuer's comments? Explain.

31. Your patient is seriously injured in a motorcycle collision. He is lying on the ground, arms folded over his abdomen, and knees drawn up. He is also showing signs of compensatory shock. Number the following steps 1–7 to show the order in which they should be performed.

_____ a. Quickly assess the patient's level of responsiveness and chief complaint.

_____ b. Perform a head-to-toe physical exam, being sure to palpate the abdomen and pelvis to assess injury.

_____ c. Ask your partner to maintain manual stabilization of the patient's head and neck.

_____ d. Apply high-concentration oxygen via nonrebreather mask.

_____ e. Check the patient's airway, breathing, and circulation.

_____ f. Size up the scene for dangers and mechanisms of injury.

_____ g. Dress and bandage a small laceration on the patient's arm.

32. You are still caring for the patient described in the question above. Write the pertinent questions you would ask yourself as you examine his abdomen.

D:

O:

T:

S:

33. From your exam, you find that the patient described above does NOT have any neck or back pain. Should you maintain manual stabilization of his head and neck? Why or why not?

Vocabulary Practice

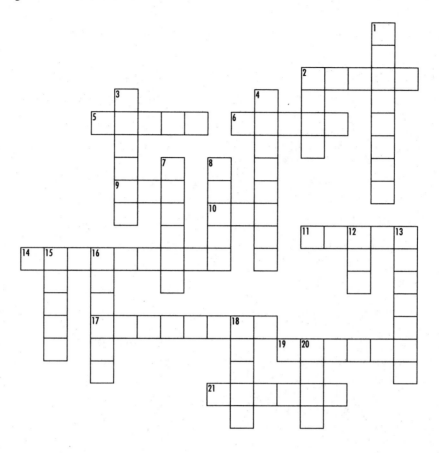

Across

2. Position in which knees are drawn up close to the body.

5. Condition that may develop as a result of trauma.

6. Male organ of copulation and urination.

9. Pneumothorax occurs when _____ from a wound enters the chest cavity.

10. Short for airway, breathing, and circulation.

11. Anterior portion of the pelvis.

14. Body cavity that contains organs of digestion and secretion.

17. Organs of reproduction.

19. Solid organ found primarily in the upper left abdominal quadrant.

21. Body cavity bounded by lower part of spine, hip bones, and pubis.

Down

1. Instinctive reaction to protect a painful abdomen.

2. For an evisceration, place this over the moist dressing.

3. Rib cage.

4. Male gonad, or testis.

7. These are exposed in an evisceration.

8. A _____ chest is a closed chest injury resulting in the chest wall becoming unstable.

12. Precautions to take to protect yourself from infection.

13. An open wound to the chest that may bubble noisily.

15. Hemothorax occurs when _____ fills the pleural space.

16. Administer this to trauma patients, if you are allowed.

18. Solid organ found primarily in the upper right abdominal quadrant.

20. Most common symptom of a broken rib.

The Call: A Bar Fight

Read this scenario and answer the questions that follow. Consider everything you have learned in this course so far.

It's 11 o'clock on a Saturday night, and you respond to reports of an assault at Rudy's Allnight Tavern. You arrive to find the scene secured by local law enforcement. Your patient, a 27-year-old man named Hank Roberts, is lying on the floor at the back of the bar. A police officer tells you that the patient was apparently attacked by three adult males after an argument broke out at the pool table. He was thrown to the floor and then kicked and beaten with pool cues. A bloody knife was taken from one of the suspects.

You move to the patient's side and you are hit immediately with the heavy smell of beer on his breath. He is clutching his chest, moaning. You can see that he is pale and having a difficult time breathing. Blood is plastered all over his hands and chest.

1. After a scene size-up, which one of the following steps should be your next action?
   a. Perform an initial assessment.
   b. Apply oxygen at 6 liters per minute by nasal cannula.
   c. Locate the patient's wounds and stop the bleeding.
   d. Remove the patient's clothing to check for hidden injuries.

2. Your physical exam finds bruising to the chest and a three-quarter-inch laceration just below the left nipple. You hear a bubbling noise at the wound site when the patient inhales and exhales. First Responder care of this injury includes
   a. continuing with the physical exam until it is complete.
   b. bandaging the wound with a 4 × 4 and an elastic bandage.
   c. immediately covering the wound with any available wrapping.
   d. immediately applying an occlusive dressing, sealed on three sides.

3. After appropriately caring for the sucking chest wound, you notice the patient becoming increasingly anxious, short of breath, and cyanotic. His neck veins are bulging. What's happening to your patient, and what action should you take to correct it?

4. This patient's vital signs initially were: respirations 20, pulse 106, BP 128/76. He is alert and his skin is pink, warm, and moist. You recheck his vital signs five minutes later and find: respirations 36, pulse 144, BP 82/48, confusion (reduced level of responsiveness), and pale, cool, moist skin. Explain why the following vital signs have changed.

   Respirations:

   Pulse:

   BP:

   Level of responsiveness:

5. This patient's rapidly deteriorating vital signs indicate he requires immediate transportation to a trauma center. List tasks that you could complete while you wait for transport to arrive.

6. You have treated the patient for his wounds and administered oxygen. Paramedics have just arrived on scene. Write a hand-off report you could give to them about this patient.

Active Learning

1. Use a red marker (with washable ink) to draw a simulated wound on the chest of a class partner or family member. Using materials you would routinely find in a home or office, create an occlusive dressing, apply it to the wound, and seal it on three sides. Time how long it takes to do this.

2. Look through the supplies used in class or where you will be working as a First Responder. Which dressings would be suitable to cover an abdominal evisceration (a dressing that will not shred, cling, or leave particles in the wound)?

21 | Burn Emergencies

Key Ideas

This chapter provides an overview of the methods of classifying burns and describes basic emergency care of burns, as well as special types of burn injuries. Key ideas include the following:

- Burns are complex injuries that can impair a number of the body's functions, including fluid balances, body temperature, and joint function.

- The severity of a burn is determined by the depth of the burn, percentage of body surface affected, location of the burn, and accompanying complications including the age of the patient.

- First Responder care for burns focuses on stopping the source of the burning, maintaining the patient's ABCs, and covering the burned area with sterile dressings.

- Inhalation injuries can cause severe, life-threatening respiratory distress caused primarily from scorched mucous membranes and swelling. In addition to respiratory burns, victims of these injuries can be poisoned by the substance that has been inhaled.

- Chemical burns require aggressive irrigation. All significant chemical burns should be treated as severe.

- The most important priority in incidents involving electrical burns is scene safety. First Responder care focuses on maintaining the patient's ABCs and should include spinal precautions.

Exam Warm-up

1. The first step in managing a burn patient is to
    a. eliminate the cause of the burn.
    b. determine the severity of the burn.
    c. remove the patient from the source of the burn.
    d. examine the patient for airway and breathing problems.

2. Which one of the following statements about the treatment of burns is TRUE?
   a. Ice may be used to cover a burn.
   b. Cover burns with wet, sterile dressings.
   c. Cover burns with dry, sterile dressings.
   d. Grease or fat may be used to cover burns.

3. Chemical burns should be flushed with water for a minimum of _____ minutes.
   a. 5
   b. 10
   c. 15
   d. 20

4. Identify all the signs and symptoms of smoke inhalation included in the list below.
   a. cyanosis
   b. noisy breathing
   c. skin rash or hives
   d. shortness of breath
   e. singed nasal hairs
   f. cough or hoarseness
   g. burns to the face
   h. carbon in the sputum
   i. difficulty speaking
   j. restricted chest movement
   k. bruising of the skin
   l. puncture/penetrating wounds
   m. abrasions or lacerations

Short-Answer Review

5. The severity of a burn depends on many factors. List four:

   a.

   b.

   c.

   d.

6. You are managing a patient who was burned in a grease fire. She has burns covering her entire anterior chest and abdomen, as well as her anterior left arm. Using the "rule of nines," calculate the percentage of her body that has been burned.

7. Decide if each patient has critical, moderate, or minor burns. Write your answer in the space provided.

_____ a. A 65-year-old patient received full-thickness burns to her hands and face from hot grease.

_____ b. A 23-year-old received superficial burns to his abdomen when he spilled a pot of boiling water.

_____ c. A 16-year-old received partial-thickness burns to her arms and chest from hot oil after her car was hit by a truck. She also suffered a fractured arm and leg.

_____ d. A 9-year-old was rescued from a burning residence. He has a rasping cough and soot in his nostrils.

_____ e. A 35-year-old received partial-thickness burns to his left forearm after leaning up against a hot metal surface at work.

_____ f. A 27-year-old received a superficial burn to the back of her left hand while tending the fire in her wood stove.

_____ g. A 17-year-old was splashed in the eyes with a mild acid solution in the chemistry lab at school.

8. Why do children under the age of 5 and adults over the age of 55 tolerate burns so poorly?

9. You have responded to a house fire. Your patient has burns and inhalation injuries. First Responder care is described below. Number the steps 1–7 to show the correct order in which they should be performed.

_____ a. Perform an initial assessment.

_____ b. Determine the history of the burn.

_____ c. Administer oxygen via nonrebreather mask.

_____ d. Remove the patient from the source of the burn.

_____ e. Stop the burning process.

_____ f. Cover the burns.

_____ g. Assess the extent and severity of the patient's burns.

10. Why is it necessary to constantly reassess a patient who has suffered inhalation injuries?

11. You are managing a patient who received burns to his arms and face following a house fire. Your partner tells you, "Remove everything on his arms and hands so that we can take care of his burns." He has rings on his fingers, a watch on one wrist, and charred clothing hanging from both arms, some of it embedded in the burns. Which of these items do you want to remove? Which do you want to leave alone?

12. You are responding to a car vs. power pole. You arrive to find two uninjured passengers still inside the car. You note that a power line is draped across the car. There appears to be no immediate danger of fire or explosion. One of the occupants is attempting to open a door to get out, but it seems to be jammed. What should these occupants do, and why?

13. List five signs and symptoms of electrical shock.

a.

b.

c.

d.

e.

14. First Responder care for a patient with lightning burns is the same care you would provide for any burn patient. What two additional treatments should you be prepared to perform?

a.

b.

Vocabulary Practice

1. Draw a line to match the signs and symptoms to the related term.

charring •   • superficial burns

red skin and swelling •

intense pain •   • partial-thickness burns

red skin and blisters •

little or no pain •   • full-thickness burns

2. Read each description. Then write whether the injury described is a superficial, partial-thickness, or full-thickness burn.

_____ **a.** A burn that results in redness and blistering; the epidermis and dermal layers of skin are usually burned

_____ **b.** A burn that involves muscle and bone

_____ **c.** A burn that appears white, dark, or charred; extends through all dermal layers and can involve subcutaneous layers

_____ **d.** A burn that involves the epidermal layer alone

The Call: An Electrocution Victim

Read the scenario and answer the questions that follow. Remember that patients who have been electrocuted may have extensive internal injuries and organ damage not immediately evident. Be sure to prioritize your care to treat the patient for life-threatening injuries first.

You arrive at a canal levy where a farmer was electrocuted by a downed power line. Bystanders tell you that the farmer was driving his tractor near the levy when he ran into a downed power line. He was electrocuted when he hopped off the tractor to investigate.

You see that the farmer is lying near his tractor. Members of the fire department, who arrived on scene before you, tell you that they removed the power line and it is safe for you to approach the patient.

1. As you cautiously move closer to the farmer, you notice that the soles of your feet begin to tingle. What is causing this, and what should you do?

2. The power company arrives on scene and deems the scene safe. You call to the farmer, but he does not respond. Based on what you know about electrocution injuries, what injuries are you expecting to find, and what equipment will you need to manage these injuries?

3. Where would you expect to find contact burns on this patient, and how will you treat them?

4. Vital signs on this patient are as follows: The farmer is unresponsive, with a pulse of 44 and respirations of 8 per minute. His blood pressure is unobtainable. You can see an ugly burn on the farmer's foot and both of his legs appear to be fractured. The two fire department crew members are busy securing the scene from curious onlookers. Which of these findings should you manage first? Why?

Active Learning

Practice using the rule of nines. Decide on the BSA burned for each patient described below.

1. A patient has burns to the anterior of both arms and the anterior torso.

2. A patient has burns to the abdomen, genitalia, and the anterior of both legs.

3. A patient has burns to the anterior chest, left arm, and face.

4. A child has immersion burns to both legs.

22 | Agricultural and Industrial Emergencies

Key Ideas

This chapter focuses on injuries that occur in agricultural and industrial settings. Key ideas include the following:

- Farming is a hazardous occupation. The number of deaths in work-related accidents exceeds those occurring in mining, construction, transportation, and public utilities.

- The top priority in responding to any farm or industrial accident is the safety of all responders.

- Farm machinery must be stabilized and shut down before the patient can be assessed and treated.

- Lifting farm equipment and disentangling a patient requires teamwork plus specialized equipment and training.

- First Responder care for farm-related injuries requires an understanding of common mechanisms of injury and the types of farm equipment involved.

- Industrial accidents may include structural collapses, toxic gas releases, hazardous materials contamination, and entrapment. All these emergencies require specially trained teams to safely rescue the patient.

Exam Warm-up

1. There are four conditions that must exist before disentanglement and rescue of a patient can begin. Identify all four in the list below.
   a. Farm equipment has been stabilized.
   b. There is time for helicopter transport.
   c. The patient has life-threatening injuries.
   d. Hazards, such as leaking fuel, are present.
   e. Engines have been shut down.
   f. The patient has been stabilized.
   g. The patient is unresponsive.
   h. Hazards have been controlled.

2. The most common cause of farm-related fatalities is the:
   a. auger.
   b. tractor.
   c. combine.
   d. power take-off (PTO) shaft.

3. What is the most common type of fatal injury associated with farm tractors?
   a. penetration injury
   b. wrapping injury
   c. crushing injury
   d. laceration

4. The first step in shutting down farm equipment is to stabilize it. Identify all the methods listed below by which this can be done.
   a. Set the parking brakes.
   b. Block or chock the wheels.
   c. Drive it to a flat surface.
   d. Tie the machine to another vehicle.

5. Do NOT stop patient care during lifting operations. Both efforts should continue at the same time.

   _____ True

   _____ False

6. It is NOT common for patients involved in a tractor rollover to have chemical burns to the eyes.

   _____ True

   _____ False

7. In any emergency involving a tractor rollover, suspect injuries to the patient's head, chest, and abdomen.

   _____ True

   _____ False

8. The best tools for lifting large, irregularly shaped machines such as tractors are
   a. cribs.
   b. power hydraulic tools.
   c. high-pressure airbags.
   d. cranes or boom trucks.

9. Airbags are most efficient during the first _____ to _____ inches of lift.
   a. 3, 5
   b. 5, 7
   c. 7, 9
   d. 9, 11

10. During any extrication of a patient from farm equipment, two rescuers should take charge. One should direct the lifting from the front and another should direct the effort from the back.

    _____ True

    _____ False

11. You should watch the patient during the lift to make sure that the part to be lifted is moving properly and that another part is not putting more pressure on the patient. If conditions change, you should
    a. lift the part that is pressing on the patient.
    b. tell the patient that it will all be over soon.
    c. advise the rescuer leading the lifting operation.
    d. take over the leader's job to make sure the patient survives.

12. Which one of the following would NOT be an appropriate method of disentangling a patient from a PTO?
    a. Cut the shaft with a power saw.
    b. Run the PTO until the patient is freed.
    c. Cut the patient's clothing with rescue knives.
    d. Uncouple the shaft and transport it with the patient.

13. Combines can cause crushing and amputation injuries when farmers get caught in which one(s) of the machine's parts?
    a. augers
    b. sprockets
    c. roller chains
    d. belts and pulleys

14. Which two of the following statements about augers are TRUE?
    a. They are used to move grain from a combine to trucks or wagons.
    b. They can cause injuries too severe to be dealt with in the field.
    c. They can be reversed to free an entrapped patient.
    d. They can be cut using a torch.

15. When rescuing a patient from a grain tank, which two of the following directives should you follow?
    a. Wear a disposable mechanical filter respirator.
    b. Use the gravity gate or auger to release the grain.
    c. Cut uniform triangular holes above the level of the grain.
    d. Secure the patient with a lifeline once he or she is exposed.

16. Which one or more of the following signs and symptoms would indicate the patient is suffering from silo gas inhalation?
    a. cyanosis
    b. coughing
    c. eye irritation
    d. nausea and vomiting

17. The top priorities for sizing up an industrial emergency include which of the following tasks?
    a. Treat the patient's airway, breathing, and circulation.
    b. Assess the patient to determine the extent of injuries.
    c. Assess the scene for the presence of hazardous materials.
    d. Call for the specialized teams needed to manage the emergency.

Short-Answer Review

18. Explain how each of the following factors contributes to the severity of farm-related injuries.

    a. Farm equipment design:

    b. Expense of new equipment:

    c. Time required to disentangle farmers from machinery:

    d. Remoteness of many farms:

19. You have responded to a farming accident in which a farmer has caught her hand in a corn picker. When you arrive, her arm is still entangled in the machinery. You note that she is bleeding profusely from the injury. Describe your strategy for controlling bleeding prior to disentanglement.

20. Some farm equipment manufacturers use color codes to help operators quickly identify controls. Describe what each color usually represents.

a. Red:

b. Yellow:

c. Black:

Vocabulary Practice

Match the following hazards or potential mechanisms of injury with their correct definitions.

pinch points   wrap points   shear points
crush points   stored energy

_____ a. Two objects move close enough together to cause a cutting action.

_____ b. Two large objects come together to cause a crushing action.

_____ c. Two objects meet to cause a pinching or pulling action.

_____ d. An aggressive component moves in a circular motion.

_____ e. All four described above remain even after the machinery has been shut down.

The Call: A Tractor Rollover

Read this scenario and answer the questions that follow. Focus on managing both the overturned tractor and the patient. Remember that scene safety must be your top priority!

You are the First Responder on the scene of a tractor rollover. The farmer, Mike Stevenson, was working on a steep hillside when his tractor rolled over sideways down the hill. As you pull up to the scene, you see that the tractor has come to rest on its side. Mike's son, Ted, witnessed the accident and states that the tractor rolled over at least twice. The tractor does have a roll bar, and Ted states that his father is wearing a seat belt. The tractor cab is wedged against the embankment. You are unable to see Mike. The tractor engine is still running.

1. The first thing you do is call dispatch. The emergency scene is at least an hour's ground-transport time from the closest hospital. Which one of the following EMS transport teams should you advise your dispatch center to send?
   a. paramedic-staffed ambulance
   b. EMT-staffed ambulance
   c. nurse-staffed helicopter
   d. nurse-staffed helicopter and paramedic-staffed ambulance

Additional rescue personnel arrive. Farming neighbors come with cables and chains, and they lock up the overturned tractor's rear wheels. The tractor engine is turned off. You climb onto the tractor and find that Mike is still seat-belted into the cab. His right leg is crushed, pinned between the tractor and the embankment. He is crying out in severe pain and appears pale and sweaty. His radial pulse is rapid and weak. He does not appear to have any other major injuries.

You determine that the tractor needs to be lifted about a foot in order to free Mike's leg. Rescue personnel at the scene have arrived with a large boom truck and hand-powered hydraulic jacks. The rescue unit outfitted with high-pressure airbags is 20 to 30 minutes away.

2. Some responders want to wait until the airbags arrive, arguing that airbags are the best tool available for lifting tractors. Others want to lift the tractor with either the boom truck or hydraulic jacks. The ground beneath the tractor is firm. What is your opinion?

3. Describe the patient care you want to initiate prior to and during rescue efforts.

You and fellow responders are able to lift the tractor, free Mike's leg, and immobilize him to a long backboard. You note that he is extremely pale, and he now responds only to painful stimuli. You are unable to feel a radial pulse, so you take his carotid pulse, which is 140 beats per minute. His leg is badly crushed. An update from dispatch indicates that the helicopter has been delayed due to mechanical problems and may not be available for some time, if at all. The paramedic ambulance has responded from the nearest hospital and is still 30 minutes away.

4. Do you want to wait on scene or begin transporting the patient in the back of a pickup truck, meeting up with the ambulance or helicopter at some point? Explain your transport plan.

Active Learning

Identify agricultural and/or industrial locations within your community. Then find out: What type of farms or industrial facilities are there? What type of machinery is used? How would you or your organization respond to calls at these locations? Are there special teams who would respond?

23 | Injuries to the Head, Face, and Neck

Key Ideas

This chapter describes the assessment and First Responder care of head-injured patients. It also describes injuries to the face and neck, which can compromise the patient's airway and signal severe facial or skull fractures and cervical-spine injuries. Key ideas include the following:

■ One of the most important clues about the severity of the patient's head injury is the degree to which the patient's condition changes over time.

■ If the mechanism of injury suggests a possible head injury, or if a trauma patient is unresponsive, suspect spine injury. Whenever you suspect head or spine injury, immediately stabilize the patient's head and neck. Maintain manual stabilization until the patient is completely immobilized.

■ Injuries to the head include skull fracture, injuries to the brain, concussion, and penetrating wounds.

■ First Responder care for head injuries includes supporting the patient's ABCs, stabilizing the patient's head and neck, and arranging for rapid transport to an appropriate medical facility.

■ Face and neck injuries can potentially compromise a patient's airway or breathing. Make airway management your emergency care priority.

■ It should be assumed that any patient with a significant face or neck injury also has a spine injury. Manually stabilize the patient's head and neck until he or she is completely immobilized.

■ Do not attempt to remove foreign objects from the ears or nose. Never pack the ears or nose when attempting to control bleeding.

■ First Responder care for injuries to the eye—including injuries to the eyelid or the bony structure around the eye—includes flushing out any foreign objects, controlling bleeding, and protecting the eyeballs from further injury.

Exam Warm-up

1. You should suspect spine injury in a trauma patient who is unresponsive.

   _____ True

   _____ False

2. Closed injuries of the head may present with which of the signs listed below?
   a. severe bleeding of the scalp
   b. clear fluid tinged pink from the nose
   c. leaking of cerebrospinal fluid from the ears
   d. swelling or depression of the bones of the skull

3. Change in patient status may be the most important sign of how a patient is doing.

   _____ True

   _____ False

4. The most frequent cause of death following a head injury is
   a. loss of pulses in the extremities.
   b. oxygen deficiency in the brain.
   c. loss of cerebrospinal fluid.
   d. unresponsiveness.

5. Your priorities while caring for a patient with a head injury are included in the list below.
   Identify all of them.
   a. Control major bleeding
   b. Protect the patient's cervical spine
   c. Administer oxygen in high concentrations.
   d. Maintain an open airway and adequate breathing

6. You should suspect a skull fracture with any significant trauma to the head.

   _____ True

   _____ False

7. Which one of the following factors most influences the severity of brain damage from a head injury?
   a. whether or not the skull is fractured
   b. the mechanism of injury and the force involved
   c. whether arteries rather than veins have been torn
   d. the length of time that elapses before the patient reaches the hospital

8. A _____ is a temporary loss of the brain's ability to function. Its key distinguishing feature is that its effects appear immediately or soon after impact.
   a. concussion
   b. skull fracture
   c. spine injury
   d. facial trauma

9. After you have stabilized an object that is impaled in a patient's skull, you should permit blood to drain from the wound.

   _____ True

   _____ False

10. Which of the following are problems that can occur with severe facial injuries?
    a. blocked airway
    b. skull fracture
    c. spine injuries
    d. severe bleeding

11. Abrasions and lacerations to the face are soft-tissue injuries. They do NOT suggest underlying fractures.

    _____ True

    _____ False

12. Management of a broken tooth includes which two of the following actions?
    a. Place the tooth in a cup of milk.
    b. Wrap the tooth in moistened gauze.
    c. Wrap the tooth in a dry, sterile gauze pad.
    d. Clean the tooth with an antibacterial disinfectant.

13. If your patient has both an eye orbit and globe injury, place cold packs over the injured eye.

    _____ True

    _____ False

14. Which one of the following eye injuries requires the most urgent and immediate care?
    a. scratched cornea
    b. fractured orbit
    c. chemical burn
    d. lacerated eyelid

15. Eyes contaminated with chemicals should be flushed with clean water for _____ to _____ minutes.
    a. 3, 5
    b. 5, 10
    c. 12, 15
    d. 30, 60

16. A patient has a pencil impaled in her eye. This injury is best protected by
    a. covering the eye and pencil with bulky dressings and roller gauze.
    b. cutting off the pencil and wrapping roller gauze around both eyes.
    c. placing a cup or cone over the pencil and securing it with roller gauze.
    d. leaving the injury alone.

17. In general, contact lenses should only be removed when
    a. there is an impaled object in the eye.
    b. there is a chemical burn to the eye.
    c. there is an injury to the face.
    d. the transport time is short.

18. Your patient is a 20-year-old woman, the driver of a car that hit a telephone pole. She was not wearing her seat belt and was thrown into the windshield. Her face and neck are badly injured and bleeding. She has gurgling respirations. One of the bystanders who extricated her from the car tells you: "We've already called 9-1-1. We've got her on her back. She looks bad." What is your most immediate concern for this patient?
    a. managing her airway
    b. controlling bleeding
    c. protecting her spine
    d. treating her for shock

19. You are still caring for the patient described in the previous question. You have managed to clear the patient's airway and have positioned a bystander to manually support the patient's head and neck in a neutral position. Your next action would be to
    a. complete a physical exam to check for other major injuries.
    b. place ice packs on the patient's face to reduce swelling.
    c. apply cravat bandages to support her jaw fracture.
    d. control the bleeding from her throat lacerations.

Short-Answer Review

20. You are assessing a patient with possible head injuries. His level of responsiveness, as well as pulses, movement, and sensation in his extremities, appear to be normal. List six special findings that could indicate this patient has suffered a head injury.

    a.

    b.

    c.

    d.

    e.

    f.

21. You have responded to a 34-year-old male who was struck in the head with a piece of lumber at a work site. He was briefly knocked unconscious. You and your partner find the patient awake but combative and vomiting. Your partner responds, "It's probably just a concussion. How bad could it be?" Do you agree with your partner's assessment? Explain.

22. You are alone with a male patient who has significant head and lower-extremity injuries. How can you stabilize his head and neck and still provide emergency care for his wounds?

23. Why should you never apply direct pressure to a head wound that is accompanied by an obvious or depressed skull fracture?

24. List three important details that should be included in the history of a head injury patient.

    a.

    b.

    c.

25. Your patient has been stabbed in the skull with an ice pick. It remains embedded. The wound is bleeding, but not profusely. How should you proceed?

26. List five signs and symptoms of injuries to the jaw.

a.

b.

c.

d.

e.

27. List five signs and symptoms of a neck injury:

a.

b.

c.

d.

e.

28. Is it appropriate to apply heavy direct pressure to control bleeding when treating a neck injury? Why or why not?

29. You are managing an unresponsive patient who received a severe laceration to her neck. She is having trouble breathing. First Responder care is listed below. Write 1–5 to show the correct order in which the steps should be performed.

_____ **a.** Apply a bulky dressing.

_____ **b.** Apply an occlusive dressing, and form an airtight seal.

_____ **c.** Apply 100% oxygen via nonrebreather mask.

_____ **d.** Open the patient's airway using the jaw-thrust maneuver.

_____ **e.** Manually stabilize the patient's head and neck.

30. Assume you are examining an eye injury patient. What questions would you ask yourself while assessing the following?

   a. Eye orbits:

   b. Eyelids:

   c. Mucous membranes:

   d. Globes:

   e. Pupils:

   f. Eye movement:

31. A patient has received a laceration to her left globe (eyeball). Why should you cover both eyes with patches?

32. List two different methods for removing foreign objects from the eye.

   a.

   b.

33. You are managing a patient who has fragments of glass lodged in his eye. Describe the appropriate First Responder care for this injury.

Vocabulary Practice

Across

1. Major features of the face.
6. Portion of the skull that encloses the brain.
7. Voice box.
9. Anatomical region of the neck.
11. An open wound to this area is an obvious sign of head injury.
12. Maneuver used to open the airway of a trauma patient.
14. Major feature of the face.
15. Major feature of the face.
16. The "A" in ABCs.
18. Eyeballs.
20. Bones that hold the eyeballs.
21. Bony framework of the head.

Down

2. Major features of the face.
3. Windpipe.
4. Check these for size, shape, equality, and reaction to light.
5. Major features of the face.
8. Short for estimated time of arrival.
9. Transparent, anterior portion of the eye.
10. Major artery in the neck.
12. Major vein in the neck.
13. Always suspect _____ injury in a patient who has a head injury.
17. Memory aid for levels of responsiveness.
19. Always take these precautions to prevent infection.

The Call: Bikers without Helmets

Read the scenario and answer the questions that follow. Focus on the correct assessment of a head-injured patient and prioritize treatment, taking into consideration available resources.

There's a "motorcycle down" on a narrow two-lane country highway. You arrive to find a "Harley Hog" wrapped around a telephone pole. Bystanders tell you that the bike, with two unhelmeted riders aboard, came around a sharp corner too quickly and slid into the telephone pole at high speed. The rider on the back of the motorcycle, a woman in her 30s, was thrown onto the blacktop. The driver, a man in his 30s, stayed with the bike until it impacted the telephone pole. He was then launched into a guard rail.

As you gather equipment, you can see that neither patient is moving. As you approach the female patient, your partner, Marco, calls for additional resources and then attends to the male patient.

The female patient is lying on her back, moaning. Her eyes are open. "What's your name?" you ask as you kneel beside her. Her eyes flicker at the sound of your voice, but she continues only to moan. You see that she is covered with abrasions and has a large head wound above her left eyebrow. Her left lower arm and left lower leg are swollen and bent at unnatural angles. They appear to be fractured. She is pale but has a strong, rapid pulse. Her breath smells of beer. A bystander approaches you.

"Can I help? I've been trained as a First Responder," she says.

"Sure," you reply, "Grab a pair of gloves from the cab of our rescue unit and I'll put you to work."

1. Which one of the following tasks would be most important for this bystander to accomplish?
   a. Gather splinting materials for the patient's fractures.
   b. Cover the patient's abrasions.
   c. Take the patient's blood pressure.
   d. Manually stabilize the patient's head and neck.

2. After you complete an initial assessment and treatment, your partner returns to your side. "The other rider is dead. He's pulseless and has brain matter showing. How bad is she?" he asks, motioning to your patient. You respond:
   a. "She appears to be moderately injured."
   b. "I'm not sure how bad she is. I need to get a set of vitals first."
   c. "She has a change in mental status and several deformed limbs."
   d. "Not too bad. She has a few broken bones and I think she's mainly drunk."

3. You perform a physical exam of the patient. She has bruising to her chest and abdomen. Her breathing is 26, pulse 120, blood pressure 116/88. You note that her breathing has a gurgling sound and discover that her mouth is filling with blood from a laceration inside the cheek. Your next action should be to
   a. suction the patient's airway.
   b. apply a cervical collar to the patient's neck.
   c. reassess the patient's level of responsiveness.
   d. apply high-flow oxygen via nonrebreather oxygen mask.

4. After stabilizing her injuries, you move your patient onto the long backboard. At that time, you notice that her respirations have dropped to six to eight breaths per minute. These respirations are very irregular and shallow. Either of two treatments would be appropriate for this patient. Which two are they?
   a. mouth-to-mask ventilation with supplemental oxygen
   b. head-tilt/chin-lift and high-flow oxygen via nonrebreather mask
   c. oropharyngeal airway and high-flow oxygen via BVM ventilation
   d. oropharyngeal airway and high-flow oxygen via nasal cannula

5. The paramedics have just arrived, and they are preparing to take over patient care. Give them a hand-off report on your patient. Make it brief.

6. As you assist the paramedics with securing the patient to the backboard, you overhear them discussing whether or not they should fly the patient to the hospital by helicopter. A helicopter was dispatched when the paramedics were requested. At this point, a helicopter would reduce the transport time by 10 to 12 minutes. What do you think? How would you transport this patient?

Active Learning

1. Injuries to one eye often require bandaging of both eyes. Have a class member bandage both of your eyes so you cannot see. Have your classmate then take your vital signs and carefully walk you around the room. How does this feel? How would you care for your blind or eye-injury patients after this experience?

2. Pretend a classmate has open injuries to various places on their head. Practice dressing and bandaging these areas. Which places are the most difficult to bandage? The easiest? Be careful not to jeopardize the spine or the airway.

24 | Injuries to the Spine

Key Ideas

This chapter focuses on spinal injuries. It covers mechanisms of spine injuries and First Responder care. Key ideas include the following:

- Injuries to the spine can affect almost any body system.

- Improper handling of a spine-injured patient can kill the patient or cause permanent disability.

- If the mechanism of injury suggests a possible head injury, or if a trauma patient is unresponsive, suspect spine injury.

- If the mechanism of injury suggests it, assume a spine injury even if your assessment finds nothing wrong with the patient.

- Signs and symptoms of a spine injury can range from mild neck tenderness to paralysis and respiratory arrest.

- The goals of managing a spine-injured patient are to support the patient's ABCs and to stabilize his or her spine until the patient is completely immobilized.

Exam Warm-up

1. The spinal column is made up of _____ vertebrae, one stacked on top of the other.
   a. 11
   b. 22
   c. 33
   d. 44

2. The cervical spine is made up of 12 vertebrae and is supported by the rib cage.

   _____ True

   _____ False

3. The section of the spine especially vulnerable to injury is the _____ spine.
   a. thoracic
   b. cervical
   c. coccyx
   d. sacral

4. If the mechanism of injury suggests it, suspect spine injury even if there are no signs or symptoms.

   _____ True

   _____ False

5. The ability to walk, move arms and legs, and feel sensation rules out spine injury.

   _____ True

   _____ False

6. While assessing a suspected spine-injured patient's neck and back, do NOT
   a. palpate the patient's spine.
   b. bare the patient's chest and back.
   c. move the head to an in-line position if you meet resistance.
   d. ask the patient if his or her spine hurts.

7. A cervical-spine injury can result in severe breathing problems, even respiratory arrest.

   _____ True

   _____ False

8. The word "neutral" in the term "neutral in-line position" means the head is
   a. flexed forward and extended back.
   b. not flexed forward but extended back.
   c. flexed forward but not extended back.
   d. neither flexed forward nor extended back.

9. The word "in-line" in the term "neutral, in-line position" means the patient's
   a. nose is in line with the chin.
   b. nose is in line with the navel.
   c. "Adam's apple" is in line with the navel.
   d. "Adam's apple" is in line with the chin.

10. If you find that the spine-injured patient's head is not in line, gently put it there, even if you feel some resistance.

    _____ True

    _____ False

11. Manual stabilization must be maintained, even when the patient is immobilized from head to toe on a long backboard.

_____ True

_____ False

12. Even the best rigid cervical immobilization devices do not eliminate movement.

_____ True

_____ False

13. Which of the following statements are NOT true?
    a. All patients with suspected spine injury must be immobilized on a short backboard.
    b. While securing the patient to the backboard, maintain manual stabilization.
    c. Rescuers may NOT move a spine-injured patient at all.
    d. Secure the patient's head first, torso next, legs last.

14. Manual stabilization may be released when a patient has been properly secured to a short backboard.

_____ True

_____ False

15. Removal of a helmet from a suspected spine-injured patient requires at least _____ rescuers.
    a. 2
    b. 3
    c. 4
    d. 5

Short-Answer Review

16. Why should you suspect a spine injury in a patient with a head injury?

17. List four emergencies in which your index of suspicion for spine injury should be very high.

    a.

    b.

    c.

    d.

18. List five signs and symptoms of a spine injury.

a.

b.

c.

d.

e.

19. Describe how you should assess pulses, movement, and sensation in all four extremities of a suspected spine-injured patient who is alert.

a. Pulses:

b. Movement:

c. Sensation:

20. Describe how you can assess movement and sensation in a suspected spine-injured patient who is unresponsive.

21. You have arrived at the scene of a side-impact motor-vehicle collision. One of the patients is a male in his 30s who was the driver of the car that was hit. He is complaining of neck pain. Another First Responder arrived on scene before you and applied a cervical collar to his neck. You note that the patient is sitting unattended on the curb, cervical collar in place. The other First Responder is getting an incident history from bystanders. What is your opinion of the care given to this patient? Does it adequately protect his possible neck injury? Why or why not?

22. You have responded to a "man down" call. You find an intoxicated patient, James, who gives you a conflicting story. He first states that he was assaulted, struck in the head with a tire iron, and thrown to the pavement. He then states that he was really just sleeping and that his assault story actually occurred a week ago. You see what may be relatively old lacerations and bruises on his head. You find that he is unsteady on his feet (from the alcohol?) and that his grip appears quite weak. During your exam, a buddy of his, Bob, walks up and tells you that James had indeed been sleeping, and that Bob called 9-1-1 because "James was breathing kind of funny." Bob also seems fairly intoxicated. Should you take spinal precautions or not? Explain your decision.

23. You are managing a patient who has suffered a possible neck injury when diving into a pool. You arrive at her side after she has been rescued from the water. She is conscious and complains of neck pain and tingling to her arms and legs. Read the following actions. Number them 1–4 to show the order in which they should be performed.

_____ **a.** Administer high-concentration oxygen to the patient.

_____ **b.** Secure the patient to a long backboard.

_____ **c.** Identify the mechanism of injury.

_____ **d.** Stabilize the patient's head and neck.

24. You have completed your initial assessment of the patient described in the previous question. Read the following actions. Number them 1–9 to show the order in which they should be performed.

_____ **a.** Perform a log roll, and place a long backboard under the patient.

_____ **b.** Perform a physical exam, including assessment of pulses, movement, and sensation in all four extremities.

_____ **c.** Reassess pulses, movement, and sensation.

_____ **d.** Pad the spaces between the patient and the board.

_____ **e.** Immobilize the patient's legs.

_____ **f.** Immobilize the patient's torso.

_____ **g.** Immobilize the patient's head.

_____ **h.** Reassess pulses, movement, and sensation.

_____ **i.** Withdraw manual stabilization.

25. The procedure called "rapid extrication" may be performed in certain emergencies. Write three examples of such emergencies.

a.

b.

c.

Vocabulary Practice

Choose from the list of words and terms to complete each sentence. Each may be used more than once.

cervical	lumbar	spinal column
brain	coccygeal	spinal cord
thoracic	vertebrae	sacral

1. The _____ _____ is responsible for sending signals

   from the _____ to the body and for receiving signals from the body and

   relaying them to the _____.

2. The _____ _____ is made up of 33 bones, one

   stacked on top of another. These bones are called _____. They fit and

   move together, so we can bend, turn, and flex.

3. The spine is divided into five regions. They are the _____,

   _____, _____, _____,

   and _____.

4. The _____ spine starts at the base of the skull where the spinal cord

   begins. It has seven _____.

5. The _____ spine is supported by the rib cage. It has

   12 _____, one for each rib.

6. The next group of five vertebrae makes up the _____ spine. These bones

   carry the weight of most of the body.

7. The last two regions of the body are the _____ and

   _____ spines. Together they form the posterior portion of the pelvis.

The Call: A Diving Accident

Read the scenario and answer the questions that follow. Focus on protecting the patient's spine while completing other tasks necessary to manage the patient.

You are enjoying a peaceful day in the mountains when you suddenly hear screams for help coming from the direction of a nearby creek. You rush over to a small, deep pool that is popular with summer hikers and find a group of people crowded around a 16-year-old boy on a sand bar. He apparently dove into the pool and struck a small outcropping of rocks with the top of his head. Fellow swimmers rescued him from the pool.

The patient, John, is lying on his back. Blood is seeping from a wound on the top of his head. One of his friends, obviously terrified, takes John by the shoulders and shakes him. "John, c'mon, get up buddy," he pleads.

"Don't touch him!" another of his friends screams. "Can't you see that he's hurt badly?"

You notice that two other ashen-faced friends are standing nearby.

1. Describe your approach to handling this situation. What might you do to get this scene under control?

2. What are your top priorities in assessing and treating John?

You find that John is awake but confused. His airway is patent. He appears to be breathing adequately, but you see that his abdomen, not his chest, moves with each breath. His pulse is 88 and strong at the wrist. His only injury appears to be the head wound. Bleeding is controlled. John is able to move his left arm slightly, which is the only extremity movement you see.

3. As you are caring for John, an onlooker says, "It looks like he can move one of his arms. That's a good sign, isn't it?" Which one of the following would be the best response to this question?
   a. "He may still have a permanent spine injury. It's too early to tell."
   b. "That sure is. Keep your fingers crossed that everything's going to be okay."
   c. "Spine injuries can get worse over time. We'll have to let the doctors sort it out."
   d. "Movement is good. Since we don't know the extent of injury, we're going to hold him very still until the paramedics arrive."

By now you have completed your initial assessment and physical exam, throughout which John's head and neck have been manually stabilized in a neutral in-line position. Now, instead of speaking in confused sentences, John has become unresponsive and his eyes don't seem to focus on anything. His pulse has dropped to 44 beats per minute, and his breathing appears more labored.

4. What can you do at this point to help John?

5. "He's getting worse!" one of his friends shouts. "Let's carry him up to the road so that he'll be closer to the paramedics when they arrive." Do you agree or disagree with this plan? Explain.

6. Paramedics have arrived. Give them a brief hand-off report about John, including information about the mechanism of injury, your assessment, and your treatment.

Active Learning

Go to the Internet address http://academic.uofs.edu/department/pt/students/charts.htm to determine which part of the spine provides innervation to the following areas: chest at nipple level; thumb; umbilicus; top of the foot; bottom of the foot.

25 | Musculoskeletal Injuries

Key Ideas

This chapter focuses on First Responder care of patients with injuries to muscles, joints, and bones. Key ideas include the following:

- Muscle, joint, and bone injuries are some of the most common injuries First Responders will encounter. They can range from minor ankle or knee sprains to life-threatening fractures of the neck or pelvis.

- Accurate assessment and aggressive treatment of musculoskeletal injuries can prevent permanent disability and death.

- Since it is not possible for a First Responder to distinguish between sprains and strains or dislocations and fractures, First Responders are to treat all musculoskeletal injuries the same way.

- Patients who have suffered critical injuries require the First Responder to arrange for rapid transport to the hospital.

Exam Warm-up

1. The musculoskeletal system is made up of more than _____ bones and over _____ muscles.
   a. 200, 600
   b. 100, 300
   c. 50, 150
   d. 25, 75

2. With an indirect force, the energy of a blow
   a. causes an injury at the point of impact.
   b. is sent in parallel paths away from the body.
   c. travels along a path away from the point of impact.
   d. turns one body part away from a connecting body part.

3. An obvious injury, like a broken leg, may actually be one of several related injuries.

_____ True

_____ False

4. In an emergency involving a musculoskeletal injury, you should stay focused on treating the patient's life-threatening injuries. Once that is done, you can turn to limb-threatening injuries.

_____ True

_____ False

5. Your patient has closed musculoskeletal injuries to the forearm. To check for a distal pulse, you must palpate the _____ pulse.
   a. radial
   b. tibial
   c. femoral
   d. brachial

6. Your patient has closed injuries to the ankle. To check for a distal pulse, you must palpate the posterior _____ or the dorsalis pedis pulse.
   a. radial
   b. tibial
   c. femoral
   d. brachial

7. The ability to move an extremity, such as wiggling fingers or toes, means that impulses from the _____ system can reach these points.
   a. nervous
   b. endocrine
   c. circulatory
   d. musculoskeletal

8. You must maintain manual stabilization of an injured limb until the patient is completely immobilized from head to toe on a long backboard.

_____ True

_____ False

9. A splint that completely surrounds an injured limb may best be called a(n) _____ splint.
   a. rigid
   b. traction
   c. improvised
   d. circumferential

10. A splint made from any available material that can immobilize an injured limb may best be called a(n) _____ splint.
   a. rigid
   b. traction
   c. improvised
   d. circumferential

11. Which one of the following splints would NOT be appropriate for immobilizing a painful, swollen, deformed forearm?
   a. board splint
   b. improvised splint
   c. circumferential splint
   d. pillow splint

12. BSI precautions are NOT necessary during a splinting procedure.

_____ True

_____ False

Short-Answer Review

13. List three major functions of the musculoskeletal system.

   a.

   b.

   c.

14. Common mechanisms of musculoskeletal injury include what three types of forces?

   a.

   b.

   c.

15. List five signs and symptoms of musculoskeletal injury.

   a.

   b.

   c.

   d.

   e.

16. Explain the following statement: "Sprains, dislocations, and fractures are all treated the same in the field."

17. Your patient is lying on the side of a two-lane road after falling from her bicycle. There is an open injury to her left leg half way between the ankle and knee. What appears to be a broken bone protrudes from the wound. Number the following actions 1–8 to show the order in which they should be performed.

_____ a. Cover the open wound at the injury site.

_____ b. Assess for distal pulse, movement, and sensation.

_____ c. Complete a scene size-up.

_____ d. Splint the injured leg.

_____ e. Complete a physical examination.

_____ f. Reassess for distal pulse, movement, and sensation.

_____ g. Complete an initial assessment.

_____ h. Manually stabilize the injured leg.

18. List five reasons for splinting a musculoskeletal injury.

a.

b.

c.

d.

e.

19. The patient has an open angulated injury to the lower leg. The First Responder decides not to remove the patient's jeans before splinting in order to avoid moving the protruding bone and making the injury worse. Do you agree or disagree? If you disagree, write your reasons.

20. List three problems that can be caused by improper splinting.

    a.

    b.

    c.

21. You are managing a 14-year-old patient who has a closed injury to her forearm. The bone appears to be bent at an angle between the elbow and the wrist. You attempt to straighten it by pulling gentle traction, but she screams, "Ow! It hurts!" What should you do?

22. You and your partner are managing a patient who has fallen and presents with an elbow injury. Your partner turns to you and states, "There's no way we can leave that elbow bent like that. We need to straighten it so that extrication will be easier." What do you think? Explain your answer.

23. Analyze the splinting strategies used to immobilize the following injuries. Decide if you agree or disagree. If you disagree, write the correct answer in the space provided.

   a. A broken humerus was splinted with a padded board that was secured with a roller bandage. A sling and swathe was used to support the arm.

   b. A broken forearm was immobilized by straightening the arm at the elbow and applying a cardboard splint that extended from below the wrist to just below the elbow.

   c. The fractured hand was splinted by flattening the palm side against a padded board splint and securing it with a roller bandage.

   d. The patient has an injured pelvis. He was secured to a long backboard with padding between his legs and a blanket on each side of his hips.

   e. The fractured tibia was splinted by securing two padded splints on either side of the leg, one extending from the hip to below the foot, and the foot was secured in place by a triangle bandage.

Vocabulary Practice

Across

1. Bone of lower leg.
4. Always take these precautions.
6. Symptom of bone or joint injury.
9. Knee cap.
13. Sign of bone or joint injury.
15. Bone of lower leg.
17. Type of splint.
18. Phalanges.
21. This is used to support an injured arm or hand and is suspended from the neck.
22. Collarbone.
23. Upper arm bone.
27. These connect muscle to bone.
28. Lower arm bone.
29. This keeps an injured arm protected and immobile against the body.

Down

2. Components of musculoskeletal system.
3. Metatarsals.
5. Sign of bone or joint injury.
7. Tarsals.
8. Device used to immobilize a body part.
10. This is used to form a sling or swathe.
11. Extremity.
12. Breastbone.
14. Phalanges.
16. Check for a distal _____ before and after splinting.
19. Shoulder blade.
20. Bone in the thigh.
22. This can help reduce pain and swelling.
23. Metacarpals.
24. Lower arm bone.
25. Carpals.
26. Joint of the leg.

The Call: An Auto vs. Bridge Abutment

Read the scenario and answer the questions that follow. Focus on prioritizing the management of musculoskeletal injuries as well as on the correct technique for splinting.

You are on a Sunday drive in the country when you notice that a sedan has just crashed head-on into a concrete bridge abutment. After reporting the incident on your cellular telephone, you approach to assess the scene and the patients. The scene appears to be safe. The car has suffered severe front-end damage. The steering wheel is not bent. The windshield has been starred on the passenger side. There are three patients in the car. The status of each follows:

Patient A: 22-year-old male, driver of the car. Was restrained with a three-point seat belt. Complains of pain and swelling to his right ankle and lower left leg. Has a small bump to his forehead where he impacted the side window. Did not lose consciousness. Appears to have strong radial pulses. Skin signs appear normal. Has good distal pulses and sensation in all extremities.

Patient B: 21-year-old male, unrestrained front-seat passenger. He was thrown against the windshield and dashboard. Presents as very combative, with a large bruise to his forehead. Has serious-looking chest injuries. Right humerus and forearm appear to be deformed. Severe pelvic pain with palpation. Has weak radial pulses. Skin is pale, cool, and moist.

Patient C: 23-year-old female, back-seat passenger. Was restrained with a three-point seat belt. Did not lose consciousness. Complains of pain and deformity to her left clavicle and wrist. Is also unable to straighten her left knee, which is swollen and painful. Has strong radial pulses. Skin is pale, warm, and dry. Has a good distal pulse and sensation in her arms. There are no pulses present at her left foot.

1. Order these patients from most severely injured (1) to least severely injured (3). Explain how you arrived at your decisions.

   _____ **a.** Patient A:

   _____ **b.** Patient B:

   _____ **c.** Patient C:

2. An EMT ambulance and two fire trucks arrive. A helicopter has also been dispatched. The patients are extricated and placed on long backboards. You move over to where rescuers are packaging Patient B for transport. You remember that his humerus appeared fractured during your exam, and you reach for splinting materials from an open first aid box. An EMT turns to you and says, "I appreciate your help, but that arm just gets strapped to his chest. Nothing more." Why would this EMT say this? Agree? Disagree?

3. You assist with Patient C. You have already splinted her wrist and are trying to apply a sling and swathe to her injured clavicle. Every time you try to apply the sling and swathe, you move her arm slightly, causing her severe pain. "Just let me hold my left arm with my good arm," she suggests. Does this seem to be an acceptable alternative? Explain your answer.

4. Another rescuer attempts to straighten Patient C's left leg, but she screams when he tries to do so. Describe a splinting strategy for this injury.

5. Describe a simple technique for splinting Patient A's ankle injury.

Active Learning

1. Have a classmate put your dominant arm (the one you use to write) in a sling. Perform some daily activities (handshakes, writing, opening doors) with the sling on. Then apply one to your partner, who should perform similar daily activities. Discuss: How does it feel? How will it affect the way you care for patients who have been immobilized?

2. Improvise a splint out of non-traditional materials (such as household or office items) to splint the following body parts (below). For each splint you apply, remember the rule of immobilizing the bone ends and adjacent joints.
   a. Finger
   b. Lower arm
   c. Lower leg

26 | Childbirth

Key Ideas

This chapter describes the basic anatomy of pregnancy, stages of childbirth, and assessment and management of both the baby and mother during and after delivery. Key ideas include the following:

- Childbirth is a natural, normal process. However, it is physically traumatic, and complications to both the baby and mother do occur, though infrequently. While emergency deliveries do occur in the field, most mothers in labor are able to deliver their babies in the hospital.

- Childbirth is divided into three stages of labor: dilation, expulsion, and placental.

- First Responders must be able to determine whether or not birth is imminent.

- The role of the First Responder is to help coach the mother through the delivery and then to support the mother's and baby's airway, breathing, and circulation.

- First Responders may at some point manage a patient experiencing pregnancy or birth complications. Most pregnancy complications can lead to shock. Pregnancy complications most commonly involve a problem with the umbilical cord or the position of the baby prior to or during delivery. Other delivery complications may involve multiple or premature births.

Exam Warm-up

1. The _____ contains a mucous plug that is discharged during labor.
   a. vagina
   b. placenta
   c. cervix
   d. perineum

2. The _____ provides nourishment and oxygen to the fetus from the mother's blood. It also absorbs waste from the fetus into the mother's bloodstream.
   a. vagina
   b. cervix
   c. placenta
   d. perineum

3. A full-term pregnancy lasts approximately _____ days.
   a. 175
   b. 280
   c. 360
   d. 420

4. At the beginning of the dilation stage of labor, contractions commonly occur 10 to 20 minutes apart and last about _____ to _____ seconds each.
   a. 1, 2
   b. 5, 10
   c. 30, 60
   d. 90, 120

5. If contractions are more than _____ minutes apart, the mother usually has time to be transported to a hospital.
   a. 5
   b. 4
   c. 3
   d. 2

6. If contractions are _____ minutes apart, the mother usually has NO time to be transported to a hospital.
   a. 12
   b. 7
   c. 8
   d. 2

7. One way to tell if you should prepare for a normal delivery of the baby on scene is to examine the mother for
   a. crowning.
   b. toxemia.
   c. rupture.
   d. dilation.

8. At what point will a woman in labor have an uncontrollable urge to push down?
   a. at any stage
   b. dilation stage
   c. expulsion stage
   d. placental stage

9. In which one of the following positions should your patient be placed while in the first and second stages of labor?
   a. supine
   b. standing
   c. left lateral
   d. position of comfort

10. To protect the baby and the mother from contamination and infection, all materials used during delivery should be sterile, or at least as clean as possible.

   _____ True

   _____ False

11. Since _____ causes muscles to tighten, to help a mother relax, have her _____ with each contraction.
   a. inhaling, exhale
   b. exhaling, exhale
   c. exhaling, inhale
   d. inhaling, inhale

12. During the expulsion stage of labor, have the mother hold her breath for _____ to _____ seconds when she bears down. Any longer will cause too much straining, broken blood vessels, and tearing of the area around the vagina.
   a. 1, 3
   b. 3, 6
   c. 7, 10
   d. 11, 15

13. To prevent an explosive delivery, you should
   a. firmly press the mother's legs together.
   b. apply firm pressure to the vaginal opening.
   c. elevate the mother's buttocks 8 to 12 inches.
   d. apply very gentle pressure to the baby's head.

14. What should you do if the baby's head delivers and you see that the amniotic sac is still intact and covering the baby's face?
   a. Leave the sac alone. It will rupture at the appropriate time.
   b. Pinch the sac, and push it away from the infant's head and mouth.
   c. Immediately place your patient in a knee-chest position.
   d. Cut the sac using a pair of sterile surgical scissors.

15. Meconium staining is NOT a life-threatening event. Just be sure to suction out the baby's airway.

   _____ True

   _____ False

16. What should you do if after the baby's head delivers, you see that the umbilical cord is wrapped around his neck?
    a. Do nothing. The baby is in no danger.
    b. Immediately cut the cord to prevent strangulation.
    c. Use two fingers to slip the cord over the baby's shoulder.
    d. Apply pressure to the baby's head to prevent it from delivering.

17. The baby has delivered, but she is not breathing. What is the first thing you should do?
    a. Suction the mouth and then the nose.
    b. Provide artificial ventilation immediately.
    c. Hold the baby by the feet and slap her buttocks.
    d. Nothing. She will breathe on her own in a few minutes.

18. The baby is still not breathing. What is the second thing you should do?
    a. Provide tactile stimulation.
    b. Provide artificial ventilation.
    c. Provide both oral and aural stimulation.
    d. Nothing. She will breathe on her own in a few minutes.

19. The baby is still not breathing. What is the third thing you should do?
    a. Suction the mouth and then the nose.
    b. Provide artificial ventilation immediately.
    c. Hold the baby by the feet and slap her buttocks.
    d. Nothing. She will breathe on her own in a few minutes.

20. After the baby has been delivered, assist the mother with delivery of the placenta in which of the following ways?
    a. Encourage the mother to bear down as the uterus contracts.
    b. Gently guide the placenta and attached membranes from the vagina.
    c. Gently tug on the umbilical cord to help the placenta pass.
    d. Massage the uterus to help it expel the placenta.

21. In a normal delivery, you can expect the mother to lose about _____ cc of blood.
    a. 500
    b. 1,000
    c. 1,500
    d. 2,000

22. Your patient has delivered both the baby and the placenta and is experiencing heavy bleeding. Management strategies for this patient include all the following EXCEPT
    a. Pack the inside of the vagina with gauze pads.
    b. Place sanitary napkins over the opening of the vagina.
    c. Encourage the mother to begin breastfeeding, if she plans to do so.
    d. Massage the lower abdomen to help the uterus contract.

23. The primary goal(s) of managing both the mother and baby after delivery include which of the following?
    a. Keep them warm.
    b. Regularly reassess the status of their ABCs.
    c. Keep them in close contact to one another.
    d. Assure both are transported immediately to be evaluated by a physician.

24. The recommended rate for assisting a newborn's ventilations is between _____ breaths per minute.
    a. 10–20
    b. 30–60
    c. 80–100
    d. 120–140

25. If the newborn's breathing and pulse are absent or if the pulse rate is less than _____ beats per minute, then start CPR.
    a. 20
    b. 40
    c. 60
    d. 80

26. For CPR on a newborn, the rate of compressions is _____ per minute and the ratio of compressions to breaths is _____.
    a. 120, 3:1
    b. 100, 5:1
    c. 100, 5:2
    d. 120, 3:2

27. What is the proper method for maintaining perfusion in the baby when a prolapsed cord occurs?
    a. Monitor the situation carefully.
    b. Immediately clamp and cut the umbilical cord.
    c. Gently push the head off the umbilical cord.
    d. Push the umbilical cord back into the vagina.

28. You are assisting with the delivery of a baby. Your partner is ready to apply gentle pressure against the baby's head as it delivers, when he says, "It's a breech birth! The baby's bottom is delivering first!" The buttocks and trunk deliver quickly, but the baby's head appears to be stuck in the vaginal canal. Your next course of action should be to:
    a. rush the mother and child to the hospital.
    b. very gently pull at the baby's torso.
    c. form an airway for the baby with your fingers.
    d. slip your hand under the baby's head and pull.

29. When managing twin births, the primary reason why you must clamp and cut the cord is to
    a. prevent bleeding to the second baby.
    b. move the first-born baby out of the way.
    c. prevent the twins from becoming entangled in it.
    d. avoid confusion about which cord belongs to which baby.

30. Which one of the following is NOT true about premature babies?
    a. A premature baby is born before the 36th week of pregnancy.
    b. Premature babies are more susceptible to infection.
    c. Premature babies cannot tolerate losing even tiny amounts of blood.
    d. Premature babies should not receive supplemental oxygen.

Short-Answer Review

31. How do the contractions a woman experiences at the beginning of labor compare to the contractions when delivery is imminent?

32. Describe the technique for measuring the length and frequency of contractions.

33. List five questions you might ask an expectant mother in order to determine if delivery is imminent.

a.

b.

c.

d.

e.

34. You are managing a patient who is in labor. She was sitting in a chair when you arrived. You had her get in a supine position on the floor, and she immediately became quite pale and lightheaded. What may have happened to this patient, and how can you remedy it?

35. Describe how you would provide a woman in labor with encouragement, support, and coaching. How could you make her feel more calm, reassured, and confident? Provide specific examples.

36. List the equipment that should be included in your obstetrical kit.

37. List five BSI precautions you should take prior to and after delivery.

    a.

    b.

    c.

    d.

    e.

38. The infant emerges with the amniotic sac still intact. There is meconium staining. You break the sac and push it away from the baby's face. What should you do next?

39. List three conditions that would require you to perform artificial ventilation on a newborn.

    a.

    b.

    c.

Vocabulary Practice

Across

2. Disk-shaped organ attached to the uterus during pregnancy.
3. Appearance of the baby's head at the opening of the birth canal.
5. Short for body substance isolation.
7. These are your top priorities for the mother and the newborn.
11. Placenta, when it delivers.
15. A woman has two fallopian _____.
17. Fetal bowel movement.
19. Process of childbirth.
21. Normal labor is divided into _____ stages.

Down

1. The cervix and this make up the birth canal.
3. The umbilical _____ may be tied or clamped after the baby is born.
4. Plural of ovum, or egg.
6. Pregnant patients in this position could develop shock.
8. Neck of the uterus.
9. The amniotic _____ is also called the bag of waters.
10. Organ that contains the developing fetus.
12. "Poisoning" of the blood during pregnancy.
13. In this type of birth, the feet deliver first.
14. Identical twins have _____ umbilical cords coming out of a single placenta.
16. The bloody _____ is a plug of mucus that is discharged during labor.
18. Start this if the newborn's pulse rate is less than 60 beats per minute.
20. Short for obstetrics.

The Call: Delivery in a Station Wagon

Read the scenario and answer the questions that follow. Keep in mind that labor is a natural process, not an illness or an injury.

You are dispatched to a "delivery in progress" on a busy expressway and arrive to find a woman in labor in the back seat of a station wagon. Her frantic husband had attempted to drive her to the hospital—which is still about 10 minutes away—but stopped and called for help when it looked like she was going to deliver her baby in the car.

Your patient is lying sideways on the back seat. She is calling out for her husband, who is nervously pacing at the front of the car. Sweat is pouring down her face, and in between contractions she moans softly.

1. What strategies would you use to gain control of the scene, your patient, and her husband?

2. You time her contractions and find that they are six minutes apart, lasting about 45 seconds each. The hospital is about 10 minutes away, and traffic is relatively light. The transporting ambulance is about three minutes away. This is your patient's first baby. Do you want to set up to deliver the baby or arrange for the ambulance to transport her to the hospital? Explain.

3. Ten minutes have passed. There is still no ambulance. Dispatch tells you that the ambulance has been caught in a heavy traffic snarl and will be delayed at least 10 more minutes. What patient exam or patient history information would help you to determine how imminent the delivery might be?

4. A gush of clear liquid splashes your patient's thighs. "Oh my! What was that?" she screams. "Is the baby coming?" Explain to your patient what has happened.

5. Your patient now tells you, "I need to push. I can't help it. I've got to push now." You check her vagina and see that the baby's head is visible. Explain what is happening.

6. The ambulance has just arrived, and so has the baby. You note that the newborn is fairly blue and limp. She is not crying. You vigorously suction, dry, and stimulate the baby, but she still remains limp and unresponsive. What is the next step in resuscitating this baby?

7. Success! The baby is now crying. She has turned from blue to pink and appears to have good muscle tone. The exuberant father wants to close the doors of the station wagon and drive his wife and child to the hospital himself. After all, he says, she is already in the car. No sense in making a mess of the ambulance, too. Do you agree or disagree with his plan? Explain your answer.

Active Learning

Explore an actual OB kit. Identify each of the pieces included within and describe when you would use them.

27 | Infants and Children

Key Ideas

This chapter identifies emotional needs of children and parents in pediatric emergencies, describes a pediatric physical assessment, and identifies treatment strategies for common pediatric emergencies. Key ideas include the following:

- When managing an emergency involving a pediatric patient, First Responders must deal compassionately with the adults who are affected by the child's illness or injury. The top priority, however, is the health and safety of the patient.

- Assessment of a pediatric patient is similar to adult assessment in many ways. However, First Responders must take into account differences in anatomy and developmental characteristics when assessing an infant or child.

- Pediatric patients compensate better for shock than adults do. They also tend to decompensate rapidly when their shock state becomes severe. Hypothermia will intensify the problems faced by a pediatric patient in shock.

- Respiratory distress is one of the most common pediatric emergencies. Treating the airway and breathing in an infant or child is the top priority for First Responder care.

- Most cardiac arrests in infants and children are caused by airway obstructions or respiratory arrest. Effective resuscitation depends on diligent airway and breathing management and effective CPR.

Exam Warm-up

1. The patient most likely to be quite fearful of separation from parents is the
   a. infant.
   b. toddler.
   c. preschooler.
   d. school-age child.
   e. adolescent.

2. At this age, the _____ is very sensitive to peer pressure and may need to be reassured that what he or she tells you will be held in confidence.
   a. infant
   b. toddler
   c. preschooler
   d. school-age child
   e. adolescent

3. At this age, the _____ is very curious, so be especially alert to the possibility of poison ingestion.
   a. infant
   b. toddler
   c. preschooler
   d. school-age child
   e. adolescent

4. At this age, the _____ is likely to cooperate and be willing to follow the lead of parents and the EMS provider.
   a. infant
   b. toddler
   c. preschooler
   d. school-age child
   e. adolescent

5. At this age, the _____ may be scared and feel that what is happening is his or her fault.
   a. infant
   b. toddler
   c. preschooler
   d. school-age child
   e. adolescent

6. When a child is injured, the First Responder should view the situation as one that involves just the child, not the whole family.

   _____ True

   _____ False

7. You have been called to the scene of an injured 6-year-old girl. Her father refuses to let you help. You should
   a. keep in mind that the parent may be correct.
   b. provide lifesaving emergency care to the child.
   c. explain how the law looks upon a neglecting parent.
   d. distract him so your partner can provide emergency care.

8. One way to assess an infant's or child's level of responsiveness is to see if the patient is oriented to time and place.

   _____ True

   _____ False

9. The single most important care you can provide for a pediatric patient is to ensure an open airway.

_____ True

_____ False

10. If an infant's respirations are less than _____ per minute or a child's are less than _____, assist ventilations.
    a. 20, 10
    b. 40, 20
    c. 60, 40
    d. 80, 60

11. When a pediatric patient is not breathing and has no gag reflex, a(n) _____ should be inserted to assist in maintaining an open airway if manual techniques fail.
    a. bulb syringe
    b. oropharyngeal airway
    c. nasopharyngeal airway
    d. tonsil-tip suction catheter

12. Pay attention to your overall impression of how the pediatric patient looks and acts. Your observations may tell you more about the status of the patient than any vital sign.

_____ True

_____ False

13. Children sometimes breathe irregularly, so monitor respirations for _____ seconds to determine the rate.
    a. 15
    b. 30
    c. 60
    d. 75

14. Respiration rates in children alter easily due to emotional or physical conditions, so an increase over a previous rate is not significant.

_____ True

_____ False

15. Which one of the following statements about pediatric vital signs is NOT true?
    a. If pulse is too rapid or too slow, assess for respiratory distress, shock, or head injury.
    b. If capillary refill takes more than two seconds, the child may be in shock.
    c. Measure an infant's pulse at the brachial pulse point.
    d. Low blood pressure is an early indicator of shock.

16. Your four-year-old patient's vital signs are respirations 36, pulse 146, and blood pressure 76/56. These measurements are within normal ranges.

_____ True

_____ False

17. Always suspect a foreign body airway obstruction (FBAO) in any short-of-breath or unresponsive infant or child.

_____ True

_____ False

18. Which one of the following is the most common cause of cardiac arrest in children?
    a. elevated pulse rates
    b. shock or scarlet fever
    c. noisy breathing and hypothermia
    d. airway obstruction and respiratory arrest

19. Which two of the following actions would NOT be appropriate when managing a child who is actively seizing?
    a. Restrain the child to prevent injury.
    b. Suction the airway using a suction device.
    c. Turn the child to one side to help clear the airway.
    d. Administer oxygen holding a mask slightly away from the face.

20. All seizures in pediatric patients, even those associated with high fever, should be considered potentially life threatening.

_____ True

_____ False

21. Which one of the following is NOT typical of a SIDS baby?
    a. is between the ages of four weeks and seven months
    b. has had several recent illnesses
    c. was asleep when he or she died
    d. was born prematurely

22. SIDS is a preventable disease.

_____ True

_____ False

23. When on the scene of a possible SIDS baby, you should
    a. try to find some concrete evidence of neglect or abuse.
    b. be careful to avoid suggesting that the parents are to blame.
    c. refuse to answer questions related to the infant's condition.
    d. avoid or keep to a minimum any interaction with the parents.

Short-Answer Review

24. Complete the chart by writing in the missing information.

Patient	Age Range in Years
Infant	
Toddler	
Preschooler	
School-Age	
Adolescent	

25. Describe one technique that you might be able to use to respond to parents who are very upset.

26. You arrive at the scene of a pediatric seizure patient. 18-month-old Katie has been running a fever for the past 36 hours and reportedly had a generalized seizure lasting about 45 seconds. She is conscious and crying. Her mother is quite upset. Between sobs, the mother tells you that Katie has been undergoing some tests to determine whether she has a chronic seizure disorder.

Your partner, impatient with the mother's tears, cuts her off and states, "Ma'am, it looks like this is a simple seizure caused by a high fever. The paramedics are here and we need to get Katie moving to the hospital." Your partner then leads the mother to the front passenger seat of the ambulance "so that the paramedics can concentrate on taking care of Katie."

Critique his behavior. What would be an appropriate response to this parent's information and behavior?

27. Generally, as part of any scene size-up, you would ask, "Why was EMS called?" and "What is the chief complaint?" What other scene size-up question should you be sure to ask the caregiver of a pediatric patient?

28. What are five signs of early respiratory distress in pediatric patients?

a.

b.

c.

d.

e.

29. One way to assess circulation in infants and children is by palpating a pulse. Complete the sentences below by filling in the appropriate pulse points.

a. Palpate an infant's _____ pulse.

b. Palpate an unresponsive child's _____ or

_____ pulse.

c. Palpate a responsive child's _____ or

_____ pulse.

30. List six SAMPLE history questions you would want answered by a sick infant's caregiver.

a.

b.

c.

d.

e.

f.

31. While caring for a five-year-old girl who has fallen feet-first about five feet onto ceramic tile, a First Responder asks the parents, "How does your daughter usually respond to pain?" Explain why the First Responder asked this question.

32. For each of the following facts, list the implications for possible injuries, illness, or treatment. The first one has been completed as an example.
    a. Young children explore their world by putting objects in their mouth.
       Answer: Young children can experience foreign body airway obstruction. Always rule out foreign body aspiration in any young child complaining of difficulty breathing.

    b. Infants have proportionately larger tongues than older children and adults.

    c. Children have proportionately larger heads than adults.

    d. Children have much less blood volume than adults.

    e. A child's skin surface is large compared to body mass.

    f. Children often have extremely short necks.

33. List five signs and symptoms of shock in the pediatric patient:

a.

b.

c.

d.

e.

34. An asthma attack in an infant or child is a serious medical emergency. Describe First Responder care.

35. List four signs and symptoms of circulatory failure in the pediatric patient:

a.

b.

c.

d.

36. You are alone, and your patient is an infant who is breathless and pulseless. Write the next two steps you should perform.

a.

b.

37. Your infant patient has just suffered a seizure. So you ask the parents if the baby has had seizures before. "Yes," the mother answers. What else should you ask immediately? List five questions.

a.

b.

c.

d.

e.

38. What do the letters SIDS stand for?

S:

I:

D:

S:

39. You find that your patient is an infant boy who is breathless, pulseless, stiff, and cold in his crib. You suspect SIDS. What questions do you need to ask? List six.

a.

b.

c.

d.

e.

f.

40. List five signs and symptoms of physical abuse in an infant or child.

a.

b.

c.

d.

e.

41. List five signs and symptoms of neglect.

a.

b.

c.

d.

e.

42. A First Responder arrives on scene to find a child with injuries that raise the possibility of child abuse. The First Responder says to the parent, "You need to know that I think you have abused your child, and I'm going to report you to the hospital staff and local law enforcement." Do you think this statement was appropriate? Why or why not?

43. To learn the reporting protocols for your EMS system in regard to child abuse and neglect, you must find out what six pieces of information?

a.

b.

c.

d.

e.

f.

44. Calls involving the injury or death of a pediatric patient have a way of affecting EMS rescuers very deeply. After the event, methods such as CISD can help. The letters CISD stand for:

C:

I:

S:

D:

Vocabulary Practice

Across

1. Child _____ is a term meaning improper or excessive action so as to injure or cause harm.
4. Abbreviation for liters per minute.
7. Common cause of seizures in children.
8. Child _____ is a term meaning insufficient attention or respect.
10. A school-age child is _____ to 12 years old.
13. These patients are infants or children.
14. A preschooler is three to _____ years old.
15. Patient for whom 120 is a normal pulse.
16. Common condition among children.
18. Technique used to deliver oxygen.
20. Take this pulse in a child.
22. Dehydration is a major cause of this in children.
23. Take this pulse in an infant.
25. Short for patient assessment triangle.

Down

2. Type of history.
3. Delayed capillary _____ suggests shock.
5. Short for airway, breathing, and circulation.
6. Short for bag-valve-mask device.
7. Soft spot on the top of an infant's skull.
9. Patient who is one to three years old.
11. Patient who is younger than one year.
12. For a pediatric patient, nothing is more important than caring for this.
17. Short for sudden infant death syndrome.
18. A _____ syringe is a type of suction device.
19. Common viral infection of the upper airway.
21. Short for critical incident stress debriefing.
24. In an infant or child, a pulse below 60 requires this.

The Call: Shortness of Breath in Kindergarten

Read this scenario and answer the questions that follow. Remember that infants and children require different levels of explanation about what is happening to their bodies and what you are doing to help them. A simple, straightforward, reassuring approach is best.

You have been dispatched to a kindergarten class at the local elementary school for a five-year-old female who is having difficulty breathing. You arrive to find Lateesha sitting at her desk in a tripod position, eyes wide with fear, audibly wheezing. Her respirations are rapid and labored, her skin appears to be pale and grayish. Her teacher tells you that her pediatrician suspects that Lateesha may be developing asthma.

1. Lateesha's initial vital signs are as follows: respirations of 36, pulse of 146, BP of 120/86. Are these vital signs low, normal, or high for a five-year-old? If they are low or high, what would be normal?

2. List five questions you would like to ask Lateesha. Be sure to state them in a manner appropriate for a five-year-old.

   a.

   b.

   c.

   d.

   e.

3. The paramedics have arrived, and you must give them a hand-off report. Write 1–8 to correctly order the information in your report to them.

_____ a. Lateesha is currently undergoing tests to determine if she has asthma.

_____ b. This is Lateesha. She is five years old. About 20 minutes ago, she became acutely short of breath.

_____ c. Lateesha's medical card states that she takes no medications and has no drug, food, or other types of allergies.

_____ d. We initially found Lateesha sitting in this chair in a tripod position, stating that she was having difficulty breathing, with labored respirations of 36, a pulse of 146, and a BP of 120/86.

_____ e. Lateesha was using some accessory muscles to breathe. She had audible wheezes and was able to talk in only two- or three-word sentences.

_____ f. We applied high-flow oxygen by nonrebreather mask. After a few minutes it appeared that Lateesha experienced some relief. However, she remains quite short of breath.

_____ g. Lateesha's mother has been called, and she should be here any minute.

_____ h. Lateesha said she became short of breath while playing chase on the playground.

Active Learning

1. What equipment that can be used on an adult can also be used on children? What equipment due to size or volume must be exclusively used for pediatric patients? Examine the pediatric equipment carried by your agency (or available in class) and compare it to similar adult equipment.

2. Practice taking vital signs of children of different ages. (Invite children you know, such as relatives or children of fellow class members, for example.) Take pulse, respirations, blood pressure, and capillary refill on the children. While you take the vitals, explain what you are doing. Then discuss: Did your explanation of what you were doing differ with different children? Why? How did you feel taking these vital signs compared to vital signs you have taken on adults?

28 | Geriatric Patients

Key Ideas

This chapter provides an overview of special considerations First Responders should be aware of when caring for elderly patients. Key ideas include the following:

- Most elderly people lead active, productive lives. It is a misconception that the elderly population as a whole is sickly, in nursing homes or extended care facilities, or frail.

- Elderly people do experience changes due to aging, including thinner, more fragile skin, decreased functioning of senses, and decreased efficiency of the cardiac and respiratory systems.

- Depression and substance abuse are common in the elderly, and they may also suffer from abuse and neglect.

- Elderly patients may have one or more preexisting medical conditions, making the patient history very important. Elderly patients may also deny signs and symptoms because of fear or denial of their condition.

Exam Warm-up

1. Which one of the following is NOT a common change due to aging?
   a. high blood pressure
   b. toughening of the skin
   c. decreased lung capacity
   d. slowing digestive processes

2. Depression is common in the elderly.

   _____ True

   _____ False

3. An elderly patient who has one or more risk factors is likely to be abused or neglected. Those risk factors include all those listed below EXCEPT
   a. requires assistance with daily activities.
   b. exhibits bizarre behavior.
   c. has lost bladder control.
   d. has difficulty hearing.

4. Which one of the following statements about assessment of the elderly patient is FALSE?
   a. Take a position at the patient's eye level.
   b. Address the patient by a full or formal name.
   c. Speak to a family member, not the patient, when possible.
   d. During scene size-up, be alert for signs of substance abuse.

5. All the following statements about the initial assessment of elderly patients are true EXCEPT
   a. curvature of the spine can make it difficult to correctly position the head.
   b. false teeth should usually be removed prior to artificial ventilation.
   c. bleeding may be harder to control if the patient is taking aspirin.
   d. a patient who has had a stroke could develop airway problems.

Short-Answer Review

6. List one change due to aging a geriatric patient may experience for each of the following.

   Respiratory system:

   Circulatory system:

   Musculoskeletal system:

   Sensory organs:

   Skin:

7. You are treating an elderly patient who appears to be in considerable pain but is minimizing her symptoms and does not want to go to the hospital.

   a. List three reasons that the patient might be refusing transport even though she has significant pain.

   b. For each of the reasons above, list one way you might convince the patient to accept care.

8. List three examples of an elderly patient at high risk for abuse by a caretaker or family member.

   a.

   b.

   c.

9. What are three of the most common causes of traumatic injury in the elderly?

   a.

   b.

   c.

10. You are treating an elderly patient who is hard of hearing but alert and oriented. Describe how you would modify your communication with the patient to deal with this situation.

Vocabulary Practice

Circle the words for the things that are affected by aging. Then write the words on the lines below the puzzle. Hint: There are exactly 33.

```
M B S S E L F E S T E E M W F Y S N S E
I O L M B W D D P W S K I N T E O E T P
A N B A E Z R E P T X Q E I I I V A E E
A P C I D L U J X G Z T N R T R T N X R
P I P O L D L Y K R S U E I E S T O T S
P E N E M I E T D A M T R N O G E R R P
E V B D T E T R T M R T N R F N E P E I
A F X W E I E Y I A U O P X U T T E M R
R R N G M P T Y Q N I N Z U G F H R I A
A A W Q F N E E E T X Z H P T T Z C T T
N Z D Q K P S N A S S B Q Z A F I E I I
C F L U E Y G N D D I T L R X K M P E O
E T G E E N I M P E I G R H Q Q H T S N
P K L N I D E O P Q N G H E E Q M I C V
V S D W R C Z E O E J C E T N A Y O F Y
Z I E O N A F Z J T W I E S B G R N D X
K H O A Q X A Z S Q B F A T T O T I H D
C C L T E A R S T F O J F S U I N H H N
F A U S L F L E X I B I L I T Y O E A G
B O Q Y A N C I R C U L A T I O N N S C
```

1. _____   12. _____   23. _____

2. _____   13. _____   24. _____

3. _____   14. _____   25. _____

4. _____   15. _____   26. _____

5. _____   16. _____   27. _____

6. _____   17. _____   28. _____

7. _____   18. _____   29. _____

8. _____   19. _____   30. _____

9. _____   20. _____   31. _____

10. _____   21. _____   32. _____

11. _____   22. _____   33. _____

The Call: Elderly Patient with a Hip Fracture

Read this scenario and answer the questions that follow. Remember that managing a patient can mean managing the patient's emotions as well as actual physical injuries.

You are called to a residence for a fall. You arrive to find a 73-year-old woman who fell down the three steps to her front porch. She complains of pain in her left hip and appears slightly disoriented. It is 3:00 P.M., and the patient thinks she may have been on the porch overnight.

1. If the overnight temperature was 64 degrees, could this patient have hypothermia? Explain your reasoning.

2. List three ways the patient's family could prevent a similar fall from happening again.

   a.

   b.

   c.

3. The patient has a previous cardiac condition. How would you determine if the patient's fall was caused by an accidental misstep or by a medical condition?

Active Learning

Do the following exercises with a partner from class or a family member. They may be able to help you develop a keener understanding of what it is like to be hard of hearing or to have difficulty seeing.

1. Place cotton or ear plugs in your ears. Have your partner ask you questions about your medical history, or simply attempt to hold a conversation.

2. Then take an old pair of eyeglasses and smear them with a light coat of petroleum jelly. Put the glasses on while your partner takes your blood pressure. With the help of your partner, try to walk around your house or classroom. (Note: Be sure to be careful and have your partner guide you to prevent injury.)

29 | EMS Operations

Key Ideas

This chapter provides a brief overview of some of the operational aspects of out-of-hospital emergency care, including the six basic phases of an emergency response and emergency vehicle safety. Key ideas include the following:

- First Responders should have equipment for airway and breathing management, bleeding control and bandaging, and patient assessment. Also, personal protective equipment is necessary.

- There are six general phases of an EMS response: preparation, dispatch, en route to the scene, arrival on scene, transfer of care, and post-run activities.

- Many First Responders spend a lot of time in traffic, both in cars and on foot at the emergency scene. A traffic safety course and refresher courses are recommended.

- Driver safety depends in large part on common sense and good judgment.

- First Responders must never compromise their own safety.

- Once inside an ambulance compartment, First Responders must protect themselves. The techniques of hanging on and bracing allow for safer movement in the compartment. Securing the patient correctly can protect both the patient and rescuer.

Exam Warm-up

1. Of all the phases of an EMS response listed below, which one is the formal beginning?
   a. preparation
   b. dispatch
   c. en route to the scene
   d. arrival on scene
   e. transfer of care
   f. post-run duties

2. During which phase will you first hear details about an emergency to which you are to respond?
   a. preparation
   b. dispatch
   c. en route to the scene
   d. arrival on scene
   e. transfer of care
   f. post-run duties

3. The emergency medical dispatcher may give specific, lifesaving instructions to the caller to perform during which phase of an emergency response?
   a. preparation
   b. dispatch
   c. en route to the scene
   d. arrival on scene
   e. transfer of care
   f. post-run duties

4. While you are en route to the scene of an emergency, you must do which three of the following?
   a. Know the exact location of the emergency.
   b. Report the number of patients and severity of injuries.
   c. Ignore the speed limits, stop signs, and yields.
   d. Notify dispatch when you begin your response.
   e. Wear seat belts at all times.

5. In which phase of an emergency response should you decide whether or not the scene is safe to enter?
   a. dispatch
   b. preparation
   c. post-run duties
   d. arrival on scene
   e. transfer of care
   f. en route to the scene

6. In which phase of an emergency response should you provide a patient hand-off report?
   a. dispatch
   b. preparation
   c. post-run duties
   d. arrival on scene
   e. transfer of care
   f. en route to the scene

7. When traveling at increased speeds, you should brake to a safe speed _____ the curve.
   a. before entering
   b. after entering
   c. after leaving
   d. before leaving

8. When traveling at increased speeds, you should stay _____ of a curve.
    a. on the outside
    b. on the inside
    c. in the middle
    d. in the fast lane

9. As you approach an emergency scene, disengage your seat belt so you can slip out of the vehicle quickly.

    _____ True

    _____ False

10. Whenever you respond to an emergency in a vehicle, use your headlights and your emergency lights, even in the daytime.

    _____ True

    _____ False

11. If you have to alert oncoming traffic while parked, leave your _____ lights on.
    a. sirens
    b. emergency
    c. headlights
    d. tail lights

12. Once you turn off your lights and siren, you are no longer driving an "authorized" emergency vehicle and you are subject to the laws meant to govern regular traffic.

    _____ True

    _____ False

13. You should park alongside the crash scene to protect injured patients from oncoming traffic.

    _____ True

    _____ False

14. When riding in the patient compartment of an ambulance, you should never have more than _____ off a stable surface.
    a. one hand or two feet
    b. two hands or one foot
    c. one hand or one foot
    d. two hands or two feet

Short-Answer Review

15. List three types of equipment you should have on hand for the management of a patient's airway and breathing.

    a.

    b.

    c.

16. List six types of equipment you should have on hand for the management of soft-tissue injuries.

    a.

    b.

    c.

    d.

    e.

    f.

17. List three items of information EMS dispatch will obtain from callers who report an emergency.

    a.

    b.

    c.

18. List four basic ways you can improve driving safety on the way to an emergency scene.

    a.

    b.

    c.

    d.

19. There are three precautions you can take to protect your hearing while riding in an emergency vehicle. List them.

   a.

   b.

   c.

20. It is midnight, and Anthony, a First Responder, is at the scene of an emergency that involved falling debris. There are multiple patients, and at first glance some of them look critical. As Anthony enters the scene, he puts on his protective gloves and takes other necessary BSI precautions. He is already wearing his jump suit and heavy-duty work boots. What other protective gear, if any, should he be wearing?

Questions 21–23 relate to the following scenario: As the first response Unit 957 arrives on scene, the First Responder is set to fling open the door and run to the patient, who is bleeding.

21. What should the First Responder do before opening the door?

22. How should the First Responder open the vehicle door? Why?

23. Should additional EMS personnel exit through their ambulance's rear door or side door? Why?

Vocabulary Practice

Circle the words or terms related to EMS equipment you should have at your disposal. Then write them on the lines below the puzzle. Hint: There are exactly 29.

```
A T V A N T I S E P T I C E T C R H S R
G O X V X Z H Q Z C M Y N H S O R K S E
B L X A O C S J T N C I G E M E S S U F
S L O Y O K T R I K L I G R T A E T C L
F P A V G N Q E I A L A A E M W L E T E
P I L N E E H Z S N D Y M T M R L T I C
R J R I K S N T E N D O E B Z I F H O T
U G V E N E V P A O N K G W O S L O N I
J O I D E T T B B A C A B Y G T A S D V
K Q Z O A X S S M O R E G E I W S C E E
I Z Z C T T T O P S S Z R O C A H O V G
B U G I E S M I B D C I D S A T L P I E
F K K M E G R P N A R I R R J C I E C A
G B L R Y A B Q G G T E S E Z H G G E R
O E A H E F Q Q H I U T S S N T H V S F
H L P W Z V S D S O Y I E S O S T C D E
F S E S B T W X J S Q Q S R I R M K G F
H Y L T R I A G E T A G S H I N S A T C
E B A C K B O A R D S J H N E E G Y P P
A D H E S I V E T A P E A W Y R S S Z S
```

1. _____   11. _____   21. _____

2. _____   12. _____   22. _____

3. _____   13. _____   23. _____

4. _____   14. _____   24. _____

5. _____   15. _____   25. _____

6. _____   16. _____   26. _____

7. _____   17. _____   27. _____

8. _____   18. _____   28. _____

9. _____   19. _____   29. _____

10. _____   20. _____

The Call: Scene Safety

Read the scenario and answer the questions that follow. Focus on scene safety.

Rescue 723 is dispatched to a motor-vehicle collision with a lamp post. The dispatcher informs the rescuers that there are three patients in the vehicle who are believed to have critical injuries to the head and chest. The scene is located at First and Division Streets in the village.

1. List at least five safety tips involved in the emergency vehicle response to the scene.

    a.

    b.

    c.

    d.

    e.

2. Once on scene, you note that police have not yet arrived to control traffic. If you were to perform that task, what would three of your goals be for rerouting traffic?

    a.

    b.

    c.

3. Describe how you would place cones or flares to redirect traffic.

Active Learning

1. Go through the response equipment checklist where you work or volunteer. Is it accurate? Are all of the supplies present and in the proper place? If you do not have an affiliation, go through your personal supplies. How many of the basic First Responder supplies do you carry personally?

2. The first few minutes of a call are critical for scene size-up and ABCs. Check your agency's or your own personal equipment. Do you have BSI equipment and airway/breathing supplies (pocket face mask)? Where is it stored? Is it immediately available to you at the scene or would it cause a delay?

30 | Hazardous Materials Incidents and Emergencies

Key Ideas

This chapter focuses on how to recognize hazardous materials at the scene of an emergency and how to respond to this threat. Key ideas include the following:

- Hazardous materials are substances that pose a threat or unreasonable risk to health, life, or property if they are not properly controlled during manufacture, storage, transportation, use, or disposal.

- With 50 billion tons of hazardous material manufactured in the U.S. annually, hazardous materials incidents caused by equipment failure, vehicle collisions, environmental conditions, or human error are inevitable.

- First Responder responsibilities in a hazmat emergency may include identifying the hazmat incident, establishing command and control zones, identifying the substance, and establishing a medical treatment sector.

- First Responders must never compromise their own safety when helping to manage a hazardous materials incident.

Exam Warm-up

1. Using the NFPA 704 system, a red placard with a "4" written on it would denote a _____ hazard.
   a. low-risk reactivity
   b. moderate-risk fire
   c. high-risk health
   d. high-risk fire

2. The NFPA 704 system was developed by the
   a. National Fire Protection Association.
   b. Natural Fire and Prevention Agency.
   c. Nation's First Protection Agency.
   d. U.S. Department of Transportation.

3. The _____ is a toll-free 24-hour emergency phone service provided by chemical manufacturers.
   a. DOT placarding
   b. MSDS
   c. CHEMTREC
   d. NFPA 704 System

4. Which one of the following information sources is NOT designed to help identify the contents and relative danger of a substance being carried on a truck?
   a. DOT placarding
   b. MSDS
   c. CHEMTREC
   d. NFPA 704 System

5. Which one or more of the following resources provide helpful information for treating patients contaminated by hazardous materials?
   a. MSDS
   b. DOT's Emergency Response Guidebook
   c. CHEMTREC
   d. regional poison control center

6. When arriving at the scene of a potential hazmat emergency, the first step is to
   a. assess the situation from a safe command position.
   b. set up a triage area for potential victims.
   c. begin evacuation from the hot zone.
   d. call for additional resources.

7. When you are called to a possible hazmat emergency, you should station yourself _____ and _____ of the scene.
   a. downhill, downwind
   b. uphill, downwind
   c. uphill, upwind
   d. downhill, upwind

8. Once you have stationed yourself, it is best to look at the possible hazmat scene through your
   a. binoculars.
   b. closed window.
   c. face mask with HEPA filter.
   d. chemical-resistant jumpsuit.

9. The area immediately outside the location of actual contamination is called the
   a. hot zone.
   b. warm zone.
   c. cold zone.
   d. outer perimeter.

10. The location for all rescuers and equipment not immediately managing the hazmat emergency is known as the
    a. hot zone.
    b. warm zone.
    c. cold zone.
    d. outer perimeter.

Short-Answer Review

11. Write the three types of dangers presented by hazardous materials.

    a.

    b.

    c.

12. Write three examples of hazardous materials commonly shipped in the U.S.

    a.

    b.

    c.

13. Complete the sentence by writing the missing word(s).

    The U.S. _____ _____ _____ requires specific hazards labels to be put on packages and containers and hazard placards to be placed on the outside of vehicles.

14. The letters MSDS stand for:

    M:

    S:

    D:

    S:

15. List the four levels of hazmat training for rescuers, and describe the level of training for each.

    a.

    b.

    c.

    d.

16. A First Responder's specific responsibilities at a hazmat incident are

    a.

    b.

    c.

    d.

17. You are out shopping when you see a delivery truck carrying bottles of compressed gas crash into a parked car and overturn. A crowd of onlookers gathers close to the truck. You have no hazmat training. What actions should you take?

18. Write three possible visual clues to the presence of a hazardous material.

    a.

    b.

    c.

19. When you report your position and the situation to dispatch, what facts should your report include?

20. You and your partner have arrived at the scene of a hazardous materials incident. A tractor-trailer jack-knifed on the highway, spilling its liquid contents all over the roadway. After sizing up the scene from a distance, you are able to identify the substance as a strong acid. You can see that the driver is still sitting in the cab. He appears badly injured. Acid is bubbling forth from a large gash in the side of the tank. The hazmat team should be at the scene in 10 to 15 minutes. What actions do you wish to take prior to their arrival?

Vocabulary Practice

Read the clues and fill in the blanks that follow. Then write the boxed letters as you find them on the "Scrambled Letters" line near the bottom of the page. Finally, unscramble the letters to find out what essential item you should have on hand for any potential hazmat incident.

1. The U.S. DOT requires hazardous materials packages and containers to be marked with these.

    ☐ __ ☐ __ __ __

2. These are required by the U.S. DOT to be placed on the outside of vehicles carrying hazardous materials.

    __ __ __ ☐ __ __ __ __

3. The driver of a vehicle that carries a hazardous material must have these papers, which identify the exact substance, quantity, origin, and destination.

    ☐ __ ☐ __ __ __ __

4. The NFPA 704 system identifies hazardous materials on its diamond-shaped symbol with colors and these.

    ☐ ☐ __ __ __ __ __

5. This abbreviation stands for the U.S. government office that helps to develop safety regulations, which include standards for hazmat training.

    ☐ __ __ __

6. This level of hazmat training teaches First Responders how to recognize a hazardous materials emergency and how to call for the proper resources.

    ☐ __ __ ☐ __ __ __ __ __

    Scrambled Letters: __ __ __ __ __ __ __ __ __ __

    Unscrambled Letters: __ __ __ __ __ __ __ __ __ __

The Call: Incident at the Packing Plant

Read this scenario and answer the questions that follow. Always remember to ensure your own safety above all other considerations.

You have responded to a possible inhalation emergency at one of the local vegetable packing plants. Dispatch originally indicated that one patient might have been exposed. You arrive to find a chaotic scene. Workers are streaming out of one packing shed, while supervisors are running around, shouting instructions to each other. You find a group of about 20 workers just outside the shed, complaining of headache, dizziness, and some difficulty breathing.

"What's going on?" you ask one of the workers.

"I think there's bad air in this packing shed," she says.

"What kind of bad air?"

"Who knows? They use different types of gases at this plant."

"Was anyone contaminated by any type of liquid?"

"No, just something in the air."

1. Your first action at this point should be to
   a. begin initial assessments of the workers.
   b. move the people away from the danger.
   c. attempt to identify the gas causing the incident.
   d. go into the building to see if there are more patients.

2. A supervisor tells you that he is pretty sure the gas in the packing shed is carbon monoxide. Based on this information, is it really necessary to establish hot, warm, and cold zones, or to have a hazmat team dispatched? Explain.

3. A packing plant supervisor tells you that the contaminated shed has been evacuated except for three workers who cannot be accounted for. Hazmat personnel are still five to seven minutes away from the incident. The supervisor and some of the workers want to reenter the shed to look for the missing workers. Do you let them in or do you deny access until the hazmat team arrives?

Active Learning

1. While around town, make a special effort to look for hazardous materials placards on vehicles and rail cars. Note the numbers on the placards.
   a. How many did you see?
   b. Using the DOT's Emergency Response Guidebook, determine what chemicals and substances you saw.

2. Look for NFPA 704 placards on buildings in your area.
   a. Did you find any with high hazard levels?
   b. Were you surprised by the hazard levels you found? Why?

3. Using the Emergency Response Guidebook, determine the type of substance, isolation distances, and emergency care for the following highway/DOT placard numbers:
   a. 1203
   b. 1993
   c. 1760
   d. 1956

31 | Multiple-Casualty Incidents and Incident Command

Key Ideas

This chapter provides an overview of ways in which EMS systems respond to multiple-casualty incidents, as well as your role as a First Responder. Key ideas include the following:

- The key to managing emergencies with multiple patients is recognizing priorities and organizing your actions.

- The Incident Command System (ICS) provides a command structure through which rescuers can manage multiple-casualty incidents.

- The EMS sector functions in a multiple-casualty incident include triage, treatment, transportation, and staging.

- In a multiple-casualty incident, First Responders size up the scene, establish command, request additional resources, and begin triage.

- Triage is a process of classifying sick and injured patients. It is used to determine the order in which each patient receives medical care and transport.

- Multiple-casualty incidents can have a severe psychological impact on both patients and rescuers. Strategies for managing this impact increase the effectiveness of rescuers and help to lessen the long-term problems associated with critical incident stress.

Exam Warm-up

1. You are the first EMS personnel to arrive at the scene of a high-speed, head-on vehicle collision involving two cars. Your first action should be to
   a. begin initial triage.
   b. request additional resources.
   c. size up the scene and establish command.
   d. block off the roadway and set out flares and cones.

2. In the START triage system, "Priority-1 Red" is given to a patient if he or she meets certain criteria. Identify all those criteria in the list below.
   a. Patient is dead.
   b. Injuries are life-threatening.
   c. Patient is not seriously injured.
   d. Patient needs minimal care to survive.
   e. Risk of asphyxiation or shock is imminent or present.
   f. Patient can be stabilized without constant care.
   g. Patient can wait for treatment without getting worse.
   h. Patient has a good chance of survival if treated and transported immediately.
   i. Patient has injuries that would be fatal even if he or she received treatment.

3. You are responsible for triaging patients using the START system. What is your first action?
   a. Assess and treat each patient's ABCs as necessary.
   b. If a patient is alert with no major bleeding, move on.
   c. Tell everyone to get up and walk unassisted to a specified area.
   d. If there is no carotid pulse, tag the patient as a "Priority-0 Black."

Short-Answer Review

4. Describe the responsibilities of each of the following officers in an Incident Command System.

   a. Triage officer:

   b. Treatment officer:

   c. Transportation officer:

   d. Staging officer:

5. You are the first to arrive at the scene of a multiple-casualty incident. Your major goals are to:

   a.

   b.

   c.

   d.

6. During scene size-up of a multiple-casualty incident, to what seven questions must you find answers?

    a.

    b.

    c.

    d.

    e.

    f.

    g.

7. When resources arrive on the scene of a multiple-casualty incident and you are relieved by someone higher in the chain of command, what five facts should you report?

    a.

    b.

    c.

    d.

    e.

8. A common three-level triage system is called START. Write what the letters stand for.

    S:

    T:

    A:

    R:

    T:

9. Use a typical three-level system to triage the following patients. Write "Priority-1 Red," "Priority-2 Yellow," "Priority-3 Green," or "no care" beside each one.

    _____ a. A patient with shortness of breath and cyanosis

    _____ b. A patient in respiratory arrest after repositioning the airway

    _____ c. A patient with a painful, swollen ankle

_____ **d.** A patient in labor with an imminent birth

_____ **e.** A patient with an open, deformed injury to the right femur

_____ **f.** A patient with swelling and deformity to both arms

_____ **g.** A patient having a generalized seizure

_____ **h.** A patient who is unresponsive with no signs of head or spine injury

_____ **i.** A patient with superficial burns to a forearm

_____ **j.** A patient with uncontrolled bleeding from the wrist

_____ **k.** A patient with full-thickness burns on the hands

_____ **l.** A patient with generalized hypothermia

_____ **m.** A patient with a two-inch laceration to a lower leg with controlled bleeding

_____ **n.** A patient with hypoglycemia

_____ **o.** A patient with inhalation burns

_____ **p.** A patient with suspected ingested poisoning

_____ **q.** A patient with burns to the legs, pelvis, and chest

_____ **r.** A patient with cuts and bruises all over the body

_____ **s.** A patient with unknown trauma to both eyes

_____ **t.** A patient who is breathing but says it is very difficult

_____ **u.** A trauma patient with rapid pulse, cool moist skin that is gray looking, and altered mental status

_____ **v.** A patient with a closed wound to the head and altered mental status

_____ **w.** A patient who is unresponsive and pulseless

_____ **x.** A patient with broken ribs and a possible pneumothorax

_____ **y.** A patient with an abdominal evisceration

_____ **z.** A patient with severe blunt trauma to the cervical spine

10. Using the START system, what is your initial assessment of the following patients? Write "Priority-1 Red," "Priority-2 Yellow," "Priority-3 Green," or "Priority-0 Black" beside each one.

_____ a. The patient's breathing is faster than 30 breaths per minute.

_____ b. You clear the airway of a patient who is not breathing and breathing does NOT resume.

_____ c. You clear the airway of a patient who is not breathing and breathing resumes.

_____ d. Respirations are 28 and the carotid pulse is weak.

_____ e. Respirations and pulse are good, but the patient only responds to voice.

11. Describe common psychological reactions that rescuers may experience after managing an MCI.

12. After the incident is over, how can rescuers get help in dealing with the stress caused by managing an MCI?

13. List three strategies for reducing the stress rescue personnel experience during management of an MCI.

a.

b.

c.

Vocabulary Practice

1. Draw a line to connect each sector officer to the correct description.

Triage Officer •

Treatment Officer •

Transportation Officer •

Staging Officer •

Safety Officer •

• arranges for ambulances and tracks the priority, identity, and destination of all patients.

• identifies potential danger on scene and takes action to prevent it from causing injury to patients and rescuers.

• releases and distributes resources when they are needed.

• sets up a medical treatment area and supervises treatment.

• supervises patient assessment, tagging, and removal of patients to a treatment area.

2. Draw a line to connect each START priority to its correct description.

Priority-1 Red •

Priority-2 Yellow •

Priority-3 Green •

Priority-0 Black •

• urgent-care category

• no-care category

• immediate-care category

• delayed-care category

The Call: Motor-Vehicle Crash on the Interstate

Read the scenario and answer the questions that follow. Remember, establishing an organized approach that correctly sets priorities is the most important determinant of a successful MCI.

You respond along with two other First Responders in a rescue vehicle to a reported head-on collision on the nearby interstate. Your communications center advises you that the closest law enforcement and ambulance responses are approximately 15 and 20 minutes away, respectively.

You arrive on scene to find all lanes of the interstate blocked by the collision. It appears that a bread truck crossed the center median and collided head-on with a station wagon carrying six occupants. There is massive damage to both vehicles. Bystanders have set out flares. As the senior member of the rescue crew, you are the initial incident commander.

1. What initial information should you gather during your scene size-up? List a series of questions you would ask to gather this information.

2. You have identified seven patients, six in the station wagon and one in the bread truck. Use a two-level system to triage them. Write "immediate" or "delayed" in the space provided.

_____ a. An unrestrained 18-month-old female who appears to be unresponsive after being thrown against the windshield of the station wagon. She presents with head and chest injuries, rapid breathing, and a faint brachial pulse.

_____ b. A 37-year-old male, driver of station wagon. Presents with an altered mental status, from repeating himself to being confused about what has happened. He is pinned by the steering column and has obvious chest injuries and leg fractures.

_____ c. A 38-year-old male, the restrained driver of the bread truck. He presents as alert with significant facial lacerations and neck pain.

_____ d. A 34-year-old female, the restrained front-seat passenger of the station wagon. She took the brunt of the bread truck's impact. She appears to be breathless and pulseless with massive head, chest, and pelvic trauma.

_____ e. A 14-year-old male, an unrestrained back-seat passenger in the station wagon. He has painful, swollen, deformed injuries to both thighs. He also has closed abdominal injuries. He is responsive and screaming.

_____ f. A 9-year-old female, an unrestrained back-seat passenger in the station wagon. She was ejected from the car on impact, and was found supine on the median with massive open head injuries and a grossly angulated neck. She is unresponsive and breathing three to four times per minute.

_____ g. A 12-year-old male, a restrained back-seat passenger of the station wagon. He has severe abdominal and chest pain, and he has painful, deformed forearms. He presents as alert and crying.

3. Which one of the patients listed above would you consider to be your top-priority patient? Why?

4. Unfortunately, there is no helicopter service available. Bearing in mind that optimally one ambulance should transport only one critical patient, how many ambulances should you request for this incident? Why?

5. Fire, law enforcement, and ambulance resources begin to arrive on scene. You relinquish incident command and take over control of the EMS sector. You notice that since the change in command, confusion has broken out. Ambulance crews are making their way directly to patients without stopping at the staging area, firefighters are running into each other as they pull equipment, and law enforcement officers are yelling at passing motorists to stop rubbernecking. All you can think is, "This MCI just got worse." What can you do to solve this problem?

6. Order has been restored. You see that patients are being extricated, packaged, loaded, and transported efficiently. You notice one responder sitting on the tailboard of a fire engine with his head in his hands, quietly weeping. Describe how you would handle this situation and what resources you would use to help him.

Active Learning

1. Using a fellow student from class, perform a patient assessment as if he or she is a trauma patient. After completing the assessment, fill out a triage tag and attach it to the patient as you would in the field. (If triage tags are not available, use a photocopy of a tag.)

2. Determine what type of incident command is used where you work or volunteer. Most organizations use some type of plan with variations based on the mission of the organization (public vs. private, industrial, fire vs. EMS third service, etc.)

32 | Water Emergencies

Key Ideas

This chapter provides an overview of water rescue and water-related emergencies. Key ideas include the following:

- Drowning is the third leading cause of accidental death in the U.S. After auto collisions, it is the most common cause of preventable death among children.

- The top priority in managing patients with water emergencies is the safety of the rescuer. The next priority is resuscitating the patient as soon as possible.

- Never attempt a water rescue unless you are a good swimmer, you are specially trained in water rescue, you are wearing a personal flotation device, and you are accompanied by other rescuers.

- Always assume that unresponsive patients have spine injuries. Patients with suspected spine injuries should have their spines stabilized while still in the water if possible.

- Barotrauma occurs when divers experience increasing underwater pressures or when they ascend from deep water improperly. Common types of barotrauma include air embolism, decompression sickness, and a phenomenon known as "the squeeze." First Responder care for these emergencies focuses on supporting the patient's ABCs and transporting the patient to an appropriate hospital. Air-embolism or decompression-sickness patients should be transported to a facility with a decompression chamber.

Exam Warm-up

1. Do not walk in fast-moving water over _____ depth, because it is not safe. It can push you over and hold you down.
   a. knee
   b. waist
   c. mid-chest
   d. shoulder

2. Which of the following items poses a hazard for water rescuers?
   a. oil or gas
   b. blood
   c. sewage
   d. electricity

3. All the scene size-up questions listed below ask about the condition of the water EXCEPT
   a. Can you see any potential hazards under or on the water?
   b. Can your feet touch the bottom so you can stand?
   c. Is the patient on the surface or is he submerged?
   d. Will the location of the patient change?

4. Your patient is unresponsive and face down in shallow water. To turn him, you should use the _____ technique.
   a. head-splint
   b. recompression
   c. reach-and-throw
   d. head-chin support

5. To turn a patient face up in deep water, you should use the _____ technique.
   a. head-splint
   b. recompression
   c. reach-and-throw
   d. head-chin support

6. You are rescuing a responsive near-drowning patient who is in safe, shallow water. Your first action should be to
   a. perform a physical exam.
   b. activate the EMS system.
   c. perform an initial assessment.
   d. administer high-flow oxygen.
   e. remove the patient from the water.
   f. conserve the patient's body heat.

7. A drowning patient is unresponsive, breathless, and pulseless in water that is shallow, cold, and moving fast. Are the following statements about this emergency true or false?

   a. Only qualified rescuers—that is, rescuers who are properly equipped and trained—may enter the water to rescue this patient.

   _____ True

   _____ False

   b. Because of the patient's critical condition, rescuers may remove him from the water without stabilizing his head and spine.

   _____ True

   _____ False

c. Rescuers must start CPR on this patient immediately, but not until the patient is removed from the water.

_____ True

_____ False

d. To immobilize this patient's spine on a long backboard, the rescuers should leave his personal flotation device in place.

_____ True

_____ False

8. Near-drowning patients should always be transported to the hospital because
   a. you may miss an important finding during your assessment.
   b. they require sophisticated tests to make sure they are okay.
   c. they always need hospitalization regardless of their status.
   d. complications can develop up to 72 hours after the incident.

9. Which one of the following would NOT be appropriate care for a spine-injured, near-drowning patient still in the water?
   a. Ventilate the patient only after removing her from the water.
   b. Keep her floating on her back until further help arrives.
   c. Support her head and neck level with her back.
   d. Do not remove the patient from the water until help arrives.

10. The force of moving water can be measured solely by its velocity.

    _____ True

    _____ False

11. A swimmer fell into fast water and experienced a foot entrapment. What can you tell him is the one best thing to do until he is rescued?
    a. Do a backstroke with feet pointed downstream.
    b. Pull out your foot in any way except the way it went in.
    c. Dive down and try to pull out your foot with your hands.
    d. Breathe through a straw that reaches the water's surface.

12. A good rule to follow for an ice rescue is: "one inch, keep off; two inches, one may; three inches, small groups; four inches, okay."

    _____ True

    _____ False

13. Air embolism usually occurs when:
    a. a diver holds his or her breath during the ascent from a dive.
    b. a diver comes up too quickly from a deep, prolonged dive.
    c. air pressure is not equalized in the body's air cavities.
    d. a diver stays submerged for too long.

14. Which one of the following is the correct position in which to place an uninjured diver who has signs of air embolism?

    a. supine
    b. sitting up, with legs in a dependent position
    c. left lateral, with head and chest lower than feet
    d. prone

15. Decompression sickness usually occurs when

    a. a diver holds his or her breath during the ascent from a dive.
    b. a diver comes up too quickly from a deep, prolonged dive.
    c. air pressure is not equalized in a body's air cavities during ascent or descent.
    d. a diver stays submerged for too long a period of time.

16. Which one of the following statements about decompression sickness is NOT true?

    a. When the diver ascends too quickly, nitrogen turns into tiny bubbles that lodge in the body's tissues.
    b. Nitrogen bubbles eventually enter the bloodstream and can cause injuries to major organs.
    c. The risk of decompression sickness increases if the diver flies in an airplane shortly after diving.
    d. The signs and symptoms of decompression sickness occur rapidly following the dive.

17. "The squeeze" usually occurs when

    a. a diver holds his or her breath during the ascent from a dive.
    b. a diver comes up too quickly from a deep, prolonged dive.
    c. air pressure is not equalized in a body's air cavities during ascent or descent.
    d. a diver stays submerged for too long a period of time.

Short-Answer Review

18. There is a significant difference between warm- and cold-water drownings. Describe the difference in the space below.

19. A First Responder should never try a water rescue without meeting four basic criteria. List them.

    a.

    b.

    c.

    d.

20. You are enjoying a sunny afternoon at a lake when you are informed that a swimmer is in trouble just offshore. You run over to where a group of people has gathered. You see a woman thrashing about in the water about 25 yards offshore. Witnesses tell you that she was floating on an inflatable raft that lost air and sank. List three techniques that can be used to rescue her.

    a.

    b.

    c.

21. Fast-moving water is dangerous, and certain river features make it even more so. Write a brief description of the dangers each one listed below may pose.

    a. Strainers:

    b. Obstructions:

    c. Recirculating currents or "holes":

    d. Low-head dams:

22. Describe how each of the following water-rescue techniques would be performed during an ice rescue.

    a. Reach and Throw:

    b. Row:

    c. Go:

Vocabulary Practice

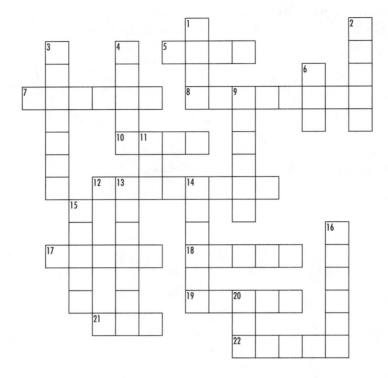

Across

5. When a _____ forms, currents can recirculate a swimmer until he tires and drowns.
7. Voice box.
8. Death from suffocation due to submersion.
10. Short for self-contained breathing apparatus.
12. Obstruction that allows water to pass through but not people or objects.
17. Do this before you throw, row, and go.
18. Artificial ventilation rate for this patient is 10–12 per minute, if a pulse is present.
19. Reach, _____, row, and go.
21. A hole, or recirculating current, can form beside this structure.
22. Fast-moving water may also be called _____ water.

Down

1. This type of water can reduce the body's need for oxygen.
2. Organs that contain thousands of alveoli.
3. Throat.
4. Decompression sickness.
6. With this type of embolism, one or more bubbles block a blood vessel.
9. Administer this to a near-drowning patient.
11. Remove the patient from the water to perform this.
13. Windpipe.
14. Artificial ventilation rate for this patient is 20 per minute, if a pulse is present.
15. Divers _____ Network is a source of free medical consultation for dive-related emergencies.
16. Make sure this is not blocking the airway.
20. Reach, throw, _____, and go.

The Call: Child in the Water, Possible Drowning

Read the scenario and answer the questions that follow. Remember that effective resuscitation of a patient depends on an accurate assessment and aggressive treatment of the patient's airway, breathing, and circulation.

You have just finished lunch at the fire station when one of the calls you dread the most is dispatched: "Child in the water, possible drowning." As you respond to a nearby resort, your dispatcher updates you, stating that lifeguards have located an unresponsive five-year-old in the lake. A paramedic ambulance is approximately 10 minutes behind you.

1. What sort of management planning could you complete with your two fellow crew members en route to this call? How might you divide the workload for this call among the three of you?

2. As you drive up to the scene, two of the resort lifeguards are exiting the water, carrying the child. One of the lifeguards is performing rescue breathing. A crowd of about 10 people converges on them, and they are lost from sight. What actions should you take to get control of this scene?

3. You have controlled the crowd and have gained access to the patient. She is unresponsive, breathless, pale, and cold to the touch. The exhausted lifeguards continue to perform artificial ventilation. You ready your airway and ventilation equipment. "Does she have a pulse?" you ask. "I think so," says one of the lifeguards. You note that a pulse has not been checked on the girl since the lifeguards reached the beach. You also note that the lifeguard's ventilations do not appear to be achieving any chest rise. What actions do you want to take at this point? Explain them in their proper sequence.

4. Your patient has a radial pulse of 50. You have cleared her airway and have taken over rescue breathing via bag-valve-mask supplied with 100% oxygen. You decided to use a jaw-thrust maneuver to open her airway, and you inserted an oropharyngeal airway. Despite several attempts, your patient has minimal chest rise with ventilation. You are somewhat concerned that she may have a spine injury, but you find yourself becoming more concerned with the lack of chest rise. List three methods you would use to open her airway and achieve adequate ventilations.

a.

b.

c.

5. One of her parents approaches you and asks, "How is Maggie doing? Is she going to be all right?" At this point, Maggie's heart rate is 50 beats per minute. She is unresponsive and still breathless. The paramedics are about one minute away. Write out a short response to this parent.

6. The paramedics have just shown up. Number the following sentences 1–7 in order to develop a coherent, efficient report.

_____ a. Maggie remains unresponsive. She is not breathing on her own, but does have a strong radial pulse of 88.

_____ b. When we arrived, Maggie was unresponsive, with a slow radial pulse.

_____ c. Maggie is an unresponsive, near-drowning victim. She was submerged for about three to four minutes.

_____ d. The lifeguards spotted her about 20 feet offshore in about three feet of water. They rescued her and began rescue breathing immediately.

_____ e. We suctioned her airway, inserted an oropharyngeal airway, and began ventilating with 100% oxygen via BVM.

_____ f. We do not find any associated trauma.

_____ g. Maggie has no medical history, takes no medications, and has no known allergies.

Active Learning

1. What bodies of water are near where you live or work? How would an emergency on the water affect your response?

2. Go to http://aappolicy.aappublications.org/cgi/content/full/pediatrics;112/2/437 to read the American Academy of Pediatrics policy statement on pediatric drowning, which includes statistics and prevention information. How can you help to prevent the drowning of a child?

33 | Vehicle Stabilization and Patient Extrication

Key Ideas

This chapter provides an overview of vehicle stabilization and patient extrication and how you can proceed safely and efficiently. Key ideas include the following:

- Safety is always the top priority when extricating a patient. Never attempt extrication or stabilization procedures that you have not been specifically trained to do.

- All EMS responders working in and around a wrecked vehicle should wear the proper personal protective equipment.

- The most important initial actions when faced with an extrication problem are to size up the scene, determine the number of patients, observe the presence of any scene hazards, and determine whether additional resources are needed for managing the extrication.

- Suspect any vehicle of being unstable until properly trained rescuers make it stable.

- Doors and windows provide simple access to patients. If complex access is required, call for rescuers who have the training and equipment.

- Spinal precautions should be taken on all patients prior to extrication.

Exam Warm-up

1. Two goals of traffic control at the scene of a vehicle wreck are
    a. stop all traffic in order to maintain scene safety.
    b. reduce the flow of traffic by routing vehicles back the way they came.
    c. route traffic in order to prevent traffic snarls and secondary collisions.
    d. clear out unnecessary vehicles so that emergency vehicles can gain access quickly.

2. Flares should be arranged by keeping in mind which of the following guidelines?
a. The danger zone extends out to a 50-foot radius around the wrecked cars.
b. Flares should lead vehicles around the scene and help to keep traffic moving.
c. If the crash occurred below a hill, the danger zone extends to the crest of the hill.
d. If the crash occurred on a curve, the danger zone extends to the start of the curve.

3. Flares should be set _____ feet apart.
a. 3–5
b. 10–15
c. 30–45
d. 100

4. Flares should extend _____ feet toward traffic.
a. 10
b. 25
c. 50
d. 75

5. Which one of the following statements about cribbing is NOT correct?
a. No more than one or two inches should be between the cribbing and the vehicle.
b. Wood is stacked in boxlike squares and wedges to keep pressure uniform.
c. Vehicles may be cribbed under the wheels or tires.
d. Cribbing is used to prop up vehicles.

6. Identify all the steps you should take to stabilize an upright vehicle that rests on all four wheels.
a. Place the gear shift in park.
b. Chock wheels tightly against the curb.
c. Crib under the frame, wheels, and tires.
d. Cut the tire valve stems so the car rests on the rims.
e. Place a solid object between the roof and the roadway.
f. Use a bumper jack to angle it against a solid object.
g. Use blocks at wheels to prevent unexpected rolling.

7. Complex access is access by which no tools are needed. Simple access is access that requires tools and specialized equipment.

_____ True

_____ False

8. An EMS responder is on the scene of an "auto vs. tree" and finds the vehicle with massive front and side damage. The patient inside appears to be unconscious with labored respirations. The EMS responder realizes that this patient needs airway and breathing management immediately. Provided the vehicle is properly stabilized, the two best methods for accessing this patient would be to
a. remove the windshield.
b. break a side or rear window.
c. attempt entry through a door.
d. cut through the top of the car.

9. If you must break a window to gain access to a patient trapped in a crashed vehicle, break the window farthest from your patient.

_____ True

_____ False

10. The correct method of disabling a car's air bag includes which two actions listed below?
    a. cutting the yellow air bag connector
    b. disconnecting the yellow air bag connector
    c. cutting the negative wires for the car's battery
    d. disconnecting the negative side of the car's battery

11. Which one of the following shows the correct order for extricating a patient in a sitting position from a stable car?
    a. apply cervical collar, apply short board, place on long board, extricate.
    b. apply short board, place on long board, apply cervical collar, extricate.
    c. apply cervical collar, apply short board, extricate.
    d. extricate, apply cervical collar, apply long board.

Short-Answer Review

12. You have responded to a vehicle collision. You drive up to find that a pickup truck has slammed into a telephone pole. The single occupant, a male in his 30s, appears awake but dazed. The windshield of the truck is starred, and the steering column is bent. There appears to be no fire danger. You radio in for a fire and ambulance response. What steps should you take to manage the scene and the patient prior to the arrival of these other resources?

13. What type of clothing should you wear when assisting with a vehicle extrication?

14. List five techniques for determining the number of patients at the scene of a vehicle collision.

a.

b.

c.

d.

e.

15. List 5 conditions that would make you assume that a vehicle involved in a crash is not stable.

a.

b.

c.

d.

e.

16. In order to gain access to your patient, you must remove one of the car's side windows. Number the following steps 1–7 in the order in which you should proceed.

_____ **a.** Cover the patient with a blanket, if possible.

_____ **b.** Draw the knife across the top and down the side.

_____ **c.** Insert the point of a linoleum knife into the molding at the midpoint of the glass.

_____ **d.** Pivot the window on its bottom edge.

_____ **e.** Loosen the short pry bar behind the glass.

_____ **f.** Remove the glass.

_____ **g.** Repeat on the other side.

17. You are at the scene of a "car vs. telephone pole." Your patient, who is the driver, is alert but cannot extricate his feet from beneath the dash. What strategy might you try first to help extricate this patient?

Vocabulary Practice

Decide whether each vehicle described below is likely to be stable or unstable. Write the word "stable" or "unstable" beside each one.

_____ 1. A compact car has impacted a tree head-on. It now rests with ignition off and standard shift in reverse at the peak of a steep driveway.

_____ 2. Two passenger vehicles collided head-on. The front end of the larger car is stacked on top of the smaller one.

_____ 3. An overturned vehicle has cribbing between it and the roadway to keep it from moving.

_____ 4. A small pick-up truck skidded on black ice and became wrapped around a telephone pole.

_____ 5. A U.S. mail truck was struck in a side impact collision and now rests solidly on its side, leaning against a concrete road divider.

_____ 6. A car that ran over a sidewalk and into the side of a building is upright, with standard shift in reverse, and chocked wheels.

The Call: Multiple-Patient Extrication

Read the scenario and answer the questions that follow. Remember that when faced with multiple-patient extrications, rescuers must prioritize the patients by the degree of injury as well as by their location in the vehicles.

You respond to a single-vehicle crash in which a sedan has collided with a bridge abutment. You arrive along with two rescuers to find a sedan with massive front and right-side damage. The sedan has come to rest with its right side wedged against the abutment. There are five occupants, two in the front and three in the back.

While one of your partners sets out flares, you size up the scene. The car appears to be stable. Radiator fluid is leaking, but there does not appear to be any fuel leakage or fire danger. The left side doors of the sedan will not open. You are unable to access the right side of the car. The windows of the car have been broken. You see that the front-seat occupants are trapped by the dashboard and steering column. They appear to have critical injuries. The back-seat occupants have moderate to severe injuries.

You update EMS dispatch, calling for additional ambulances and the heavy rescue unit.

1. Use a two-level triage system to prioritize your patients. Write "immediate" or "delayed" beside each one. Then order them 1–5 to indicate the sequence in which you wish to manage these patients.

   _____ **a.** Chris: 25-year-old restrained male, driver, trapped by steering column and dashboard; appears unconscious with gurgling, snoring respirations; has major head and chest injuries.

   Priority: _____

   _____ **b.** Jim: front-seat passenger, 23-year-old restrained male, also trapped by the dashboard; appears to be alert, with major abdomen, pelvic, and leg injuries.

   Priority: _____

   _____ **c.** Sherri: back-seat driver's-side passenger, 22-year-old restrained female; conscious with lacerations, bumps and bruises, neck and back pain.

   Priority: _____

   _____ **d.** Michael: back-seat middle passenger, 27-year-old restrained male; conscious with large bump to the head, neck pain, and a swollen, deformed left forearm.

   Priority:_____

   _____ **e.** Holly: back-seat passenger's side, 26-year-old restrained female; major facial lacerations, swollen and deformed jaw, swollen, deformed right collarbone, neck pain.

   Priority: _____

2. No additional emergency services personnel are on scene yet. One of your crew is still setting out flares and diverting traffic around the scene. You and your remaining crew member have pulled out your medical equipment. What assessment and treatment tasks should the two of you attempt to accomplish?

3. Additional personnel have arrived. Law enforcement takes over traffic control. You have a newly arrived First Responder set up a staging and treatment area for the incoming rescue units and ambulances. The captain of the heavy rescue unit tells you that it will require heavy rescue tools to extricate your patients. He tells you that he can have the left rear door of the sedan opened in about five minutes, but that it will take 20 to 30 minutes to pull the steering wheel and dashboard off the front-seat occupants. Given this information, describe the order in which you wish to extricate the patients.

4. While the front-seat patients are being extricated, what type of assessment and treatment do you want to perform on them?

5. The rescue crew frees Chris from behind the steering wheel of the car. Describe how you would extricate him and what type of equipment you would use.

Active Learning

1. Go to http://www-nrd.nhtsa.dot.gov/departments/nrd-30/ncsa/AvailInf.html and download the traffic statistics for the most recent year. Read them and then discuss them with a classmate. Does anything surprise you?

2. Some fire departments carry extensive equipment for vehicle rescue and disentanglement. Determine what vehicle rescue equipment is carried by your agency (if any).

34 Special Rescue Situations

Key Ideas

This chapter provides an introduction to special rescue situations and hazards. Key ideas include the following:

- Lack of understanding about scene hazards can result in injury or death.

- Confined spaces pose hazards such as engulfment, suffocation, poisoning, electrocution, and drowning.

- In a trench collapse, a special team is necessary for the rescue. Note that one trench collapse carries a high potential for a secondary collapse.

- Prepare for a litter carry. A total of 18–20 rescuers are necessary to properly effect a carry over one mile. This allows teams to rotate positions and rest.

- Rough terrain increases the risk that a patient will be dropped or a rescuer injured. Identify low-angle or high-angle rescue situations and call for specially trained personnel.

- Helicopters can be called for either operational reasons or medical reasons. In both cases, the patient's condition indicates a need for rapid transport or transport to a specialized facility.

Exam Warm-up

1. As a First Responder, your responsibility in a confined-space emergency is to quickly:
   a. recognize it and call for specialized help.
   b. provide lifesaving emergency care to the patient.
   c. make sure the responders on scene are wearing SCBAs.
   d. lock and lag out all related electrical systems.

2. Ray is a First Responder who does NOT have specialized rescue training. The tasks he should perform during a size up of a confined-space emergency are listed below. Identify the one task he should NOT perform.
   a. Call for a specialized rescue team.
   b. Determine what the hazards are.
   c. Establish safety zones.
   d. Obtain a copy of the permit for the site.
   e. Perform an emergency move of the patient.
   f. Determine how many workers are involved.

3. To avoid unnecessary emergencies, OSHA requires a "trench box" or "shoring" in any trench that is deeper than _____ feet.
   a. 3
   b. 5
   c. 7
   d. 9

4. In a cave-in emergency, the weight of two feet of soil on the patient's chest can equal about _____ pounds.
   a. 10,000
   b. 1,000
   c. 100
   d. 10

5. No matter how a cave-in occurs, if the trench is more than _____ deep, a specialized trench rescue team is required.
   a. ankle
   b. knee
   c. waist
   d. chest

6. In a rough-terrain evacuation, it takes about _____ people to carry a patient on a portable stretcher for one mile.
   a. 18–20
   b. 14–16
   c. 10–12
   d. 6–8

7. Identify two items listed below that do NOT describe a high-angle rescue.
   a. The rescuers' hands are needed for balance.
   b. The slope forms more than a 40-degree angle.
   c. Rappelling is required to get down the slope.
   d. A fall would likely result in serious injury or death.
   e. The slope forms less than a 40-degree angle.

8. A helicopter landing zone should be at least _____ feet.
   a. 25 × 25
   b. 50 × 50
   c. 75 × 75
   d. 100 × 100

Short-Answer Review

9. Define the term "*confined space.*"

10. List three examples of confined spaces.

   a.

   b.

   c.

11. List three operational reasons for calling a helicopter to the emergency scene.

   a.

   b.

   c.

12. One of the medical reasons for utilizing a helicopter for evacuation is a serious mechanism of injury. Write five examples of serious mechanisms of injury.

   a.

   b.

   c.

   d.

   e.

13. In addition to being flat, a helicopter landing zone must meet four additional criteria. List them.

   a.

   b.

   c.

   d.

14. Describe the correct procedure for approaching a helicopter.

The next two questions refer to Andrew, who has been injured while hiking in the mountains. He is currently lying on a ledge that has a slope of 60 degrees. The ledge is approximately one mile from the nearest road.

15. Will any special teams be needed to remove Andrew from the ledge? If so, which ones? Explain your answer.

16. Write a plan for removing Andrew by stretcher to the roadway for transport.

Vocabulary Practice

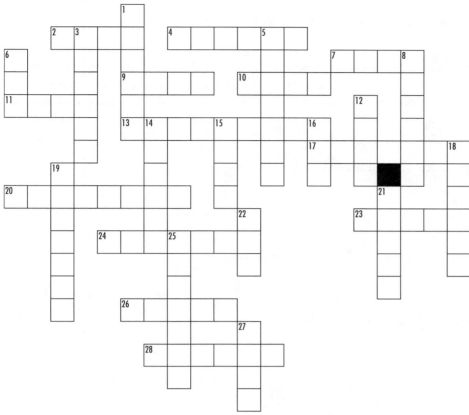

Across

2. Short for self-contained breathing apparatus.
4. Approach or enter.
7. Confined space used to store solid agricultural materials.
9. Eighteen to twenty people can carry a litter for one _____.
10. In a high-angle rescue, the slope forms _____ than a 40-degree angle.
11. Short for rescue helicopter's special insertion and extrication line.
13. Use of violence to provoke fear and influence behavior.
17. Confined space, such as a drain crossing under a road or embankment.
20. A _____ space is one with limited access and not designed for human occupancy.
24. Confined space, such as a tank for storing rainwater.
26. Minimum pilot's night visibility is _____ mile(s).
28. Another name for a portable stretcher.

Down

1. Short for hazardous material.
3. Collapse.
5. Materials propped against a structure to provide support.
6. Short for landing zones.
8. Low level of this is a common hazard in confined spaces.
12. Confined space dug deep into the earth to obtain water, gas, or oil.
14. Exit or path for going out.
15. Short for U.S. Occupational Safety and Health Administration.
16. Short for multiple-casualty incident.
18. Deep furrow or ditch.
19. When lifting the stretcher, a First Responder will need help from _____ rescuer.
21. Confined space, usually underground, with arched walls and ceiling.
22. Minimum for pilot's day visibility is _____ mile(s).
25. Rock climbing is an example of a rough _____ sport.
27. In a low-angle rescue, the slope forms _____ than a 40-degree angle.

The Call: Truck vs. Tree

Read this scenario and answer the questions that follow. Always remember to ensure your own safety above all other considerations.

You have arrived at the scene of a "truck vs. tree" on a very rural stretch of Route 202. As you approach the collision scene on foot, you see that the tree is broken off approximately four feet up from the ground and leaning precariously. The vehicle has sustained extensive front-end damage. Even from a distance, you can see that the steering wheel is bent down toward the driver's chest. You can hear her call out for help.

1. What additional resources will you need? Why?

2. Describe how to set up a landing zone for the helicopter.

3. Once the tree is stabilized and no other hazards exist, what care can you provide to the patient while you wait for the EMTs to arrive?

Active Learning

1. Identify locations in your area that might require a response from a special rescue team. For each location, determine what team or unit would respond.

2. Identify locations in your area that might create operational reasons for a helicopter to be dispatched for transport. Determine what agency calls for the helicopter. Determine appropriate landing zones for each of the areas located.

Appendix 1 | First Response to Terrorist Incidents

Key Ideas

This appendix gives an overview of a First Responder's role during a suspected terrorist incident. Key ideas include the following:

- A terrorist attack can be committed by an individual or a group and is meant to cause a psychological impact.

- Weapons of mass destructions are intended to kill and injure significantly more people than their actual size would allow. These include chemical, biological, radiological and nuclear weapons.

- There are several indicators to lead a First Responder to suspect a terrorist incident. They include unusual or unexpected events, high interest targets, psychologically significant dates, greater than usual number of patients and unusual signs and symptoms in groups of people.

- First Responders should utilize the "Five Ss" when planning a response to a suspected terrorist attack.

Exam Warm-up

1. A weapon containing anthrax, botulism, smallpox, or Ebola virus would be a _____ weapon.
   a. chemical
   b. biological
   c. radiological
   d. nuclear

2. What is the most common device for a terrorist to use during an attack?
   a. explosive weapon
   b. chemical weapon
   c. biological weapon
   d. nuclear weapon

3. Name three factors a First Responder should consider when implementing the "self" plan of action in the "Five Ss."

4. The scene size up should contain all the following EXCEPT:
   a. entering the hot zone.
   b. determining the number of patients.
   c. determining if hazardous materials are involved.
   d. determining the necessary resources.

5. The third S in the "Five Ss" stands for:
   a. Self
   b. Size Up
   c. Send Info
   d. Stabilize

6. Where are the most critical patients likely to be in a multi-casualty incident?
   a. In the cold zone
   b. In the warm zone
   c. In the hot zone
   d. In the impact zone

7. Name two pieces of information that would be important to report to a hospital during a suspected terrorist attack

8. Why is it important to stabilize a scene as soon as possible?

The Call

You are dispatched to the local water treatment plant. It is reported that suddenly several people are feeling ill and one patient has started seizing. Dispatch can-not obtain any further information due to trouble keeping a phone connection.

Do you suspect a terrorist attack? Why or why not?

What would your plan be to keep yourself and other First Responders safe?

What additional resources would you have dispatched?

Appendix

2 | Skill Summary Sheets

Work in small groups to practice caring for patients until each member of your group achieves a "perfect score." Note that the daggers (†) below indicate skills supplemental to the DOT's "First Responder: National Standard Curriculum" and may not be required of First Responders in your EMS system. Be sure you learn and follow all state and local protocols.

FIRST RESPONDER: A SKILLS APPROACH
SKILL SUMMARY SHEETS

MANUAL STABILIZATION
OF A TRAUMA PATIENT'S HEAD AND NECK

SKILL SUMMARY	Check If Performed
1 Take BSI precautions.	
2 Tell the patient to stay very still.	
3 Place your hands on both sides of the patient's head and hold it firmly and steadily in a neutral, in-line position.	
4 Maintain manual stabilization until the patient is completely immobilized.	
NOTE: If your patient's head is not already in a neutral, in-line position when you begin, gently guide it there. If there is any pain or if you feel resistance, stop immediately and stabilize the head in the position in which it was found.	

SUCTIONING

SKILL SUMMARY	Check If Performed
1 Take BSI precautions.	
2 Prepare the suction device.	
3 Select the correct type of catheter for your patient.	
4 Without suction, insert the catheter to the base of the patient's tongue.	
5 Apply suction while moving the catheter from side to side.	
6 Suction for up to 15 seconds in an adult (10 seconds in a child and 5 seconds in an infant).	
NOTE: If decreased heart rate is observed in an infant you are suctioning, stop and reapply oxygen or ventilate for at least 30 seconds prior to suctioning again.	

FIRST RESPONDER: A SKILLS APPROACH
SKILL SUMMARY SHEETS

THE OROPHARYNGEAL AIRWAY

▼ SKILL SUMMARY	Check If Performed
1 Take BSI precautions.	
2 Select the proper size airway.	
3 Open the patient's mouth. If necessary, use the cross-finger technique.	
4 In an adult, insert the airway upside down, with the top pointing toward the roof of the patient's mouth.	
5 Advance the airway gently until you meet resistance.	
6 Rotate the airway 180° clockwise while you continue to advance it, until the flange rests on the patient's front teeth.	
NOTE: In an infant or child, use a tongue depressor and insert the airway in its normal upright position. Do not rotate it.	

THE NASOPHARYNGEAL AIRWAY

▼ SKILL SUMMARY	Check If Performed
1 Take BSI precautions.	
2 Select the proper size airway.	
3 Lubricate the device with a sterile, water-soluble lubricant.	
4 Insert the airway posteriorly, with the beveled end toward the septum when it is inserted in the right nostril.	
5 Advance the airway gently and close to the midline along the floor of the nostril and straight back into the nasopharynx.	
NOTE: If the airway cannot be inserted in one nostril, try the other nostril.	

Student's Name _____ Date _____

OXYGEN ADMINISTRATION

SKILL SUMMARY	Check If Performed
1 Take BSI precautions.	
2 Identify the cylinder as oxygen, and remove the protective seal from the tank.	
3 Crack the main cylinder for one second to remove dust and debris.	
4 Place the yoke of the regulator over the cylinder valve and align the pins.	
5 Hand-tighten the T-screw on the regulator.	
6 Open the main cylinder valve to check the pressure.	
7 Attach the proper delivery device (nonrebreather mask or nasal cannula) to the regulator.	
8 Adjust the flow meter to the appropriate liter flow (nonrebreather mask—15 liters per minute; nasal cannula—no more than 6 liters per minute).	
9 Apply the oxygen delivery device to the patient.	
NOTE: When you are ready to discontinue oxygen administration, remove the device from the patient. Then shut off the control valve until liter flow is at zero. Shut off the main cylinder valve. Then bleed the valves by leaving the control valve open until the needle or ball indicator returns to zero.	

FIRST RESPONDER: A SKILLS APPROACH
SKILL SUMMARY SHEETS

EXTERNAL BLEEDING CONTROL

SKILL SUMMARY	Check If Performed
1 Take BSI precautions.	
2 Apply direct pressure to the bleeding wound. Use a sterile dressing, if available.	
3 Elevate the extremity, but only if there is no major injury to the underlying muscle or bone.	
4 Reassess bleeding. If bleeding has not stopped, then apply additional pressure as needed.	
5 If bleeding continues, apply pressure to the arterial pulse point above the wound on the injured extremity.	
6 Reassess bleeding. When bleeding is under control, bandage the wound appropriately.	

SHOCK MANAGEMENT

SKILL SUMMARY	Check If Performed
1 Take BSI precautions.	
2 Maintain an open airway in the patient. If breathing is adequate, administer oxygen by way of a nonrebreather mask. Be prepared to provide artificial ventilation, if needed.	
3 Prevent any further blood loss.	
4 Position the patient properly.	
5 Keep the patient warm, but do not overheat him or her.	
6 Provide care for specific injuries while waiting for EMS crews to arrive.	
NOTE: Comfort, calm, and reassure the patient while you wait for transport. Be sure to withhold all food and drink.	

FIRST RESPONDER: A SKILLS APPROACH
SKILL SUMMARY SHEETS

SPLINTING

SKILL SUMMARY	Check If Performed
1 Take BSI precautions.	
2 Instruct another First Responder or a helper to apply manual stabilization to the injured extremity.	
3 Assess pulse, movement, and sensation below the injury site.	
4 Cut away clothing to expose the injury to the extremity.	
5 After controlling bleeding, place a sterile dressing over open wounds, if any.	
6 If there is severe deformity, absence of a pulse, or cyanosis in the extremity, align it with gentle manual traction. Maintain it until the limb is completely immobilized.	
7 Measure the splint, and pad it appropriately.	
8 For a long-bone injury, apply the splint so that the joints above and below the injury site are immobilized. For a joint injury, apply the splint so the bones above and below the injury site are immobilized.	
9 Secure the injured extremity to the splint.	
10 Reassess pulse, movement, and sensation in the extremity every 15 minutes and record your findings.	
NOTE: If the limb is severely deformed by the injury, or if the limb has no pulse or is cyanotic below the injury site, then align it with gentle manual traction. If there is pain or grating, stop pulling immediately.	

Appendix
3
Practice Scenarios

Bring together all the knowledge and skills you have acquired in this course. Work with partners or in small groups to decide what you would do for each scenario below.

1. Your patient is in bed, unresponsive. There is shortness of breath, unusually slow pulse, and bluish, cool, damp skin. After you are told the patient is terminally ill, you are given a DNR order by his son.

2. The alarmed parents say the infant is "too quiet." The babysitter noticed nothing unusual, they report. The baby appears to you to be sleepy and pale.

3. Your partner has been exceptionally irritable lately. He seems to be either snapping at someone—including patients—or daydreaming. He has been late to the job several times and refuses to break with the rest of the crew.

4. Your adult patient has a painful, swollen, deformed injury to the lower right arm with pulselessness below the injury site.

5. A 40-year-old woman is unconscious. She has old and new bruises on her face, arms, chest, stomach, and legs. Her husband, who is nearby, appears to be unable to stand still or meet your partner's eyes.

6. The eight-year-old boy has been lost on the mountain in the woods for nine hours. Sunset was five hours ago. When you find him, he is wearing only a tee shirt and shorts.

7. Your 35-year-old patient has been sunning all day on the beach. When you reach her, you find that her skin is dry and hot and she is unresponsive.

8. A 10-year-old girl steps on a rusty five-inch nail, which goes completely through her foot.

9. Your patient was ejected through the windshield of a moving vehicle. She is now unresponsive and showing signs of breathing difficulty.

10. Your patient is an 18-year-old woman who, 15 minutes before, opened her front door, stepped onto a sheet of ice, and fell down five concrete steps. She said she landed on her "tail bone," which was and is still very painful.

11. The patient is a five-year-old boy with severe breathing difficulty. You suspect a partial foreign body airway obstruction.

12. Your 18-year-old patient has a stab wound to the neck. He is bleeding profusely.

13. Your patient has sliced off the index finger of her left hand and partially severed the thumb with a jigsaw. She is bleeding profusely.

14. It is summer and you and your partner are patrolling the lake's public beach when you see an adult male swimmer who appears to be having difficulty in the water about 50 feet from shore.

15. Your patient has been shot in the chest in a gang incident. The bullet wound entered through his back just below the scapula.

16. The patient fell, feet first, approximately 18 feet onto concrete. He is pale and unresponsive with obvious deformity to his right thigh.

17. Your 30-year-old patient was in a car crash. Both forearms are painful, swollen, and deformed. She also has suffered a blow to her forehead. On the AVPU scale, your patient is verbal. Radial pulse is weak. Skin condition is pale, cool, moist.

18. Your patient is a 19-year-old male who was thrown from a pickup truck that rolled over several times. The driver is dead. Your patient says he is fine and wants to go home now.

19. You are restocking your supplies when you are called to respond to a "fist fight" in front of the bar on the corner of Main and Connor. You must decide quickly on the personal protective equipment to take with you.

20. An 88-year-old woman tripped over her telephone cord and fell on the floor. She is complaining of severe pain in her left hip and thigh.

21. Suddenly the firefighters present you with a 70-year-old woman who has partial-thickness burns on her arms and chest. The patient has soot around her nostrils and mouth.

22. Your patient's face and neck have been slashed with a razor. There is profuse bleeding from the neck.

23. You are called to a "delivery in progress." When you arrive on scene, you are told that the baby is not due for another six weeks.

24. You are watching a game of stick ball when you see a speeding car sideswipe one of the players and race away. The boy—10 years old—was spun into the air, hit the hood of a parked car, and slid to the ground.

25. A diner performs abdominal thrusts on a man who is choking. After several thrusts, you see the patient lose consciousness and drop to the floor. No one is doing anything to help him.

26. The weather is overcast and cold at the triathlon. The contestants finished the swim portion of the race, and they are getting on their bikes to start the second event. One contestant, however, is sitting on the ground, shivering and pale.

27. A farm worker has been found unresponsive in the immediate area of a manure pit.

28. You are shopping at Macy's when you see a man clutch at his left arm and fall to the ground unconscious.

29. A 20-year-old female has just given birth. The infant is blue and limp, and the mother appears to have lost an excessive amount of blood.

30. You are exiting the "Y," where you are a swim instructor when a very young woman in obvious distress is carried through the door by an older male. He looks at you and says, "Help, the baby is coming!"

31. A woman is 22 with contractions that are four minutes apart and 45 seconds each. This is her first baby. She is 30 minutes from the nearest medical facility.

32. You are dispatched to the skateboard park for a 13-year-old male who fell off one of the ramps directly onto his head. He is complaining of neck pain.

33. You are caring for a 13-year-old girl who caught her fingers in a car door as it was slammed shut. The girl is screaming in pain. Her parents, who are trying to comfort her, are very upset. Her hand appears to be swelling and bleeding, and the fingertips are blue. There is a large puncture wound on the upper palm.

34. You have just helped a new mother deliver her baby. The newborn's pulse rate is less than 100 beats per minute.

35. Your patient is short of breath. His breathing is rapid, and he is experiencing tingling around his mouth and fingertips.

36. You are called to the scene of a drowning. When you arrive, you see an adult male performing CPR incorrectly on a supine, six-year-old child.

37. You are called to an industrial plant with a report of a gas leak and five workers down. You will arrive on the scene about five minutes before the fire service and hazmat teams.

38. You are called to an "auto versus pole." The 82-year-old driver is alert but has pain in her chest from striking the steering wheel. She has no memory of how the crash occurred.

39. You are called to a baby who appears to be dead in her crib. Her parents are demanding that you do something to help her.

40. You are called to a "man having an asthma attack." He tells you that he just has to "get a shot" at the hospital "like last time."

41. You are approaching the scene of a vehicle collision involving a tanker truck and a small pickup. Dispatch reports that the crash may involve a hazardous materials spill.

42. You have been called to a "man down" in an alley behind a high-rise office building. He smells of alcohol and cannot be roused when you call out to him.

43. Your patient is a 66-year-old male who is having chest pain. He is pale and sweaty. He has already taken several nitroglycerin tablets.

44. Your patient is 8 years old. Her mother says she is having an acute asthma attack. The child has irregular breathing, high-pitched breathing sounds, and a rapid pulse.

45. A 46-year-old male has abdominal pain. He suddenly vomits a large amount of bright, red blood and becomes pale and sweaty.

46. You are alone on the scene of a vehicle collision involving 20 or more people. Rescue vehicles will have a difficult time getting through the traffic.

47. It is a hot, sunny day. You are patrolling the shopping mall parking lot when you see a baby locked alone in a car. The baby—about one year old—is wearing a buttoned up sweater over a long-sleeve shirt, long pants, socks, and shoes. The baby appears to have hot, moist skin.

48. Your patient is a 40-year-old woman who has just been beaten and robbed. You suspect she also may have been raped.

49. Your 21-month-old patient has ingested an unknown quantity of aspirin tablets. The child has a white powder around his mouth. He is alert, happy, and interacting normally with his mother and his environment.

50. Your patient was chopping wood into tinder when "something" flew into his left eye. He has been running tap water over his eye. He can no longer open it.

51. An adult male is reported to have had sharp abdominal pain for several hours. He has taken several doses of an over-the-counter antacid but has had no relief. He is in mild distress. His skin is cool and moist.

52. An adult female, possibly in her 30s, has been found lying in bed, cyanotic, and unresponsive, with a slow respiratory rate. There is drug paraphernalia nearby.

53. An 86-year-old man awoke with shortness of breath one hour ago. He is sitting straight up and appears to be in severe distress. He looks fatigued and is unable to speak.

54. You have just arrived with the fire department on the scene of a fire in an office building. It appears that over 50 people have been injured by smoke inhalation, burns, or falls while trying to escape.

55. After starting a new prescription for a urinary tract infection, a woman complains of nausea, vomiting, abdominal cramps, and diarrhea.

56. A teenager was checking the engine radiator when a jet of boiling hot steam and water hits her face. Her mother is frantic as she pulls you to the back of the house where you hear screams of pain.

57. A man in a wheelchair is whooping loudly as he careens up and down the street, bashing into parked cars, and generally terrorizing the neighborhood. As you watch, the man speeds toward a passerby, misses hitting her only by inches, and U-turns back towards you.

58. A day-care-center supervisor reports that six children are vomiting and appear to have abdominal pain and cramping. The teaching assistant also does not feel well.

59. You have responded to a motor-vehicle collision. Your unresponsive patient's midsize car has been hit from the rear in traffic that was moving at about 30 mph. He is still wearing his lap belt. There appears to be no headrest.

60. A 70-year-old woman was found by her sons in bed, unable to speak and unable to move the right side of her body. She has a slow pulse and rapid respirations.

61. A 63-year-old is mowing the lawn when very suddenly she finds that she "can't breathe."

62. A 35-year-old male is "vomiting blood." The patient is very pale and says he is dizzy and might "pass out."

63. A 31-year-old male fell off his bicycle during a road race. The patient is standing, cradling his right arm close to his body. It appears that there is some deformity of the right clavicle.

64. A 30-year-old woman has fallen from the roof of her two-story home onto newly turned earth. She is flat on her back and unresponsive.

65. A 30-year-old male accidentally shot himself with his own hand gun. He has a small entry wound in the upper right thigh. He is awake and alert but appears to be getting pale.

66. A 27-year-old male, reported to have a seizure, seems unable or unwilling to speak. He is slightly combative and uncooperative.

67. A 22-year-old athlete complains of chest pain about 20 minutes after a basketball game. She feels short of breath and markedly anxious.

68. A 17-year-old female has "slashed her wrists" in the locker room of the high school gym. She is upset, crying, and uncooperative. She will not answer any of your questions.

69. A 13-year-old and his father are eating hot dogs "with the works" when the youngster has a sudden onset of shortness of breath and facial itching, flushing, and swelling. He also has a cough, hoarseness, and noisy breathing.

70. A 70-year-old woman tells you she was taking a shower when she realized her left arm and hand were—and still are—completely numb. She appears to be lethargic and slightly confused. She is wearing a Medic Alert bracelet that indicates she has diabetes.

Workbook Answer Key

Chapter 1: Introduction to the EMS System

Exam Warm-up/Short-Answer Review

1. **b** *(p. 2)*   2. **b** *(p. 4)*
3. **b** *(p. 7)*
4. **a, b, c, e, f.** Enter a crime scene only after it has been controlled by the police. *(p. 8)*
5. True *(p. 9)*   6. **a** *(p. 9)*
7. False *(p. 9)*   8. True *(p. 9)*
9. Answers may include the following: *(p. 7)*
   a. Regulation and policy—Each state must have laws, regulations, policies, and procedures that govern its EMS system. It also is required to provide leadership to local jurisdictions.
   b. Resources management—Each state must have central control of EMS resources so all patients have equal access to acceptable emergency care.
   c. Human resources and training—All personnel who staff ambulances and transport patients must be trained to at least the EMT-Basic level.
   d. Transportation—Patients must be safely and reliably transported by ground or air ambulance.
   e. Facilities—Every seriously ill or injured patient must be delivered in a timely manner to an appropriate medical facility.
   f. Communications—A system for public access to the EMS system must be in place. Communication among dispatcher, ambulance crew, and hospital also must be possible.
   g. Public information and education—EMS personnel should participate in programs designed to educate the public. The programs are to focus on the prevention of injuries and how to properly access the EMS system.
   h. Medical oversight—Each EMS system must have a physician as a medical director.
   i. Trauma systems—Each state must develop a system of specialized care for trauma patients, including one or more trauma centers and rehabilitation programs. It must also develop systems for assigning and transporting patients to those facilities.
   j. Evaluation—Each state must have a quality improvement system in place for continuing evaluation and upgrading of the state's EMS system.
10. The four levels of out-of-hospital care providers are: First Responder, EMT-Basic, EMT-Intermediate, and EMT-Paramedic. *(p. 4)*
11. In your role as a First Responder, you must: *(p. 8)*
   a. Protect your safety and the safety of your crew, the patient, and bystanders.
   b. Gain access to the patient.
   c. Assess the patient in order to identify life-threatening problems.
   d. Alert additional EMS resources, when needed.
   e. Provide emergency medical care to the patient based on assessment findings.
   f. Assist other EMS personnel when requested.
   g. Participate in record keeping and data collection as required.
   h. Act as liaison with other public safety workers.

12. a. Direct medical control occurs when the medical director or another physician directs an EMS rescuer at the scene of an emergency by way of a telephone, radio, or in person.
    b. Indirect medical control includes such things as system design, quality management, and protocols. *(p. 9)*

Vocabulary Practice

Crossword solution (across): 4. ORDERS · 6. PERINATAL · 9. PHYSICIAN · 11. AGENTS · 14. INTERMEDIATE · 19. DOT · 21. PARAMEDIC · 22. GOLDEN

The Call

1. You must alert additional EMS resources, provide care based on continued assessment, and participate in record keeping as required by your state or agency. Be sure to also maintain a caring attitude. *(pp. 8–9)*
2. Any three: Assist other EMS agencies as requested. Report what you found in your assessment, what you did, and if it worked. Maintain a caring attitude. Maintain a professional appearance and attitude. *(pp. 8–9)*

Chapter 2: Well-Being of the First Responder

Exam Warm-up/Short-Answer Review

1. **a–g.** High-stress situations include incidents in which there are multiple casualties or that involve injury to an infant or child, death of a patient, an amputation, violence, abuse, or injury or death of a coworker. *(pp. 28–29)*
2. **d** *(p. 26)*
3. **b** is correct. However, family members should express their grief in a way that is not dangerous to you or others. *(pp. 26–27)*
4. **a** *(pp. 26–27)*   5. **b** *(p. 29)*

6. a *(p. 29)*   7. b *(p. 29)*
8. d *(p. 29)*   9. b *(p. 16)*
10. c *(pp. 17–18)*   11. d *(p. 18)*
12. a *(p 18)*   13. c *(p. 18)*
14. a, e *(p. 18)*   15. b *(pp. 18–19)*
16. d *(p. 18)*

17. False. Always take BSI precautions. *(pp. 17, 18)*

18. You can remind yourself that the patient desperately needs you and your skills; close your eyes, take several deep breaths, and when you feel more in control, return to giving emergency care; change your thought patterns, such as quietly hum or mentally sing a peaceful song; eat properly to maintain your blood sugar during a call. *(p. 28)*

19. Certain foods increase the body's response to stress. So you might cut down on sugar and caffeine (watch out, soft drinks as well as coffee and tea may have caffeine). Avoid fatty foods, and eat more low-fat carbohydrates. While at work, eat often but in small amounts. Avoid alcohol and other kinds of self-medication. Exercise regularly, and learn to relax. If at all possible, a First Responder might also request work shifts that allow for more time with family and friends or ask for a rotation of duty to a less stressful assignment. *(p. 28)*

20. A rescuer's family may suffer from stress factors such as a lack of understanding, fear of separation or of being ignored, worry about on-call situations, and a frustrated desire to share. *(p. 28)*

21. You would request a CISD if you have been involved in the serious injury or death of a rescuer in the line of duty; a multiple-casualty incident; the suicide of an emergency worker; an event that attracts media attention; the injury or death of someone you know; or any disaster. Also initiate a CISD after any event that has unusual impact on you, such as an incident in which injury or death of a civilian was caused by a rescuer, the death of one of your patients occurred, child abuse or neglect was suspected or confirmed, an event that threatens your life, or an incident that involves distressing sights, sounds, or smells. *(p. 29)*

22. You should always put on protective gloves before you approach your patient. In addition, the appropriate personal protective equipment for each circumstance described is as follows: *(pp. 20–21)*
    a. protective gloves.
    b. eye protection, gloves, gown, mask.
    c. protective gloves.
    d. protective gloves, plus a pocket face mask with one-way valve to perform artificial ventilation during CPR. Eye protection may also be wise, since patients who are resuscitated may vomit.
    e. protective gloves.

23. a. No—A downed power line does not need to look "hot" to be a potential source of electrocution. Call for specialists to secure the scene before you enter. *(p. 23)*
    b. No—Crowds of people can be very dangerous, especially when violence has occurred. Call for police assistance. *(p.23)*
    c. No—This emergency requires trained crews wearing specialized safety equipment. *(p. 23)*
    d. Yes—You may enter a scene the police tell you they have secured. *(p. 23)*
    e. No—You do not know enough about the hazardous material to approach the scene. Have the firefighters bring you the patient after they have decided he or she is free of contaminants. *(p. 23)*

Vocabulary Practice

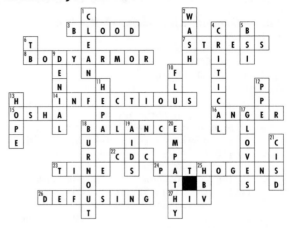

The Call

1. You should be concerned about the bloody vomit on his clothing as well as his infected sputum and other fluids related to his respiratory problem. *(pp. 18–21)*

2. Wear gloves, as you always should. Because of the potential for more vomiting, also wear eye protection, a mask, and possibly a gown. *(pp. 18–21)*

3. This First Responder is obviously not being careful about protecting her own well-being. Though she may not be able to contract HIV from touching the patient's vomit, she should know that other contagious diseases can be contracted by doing so. While there may be only a small amount of bloody vomit to avoid, it is always best to go into a scene prepared for the worst. After all, the patient may start vomiting again and more profusely. *(pp. 18–21)*

4. Practice thorough handwashing with soap and hot water, and change any soiled clothing. This clothing should be bagged and then washed in hot soapy water for at least 25 minutes. Take a hot shower yourself and rinse thoroughly. *(pp. 18–21)*

Chapter 3: Legal and Ethical Issues

Exam Warm-up/Short-Answer Review

1. b *(p. 35)*   2. b *(p. 36)*
3. c *(p. 36)*   4. c *(p. 36)*
5. a *(p. 36)*   6. d *(p. 37)*
7. b *(p. 36)*   8. a *(p. 39)*
9. d *(p. 39)*   10. c *(p. 39)*
11. c *(pp. 42–43)*   12. c *(p. 41)*
13. b *(p. 42)*   14. d *(p. 42)*
15. b *(p. 42)*

16. Your response may include the following: Make the physical and emotional needs of the patient a priority. Serve those needs with respect for human dignity and with no regard to nationality, race, gender, creed, or status. Practice your skills to the point of mastery. Show respect for the competence of other medical workers. Continue your education, take refresher courses, and stay on top of changes in EMS. Help define and uphold professional standards.

Critically review your performance and seek ways to improve response time, patient outcome, and communication. Report with honesty. Hold in confidence all information obtained in the course of your work, unless required by law to share it. Work in harmony with other First Responders, EMTs, and other members of the health-care team. *(p. 35)*

17. First tell the patient who you are. Identify your level of training, and then carefully explain your plan for emergency care. Make sure you identify both the benefits and the risks. To make sure the patient understands, question him or her briefly. *(p. 36)*

18. Provide emergency care as you would for any patient who needs it. In the absence of a valid advance directive, you have no other choice but to assume implied consent. *(p. 37)*

19. Try one last time to persuade the patient to accept treatment or transport. Be sure the patient is able to make a rational, informed decision. Consult medical direction as required by local protocol. Have the patient and a witness sign a refusal or "release from liability" form. Encourage the patient to seek help if certain symptoms develop. Advise the patient to call EMS again immediately if he or she has a change of mind. *(pp. 37–39)*

20. Yes, he is employed as a First Responder, and he is on the job. He must provide the emergency care he's trained and contracted to provide. *(pp. 39–40)*

21. No, he does not have a duty to act. He's not on call and, even if he was, his contract is with his employer, not the general public. *(pp. 39–40)*

22. Suspected child, elder, or spouse abuse; any injury that may be the result of a crime; all suspected infectious disease exposure. *(p. 42)*

Vocabulary Practice

1. consent *(p. 36)*
2. abandonment *(p. 39)*
3. advance directive *(p. 37)*
4. competent *(p. 36)*
5. duty to act *(pp. 39–40)*
6. standard of care *(p. 42)*
7. negligence *(p. 39)*
8. scope of care *(p. 35)*
9. implied consent *(p. 36)*
10. expressed consent *(p. 36)*

The Call

1. Absolutely. You have no way of knowing if the chest pain is serious or not. A physician needs to examine the patient before such a decision can be made. *(p. 36)*

2. You might explain to Mr. Boyd that he may have had or may be having a heart attack. If so, it is imperative that he be seen immediately to reduce the chance of permanent damage to his heart. Also, if he is having a heart attack, a delay in treatment could be very serious, even fatal. You might also suggest to Mrs. Boyd that she speak to her husband. He may listen to her. *(p. 37)*

3. You shouldn't agree with that strategy. Mr. Boyd has the right to refuse treatment and transport. He is fully alert and in control of his mental faculties. There is no sign of intoxication, no history of mental illness, and he generally appears to be rational. He is allowed to disagree with any medical opinion of his condition. As long as he understands that he

may be having a heart attack, as well as the risks involved with delaying treatment, EMS personnel have no recourse. *(p. 39)*

Chapter 4: The Human Body

Exam Warm-up/Short-Answer Review

1. a *(p. 50)*
2. c *(p. 50)*
3. d *(p. 50)*
4. c *(p. 50)*
5. b *(p. 50)*
6. a *(p. 50)*
7. c *(p. 50)*
8. d *(p. 50)*
9. a *(p. 50)*
10. d *(p. 52)*
11. c *(p. 52)*
12. d *(p. 52)*
13. a *(p. 52)*
14. c *(p. 54)*
15. a *(p. 54)*
16. a *(p. 54)*
17. a *(p. 54)*
18. c *(p. 56)*
19. b *(p. 54)*
20. c *(p. 54)*
21. a *(p. 54)*
22. c *(p. 56)*
23. f *(p. 56)*
24. a *(p. 56)*
25. a *(p. 56)*
26. d *(p. 58)*
27. b *(pp. 61–62)*
28. a *(p. 62)*
29. b *(p. 62)*
30. d *(p. 63)*

31. Skeletal muscles are voluntary muscles that shape the body, form its walls, and make possible all deliberate acts such as walking and chewing. Smooth muscles are involuntary muscles found in the walls of organs, ducts, and blood vessels. A person has little or no control over smooth muscle. *(p. 56)*

32. *(pp. 57–58)*
    a. smaller
    b. more
    c. more
    d. more, softer

Vocabulary Practice

1. anatomical—standing, arms down, palms out. lateral recumbent—lying on the side. prone—face down, lying on the stomach. supine—face up, lying on the back. *(p. 50)*

2. cervical vertebrae—neck bones. clavicle—collar bone. humerus—bone of the upper arm. femur—bone of the upper leg. fibula—bone of the lower leg. *(pp. 54, 56)*

3. scapula—shoulder blade. patella—knee cap. radius—bone of the forearm. orbit—eye socket. ilium—hip bone. *(pp. 54, 56)*

4. carotid—neck. femoral—thigh. brachial—upper arm. radial—wrist. dorsalis pedis—foot. *(p. 58)*

The Call

1. The liver, gallbladder, colon, and pancreas may be injured. The right kidney is behind these organs, so it is much less likely to be injured from a blow to the anterior thorax. *(p. 54)*

2. Her confusion may be the result of an injury to the nervous system, specifically her brain. She has a bruised forehead and was not wearing a helmet. Any significant impact to the head can cause a patient's thinking to become confused. *(p. 59)*

3. Treat the breathing problem before the other injuries. A body can survive only a few minutes without oxygen. Any significant injury to the respiratory system can cause an immediate threat to life. Scraped skin and abdominal pain can wait. *(p. 56)*

4. The patient appears to have a fractured tibia just distal to the knee, which has caused the lower leg to rotate laterally. *(p. 50)*

Chapter 5: Lifting and Moving Patients

Exam Warm-up/Short-Answer Review

1. c *(p. 75)*
2. c *(p. 75)*
3. a *(pp. 75–76)*
4. d *(pp. 76–77)*
5. d *(p. 78)*
6. d *(p. 78)*
7. False. In general, when there is no threat to life, do not move the patient. Provide First Responder care and wait for the EMTs to move the patient. *(p. 79)*
8. True. *(p. 79)*
9. False. The extremity lift should be used only when the patient has no injuries to his arms or legs. *(p. 82)*
10. a, c *(p. 84)*
11. b *(p. 86)*
12. a *(p. 87)*
13. a, b, c, d *(p. 78)*
14. Use your legs to lift, not your back. Keep the weight of the object as close to your body as possible. Align shoulders, hips, and feet. Reduce the height or distance you need to move the object. *(p. 75)*
15. An emergency move may be necessary if there is fire or threat of fire, explosion or threat of explosion, inability to protect the patient from other hazards at the scene, inability to gain access to other patients who need life-saving care, or inability to give life-saving care because of the patient's location or position. *(p. 79)*
16. 5, 1, 3, 2, 4 *(p. 79)*
17. Two 7- or 8-foot poles and a blanket, piece of canvas, brattice cloth, a strong sheet, cloth bags or sacks, coats or jackets. *(p. 86)*

Vocabulary Practice

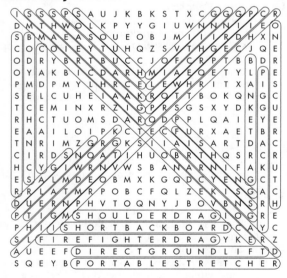

alignment
backboard
blanket drag
body mechanics
carrying
cradle carry
direct ground lift
drags
firefighter drag
fitness
immobilization device
improvised stretcher

piggyback carry
portable stretcher
posture
power grip
pulling
pushing
reaching
scoop stretcher
sheet drag
shirt drag
short backboard
shoulder drag

lifting
moving
one-rescuer crutch
orthopedic

slouch
stair chair
swayback
teamwork

The Call

1. Among your responsibilities are to guard your personal health and safety, to maintain a caring attitude, and to maintain your own composure. *(Chapter 1)*
2. You would need to consider if there is an immediate danger to the patient. In this case, a determining factor may be whether or not the structure is stable. *(p. 79)*
3. a. No. Do not move this patient. There appears to be no immediate threat to life.
   b. Yes, you probably should move patient #2 and patient #3 in order to gain access to patient #4, because Patient #4 may need life-saving emergency care (artificial ventilation or CPR). If she does, you also may have to move her into the correct position.
   c. No, do not move this patient. There appears to be no immediate threat to life. *(p. 79)*

Chapter 6: Breathing and Ventilation

Exam Warm-up/Short-Answer Review

1. a, b, c *(p. 96)*
2. a, b, d *(p. 96)*
3. b *(p. 97)*
4. b *(p. 97)*
5. b *(p. 97)*
6. c *(p. 99)*
7. c *(p. 97)*
8. b *(p. 99)*
9. d *(p. 98)*
10. c. *(p. 99)*
11. False *(p. 100)*
12. False *(p. 102)*
13. b *(pp. 102–103)*
14. c *(p. 103)*
15. a *(p. 106)*
16. b *(p. 107)*
17. c *(p. 107)*
18. a *(p. 107)*
19. a, b, c, d, e, f, i, j, k, l, m *(pp. 102–103)*
20. b, c, d *(p. 107)*
21. True. *(p. 107)*
22. b *(p. 109)*
23. d *(p. 110)*
24. a *(p. 111)*
25. a *(p. 111)*
26. b *(p. 112)*
27. b *(p. 112)*
28. c *(p. 112)*
29. 5, 2, 1, 3, 4 *(p. 95)*
30. Adult—12–20 breaths per minute. Child—15–30 breaths per minute. Infant—25–50 breaths per minute. *(p. 96)*
31. Place the hand closest to the patient's head on the patient's forehead. Apply firm, backward pressure with the palm of your hand to tilt the head back. Place the fingertips of your other hand under the bony part of the lower jaw. Lift the chin forward, and, at the same time, support the jaw and tilt the head back. Continue to press the other hand on the patient's forehead to keep the head tilted back. *(pp. 98–99)*
32. Look for the rise and fall of the patient's chest. Listen for air coming out of the patient's mouth and nose. Feel for air coming out of the patient's nose and mouth. *(pp. 101–102)*
33. Adult – less than 8 breaths per minute
    Child – less than 10 breaths per minute
    Infant – less than 20 breaths per minute *(p. 102)*
34. Any four: Rate of respiration is adequate. Force of air is consistent. Force of air is also sufficient to cause the chest to rise during each ventilation. The patient's heart rate decreases or returns to normal. The patient's color improves. *(p. 106)*

35. The chest does not rise and fall with each ventilation. The ventilation rate is too fast or too slow. The patient's heart rate does not decrease or return to normal. *(p. 106)*
36. Position the mask, and create a seal. Open the patient's airway, and deliver two slow breaths. Determine if the ventilations are adequate. If successful, continue ventilations at the proper rate. If unsuccessful, reposition the patient's head and try again. If still unsuccessful, treat for a foreign body airway obstruction. *(pp. 107, 109)*
37. Adult—10–12 breaths per minute at 1 second each. Child—12–20 breaths per minute at 1 second each. Infant—12–20 breaths per minute at 1 second each. Newborn—30–60 breaths per minute at approx. 1 second each. *(p. 109)*
38. a. Be gentle when you open the infant's airway. Position the head carefully. Keep the baby's head in a neutral position. Remember the airway is more flexible than an adult's and can be easily overextended. *(p. 109)*
    b. The rescuer may be able to form a seal with his or her mouth over the infant's mouth and nose. If a pocket mask is being used, place it on the infant's face in an upside-down position. *(p. 109)*
    c. Deliver 12–20 breaths per minute, each breath lasting 1 second. *(p. 109)*
39. hold the mask in place *(p. 112)*

The Call
1. Even though you understand how upset the family is, you must place safety and the needs of the patient first. Get control of the scene. Move people out of the way so that you can take care of Gracie. *(p. 95)*
2. No. Your first step is to assess and open Gracie's airway. Before a patient can receive artificial ventilation, he or she must have an open airway. *(p. 96)*
3. c, b, a *(pp. 107, 109)*
4. Reduce the force of your ventilations. Check to be sure the patient's head is in a neutral position. Be sure to allow the patient to exhale fully between ventilations. *(p. 111)*
5. Reassess Gracie's airway, breathing and circulation. Always reassess your patient whenever there is a status change.

Chapter 7: Airway Care and Maintainance

Exam Warm-up/Short–Answer Review
1. a *(p. 123)*   2. d *(p. 123)*
3. a *(p. 124)*   4. a *(p. 124)*
5. c *(p. 124)*   6. d *(p. 125)*
7. c *(p.127)*   8. c *(p. 134–135)*
9. a *(p. 136)*   10. False *(p. 136)*
11. d *(p. 138)*   12. e, f, g *(p. 138)*
13. False *(p. 139)* 14. False *(p. 139)*
15. c *(p. 140)*
16. Any three: poor skin color, unresponsiveness, cool and clammy skin, difficulty breathing, or blood loss. *(p. 127)*
17. 2, 1, 4, 5, 8, 9, 3, 7, 6 *(pp. 128–132)*
18. Get into position behind the patient; position your hands on the patient's abdomen; perform abdominal thrusts until the object is expelled or the patient becomes unresponsive. *(pp. 137–138)*
19. d, a, c, b, e   20. c, a, e, b, d
    (p.140)   *(pp. 140–141)*

Vocabulary Practice

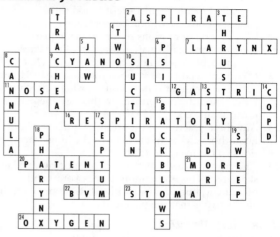

Chapter 8: Circulation

Exam Warm-up/Short-Answer Review
1. a, d *(p .147)*   2. a, b, c, d *(pp. 147–148)*
3. a, c, d *(p. 148)*   4. c *(p. 148)*
5. d *(p. 149)*   6. b *(p. 149)*
7. a *(p. 149)*   8. c *(p. 158)*
9. d *(p. 158)*
10. False. Attempt to resuscitate an infant for two minutes before activating the EMS. *(p. 158)*
11. b *(p. 160)*
12. Early access, early CPR, early defibrillation, early advanced care. *(pp. 148–149)*
13. The rescuer is exhausted and is unable to continue. The patient is turned over to another trained rescuer or to the hospital staff. The patient is resuscitated. The patient has been declared dead by a proper authority. *(p. 149)*
14. Step 2: Activate the EMS system.
    Step 4: Open the patient's airway.
    Step 5: Determine breathlessness.
    Step 7: Determine pulselessness. *(pp. 150–151)*
15. unresponsive, breathless, pulseless *(p. 149)*
16. a. 30:2
    b. 30:2
    c. 30:2
    d. 30:2 *(p. 163)*
17. a. Two or three fingers on lower half of sternum.
    b. Heel of one or two hands on lower half of sternum.
    c. Two hands on lower half of sternum.
    d. Two hands on lower half of sternum. *(p. 163)*
18. *(p. 163)*

	Infant	Child	Adult
Compression Rate	at least 100 per minute	at least 100 per minute	100 per minute
Compression Depth	$\frac{1}{3}$ to $\frac{1}{2}$ the total chest depth	$\frac{1}{3}$ to $\frac{1}{2}$ the total chest depth	$1\frac{1}{2}$ to 2 inches

19. e, b, a, f, d, c, g *(p. 151)*
20. Disagree. This student's hand placement could easily result in injuring the patient's liver. His hand placement should be two fingers' distance above the xiphoid process. *(p. 159)*

21. Chest compressions need to be smooth in order to provide the best circulation of blood through the patient's body. Providing compressions with jabbing or jerking motions results in inadequate chest compression, inadequate relaxation of the chest, and probable lowering of cardiac output. *(p. 152)*

22. CPR may need to be stopped for more than 10 seconds if the patient is in a position where effective CPR cannot be performed. In this case the patient must be moved. *(p. 156)*

23. Any three: fracture of the sternum, pneumothorax, hemothorax, cuts and bruises to the lungs, lacerations to the liver. *(p. 158)*

24. The crunch usually means the patient's rib cartilage separated. This is common. Check your hand placement, but continue with CPR. Remember, the alternative is that the patient dies. *(p. 158)*

Vocabulary Practice

1. a. lungs   b. sternum
   c. two-sided   d. left
   e. right   f. pressure
   g. pulse
2. a. artery   b. brachial
   c. carotid   d. radial

The Call

1. Your first action should be to introduce yourself to the person who is providing CPR. Tell him you are a First Responder, a trained EMS rescuer. Evaluate the CPR being performed by the bystander to ensure it is being done correctly. If it is, he may continue.

2. Assist by getting in position at the patient's head. Then check the patient's pulse while a compression is being performed. When the compression is complete, provide two ventilations and check the patient's pulse. Then, if necessary, you may take over and resume CPR. *(p. 154)*

3. This person needs some coaching. He needs to reposition his hands so that he is compressing the lower half of the patient's sternum, two finger-widths above the xiphoid process. He needs to compress the chest more forcefully—$1\frac{1}{2}$ to 2 inches in depth. Finally, he needs to compress the patient's chest at a rate of 100 compressions per minute. *(p. 163)*

Chapter 9: Automated External Defibrillation

Exam Warm-up/Short-Answer Review

1. a *(p. 167)*   2. c *(p. 171)*
3. c *(p. 173)*
4. Defibrillation is the application of an electric shock to the chest of an unresponsive, breathless, pulseless patient. *(p. 167)*
5. Begin CPR first. Current ECC standards indicate that if the down time of the patient was longer than 4–5 minutes, the First Responder should initially provide 5 cycles of 30:2 compressions/ventilations (approximately 2 minutes worth of CPR) prior to using the AED. Remember though, if using the AED on a patient between the ages of 1–8 years of age, be sure to use a dose attenuating circuit. *(p. 169)*
6. The AED should not be applied to any patient who has a pulse or is conscious. A shock should not be delivered because this patient is breathing and has a pulse, and to do so can actually cause cardiac arrest

to occur. The AED is only applied to breathless, pulseless patients. *(p. 169)*
7. a. Yes. With a dose attenuating curcuit.
   b. Yes. With a dose attenuating curcuit.
   c. Yes.   d. Yes. *(p. 169)*
8. If the patient goes into cardiac arrest in front of the First Responder or within 4–5 minutes of the First Responder's arrival, then the AED should be utilized prior to the initiation of CPR. If however, the patient's down-time was longer than 4–5 minutes prior to the First Responder arrival, then the First Responder should provide 2 minutes of CPR (5 cycles of 30:2) first. This is so that the heart can be perfused with oxygenated blood prior to defibrillation attempts, which makes the defibrillation attempts more successful. *(p. 171)*
9. d, a, f, b, e, c *(p. 171)*

Vocabulary Practice

The Call

1. Remove the patch and wipe off the chest with a towel. *(p. 171)*
2. Make sure no one touches, or is in contact with the patient or the AED. *(p. 171)*
3. Assist with ventilations at a rate of 10–12 per minute, delivering each breath over one second. *(p. 173)*
4. a. Place him in a recovery position.
   b. Apply high-concentration oxygen, if you are allowed to do so.
   c. Keep the AED attached to the patient, and continue to assess his condition until you transfer care to more highly trained EMS personnel. *(p. 173)*

Chapter 10: Scene Size-up

Exam Warm-up/Short-Answer Review

1. d *(p. 182)*   2. c *(p. 182)*
3. b *(p. 182)*   4. b *(p. 183)*
5. c *(p. 183)*   6. True. *(p. 183)*
7. True. *(p. 183)*   8. True. *(p. 183)*
9. False. *(p. 183)*   10. a *(pp. 183–184)*
11. a, b, c, d *(pp. 185–186)*   12. c *(p. 187)*
13. d *(p. 188)*   14. c *(p. 189)*
15. False. A low-velocity impact, such as a knife wound, causes injury to the immediate area of

impact. A high-velocity injury also affects tissues far from the site of impact. *(pp. 189–190)*

16. False. A high-velocity injury will affect tissues far from the site of impact. *(p. 190)*
17. c *(p. 190)*
18. Any two: wear safe clothing, prepare equipment properly, carry a portable radio, plan your safety roles ahead of time. *(p. 180)*
19. a. Any indication that violence has taken or may take place should be considered a sign of potential danger.
    b. When people use alcohol or drugs, their behavior can be unpredictable.
    c. Emergencies are usually very active events. "Absolute silence" is unusual. Anything unusual should be considered a cause for caution. *(pp. 181–182)*
20. Retreat, radio, and reevaluate. *(p. 182)*
21. The car impacts the tree. The occupant impacts the interior of the car. The occupant's organs impact on the surfaces inside the body. *(p. 183)*
22. Up-and-over pathways of motion tend to cause major head, neck, chest, and abdominal injuries. Down-and-under pathways of motion tend to yield more injuries to the legs and pelvis. *(pp. 184–185)*
23. Driver of the sedan: This patient would probably have few injuries. The combination of safety devices he used is specifically designed to minimize injury resulting from a head-on crash. Aside from some bumps, bruises, strains, and sprains, and possibly a few minor burns from the deployment of the air bag, this patient should be relatively unhurt. Driver of the pickup: Expect this patient to have severe injuries. While the lap belt may have kept him from being ejected, this patient could have severe injury to his spine as well as major head, neck, chest, and abdominal injuries. *(p. 187)*
24. Yes. While it does not meet the 15-foot requirement for a severe fall, it is close. Plus, the surface the patient landed on is hard, and the patient fell on his chest, which is a region that can incur life-threatening injuries. If ever you have trouble deciding whether or not a mechanism of injury is severe, err on the side of the patient. It is always better to overtreat a patient than to undertreat him. *(p. 189)*

Vocabulary Practice

1. rear 2. car seat
3. head-on
4. Either acceleration or deceleration is correct.
5. ejection 6. side impact
7. sternum 8. blast
Scrambled letters: A S E E L T S T B
Unscrambled letters: SEAT BELTS

The Call

1. Either up-and-over (where the patient's head, chest, and abdomen impact the windshield and steering wheel) or down-and-under (where the patient slips beneath the steering wheel with resulting injuries primarily to the legs and pelvis). *(pp. 183–184)*
2. Probably not. Many cars have front-end airbags that would not deploy with side collisions. Newer cars have side-impact airbags in the sides of the seats or in the doorposts; these would deploy in a collision such as this. *(p. 187)*

3. 4, 2, 1, 3. The sedan driver is the most injured. The station-wagon driver is likely to have major head, chest, and abdominal injuries. The compact-car driver is next in rank; since the concrete barrier did not intrude into the passenger space, and damage to the car was minimal, injuries should only be mild to moderate. For the pickup-truck driver likeliness of injury is low, plus he had his headrest up. *(pp. 183–187)*
4. a. compact car b. pickup truck
   c. sedan d. station wagon *(pp. 183–187)*

Chapter 11: Introduction to Patient Assessment and Vital Signs

Exam Warm-up/Short-Answer Review

1. True. *(p. 200)* 2. c *(p. 201)*
3. b *(p. 201)* 4. d *(p. 201)*
5. e *(p. 201)* 6. b *(p. 201)*
7. b *(p. 202)* 8. c *(p. 202)*
9. d *(p. 202)* 10. b *(p. 202)*
11. c *(p. 205)* 12. c *(p. 205)*
13. Scene size-up, initial assessment, physical exam, patient history, ongoing assessment, patient hand-off. (p. 198)
14. Respiration, pulse, skin, pupils, and blood pressure. (p. 200)
15. a. Cool skin may mean the patient is suffering from shock, heat exhaustion, or exposure to cold.
    b. Hot skin may be the result of fever or heat stroke.
    c. Pale skin may be caused by shock, heart attack, fright, faintness, emotional distress, impaired blood flow.
    d. Blueness is caused by reduced levels of oxygen as in shock, heart attack, or poisoning.
    e. Black-and-blue mottling is the result of blood seeping under the skin, which is usually caused by a blow or severe infection. *(pp. 202–203)*

Vocabulary Practice

The Call

1. a. scene size-up b. scene size-up
   c. initial assessment d. patient history

e. initial assessment   f. physical examination
g. patient hand-off *(p. 198)*

2. Make every effort you can to obtain a history from the patient's family members or friends at the scene or from medical identification devices, such as a medical bracelet or medallion. In some cases, you may not be able to obtain a medical history. *(Chapter 4)*

3. supine position *(Chapter 4)*

4. Include all your findings, but make your report brief and to the point. Generally, you would be required to include: the patient's age and sex (male in his 20s); the chief complaint (why EMS was called); the patient's level of responsiveness (in this case, unresponsive); the patient's airway, breathing, and circulation status; physical exam findings (bruise on the chest and deformity to the right hip and femur); medical history, if any; and, finally, what you did to help the patient and the patient's responses to your interventions.

Chapter 12: Patient Assessment

Exam Warm-up/Short-Answer Review

1. a *(p. 214)*
2. c, d, f, g h, i *(pp. 214, 216)*
3. c. This patient needs to be ventilated immediately. Her respirations will not supply her with enough oxygen to survive. *(pp. 218–219)*
4. a *(pp. 214–215)*   5. b *(pp. 216–217)*
6. b *(pp. 216–217)*
7. b. Remember: Airway! Airway! Airway! This patient needs a clear, open airway if she is to survive. Use a jaw-thrust maneuver if the mechanism of injury suggests spine injury. Then clear the airway using suction or a gloved finger. *(pp. 217–218)*
8. b *(pp. 218–219)*   9. b *(p. 219)*
10. a *(p. 219)*   11. c *(p. 219)*
12. d *(pp. 219–220)*   13. b *(p. 220)*
14. a. The other three injuries can wait. Patients with neck pain require immediate spinal precautions. *(pp. 215, 223–224)*
15. b *(p. 224)*
16. a *(p. 226)*
17. b *(p. 229)*
18. Scene size-up, initial assessment, physical exam, patient history, ongoing assessment, patient hand-off. *(Chapter 11 and p. 214)*
19. 3, 8, 6, 7, 2, 1, 4, 5 *(pp. 214–221)*
20. A — The patient is "alert" and oriented to his or her surroundings.
V — The patient is "verbal," or disoriented but responds when spoken to.
P — The patient only responds to "painful" stimuli.
U — The patient is "unresponsive" or does not respond to any stimuli. *(pp. 216–217)*
21. Try to find out from the family if there has been a change. That is, the patient may normally be somewhat confused, but has it worsened with this last episode? *(pp. 216–217)*
22. Expect a responsive child of this age to recognize his or her parents, want to go to them, and probably react negatively to your assessment and treatment. *(p. 217)*
23. Adequate breathing is characterized by adequate rise and fall of the chest, ease of breathing, and adequate respiratory rate. *(p. 218)*

24. Your update report to EMS should include the patient's age and sex, chief complaint, level of responsiveness, plus airway, breathing, and circulation status. *(pp. 220–221)*
25. 6, 3, 1, 5, 4, 2 *(p. 221)*
26. a. Yes   b. No   c. Yes *(p. 221)*
27. Inspection (looking), auscultation (listening), and palpation (feeling). *(p. 222)*
28. D = deformities, O = open injuries, T = tenderness, S = swelling. *(p. 223)*
29. S = signs and symptoms, A = allergies, M = medications, P = pertinent past history, L = last oral intake, E = events. *(p. 227)*
30. A sign is something that is observable by another person. A symptom cannot be observed by anyone but the patient. So this patient's complaints are symptoms. *(p. 227)*
31. Any question related to signs and symptoms would be appropriate, such as "Describe what you feel" or "Where do you feel the worst?" *(p. 227)*
32. Any question related to allergies would be appropriate, such as "Are you allergic to anything?" "Do you have any allergies to medications?" "Do you have any food allergies or allergies to pollen or dust?" *(p. 228)*
33. Any questions related to medication the patient is currently taking or has recently taken are appropriate. You might ask, for example, "Do you take prescription medication?" or "Have there been any changes in your medications lately?" *(p. 228)*
34. Any question related to the patient's pertinent past history would be appropriate. For example, you might ask questions like "Do you see a doctor for anything?" or "Have you ever been admitted to a hospital? For what?" Or you might ask "Have you ever had chest pain before? When? What was done for it?" *(p. 228)*
35. The nine elements of the patient hand-off report are: patient age and sex, chief complaint, level of responsiveness (AVPU), airway status, breathing status, circulation status, physical exam findings, patient history, and interventions and the patient's response to them. *(p. 230)*
36. The patient history was omitted. *(p. 230)*

Vocabulary Practice

The Call

1. **a.** The ABCs are always first. *(p. 214)*
2. a *(Chapter 6 and pp. 217–218)*
3. The patient appears to be verbal. *(pp. 216–217)*
4. Immediately reassess the patient's airway, breathing, and circulation. Any time your patient has a dramatic change in level of responsiveness, recheck his or her ABCs. *(pp. 216, 229–230)*
5. D — Inspect and palpate the skull, face bones, and jaw for signs of deformity, including loose teeth.
   O — Inspect for open injuries, especially any injury that bleeds into the airway. Also look in the hair for injuries that may be hidden.
   T — Palpate the head for pain or tenderness, even where there is no obvious injury.
   S — Inspect injuries to the skull and to facial structures such as areas around the eyes, nose, and mouth for swelling. *(p. 223)*
6. D — Inspect the trachea to see if it is deformed or if it has shifted. Palpate the vertebrae in the posterior (back) of the neck.
   O — Inspect for open injuries, and bandage them immediately with occlusive dressing.
   T — Palpate the soft tissues, trachea, and vertebrae for tenderness.
   S — Inspect for swelling and listen for a popping or crackling sound under the skin. *(pp. 223–224)*
7. D — Palpate the rib cage for signs of deformity. Do not move the patient in order to examine the back until appropriate spinal precautions have been taken. Palpate the sternum. If the patient is responsive, ask him to take a deep breath to determine if it causes pain.
   O — Inspect for open injuries. If a wound extends into the chest cavity, bandage it immediately with an occlusive dressing.
   T — While palpating the chest, ask the patient if he feels any pain to examine for possible internal injuries.
   S — Inspect for swelling or any other sign of underlying breathing problems. *(p. 224)*
8. D — Palpate for rigidity or distention.
   O — Inspect for open injuries.
   T — Palpate each quadrant of the abdomen, but palpate the quadrant where the patient complains of pain last.
   S — Inspect for swelling or discoloration of the skin. Check the flanks for pooling of blood. *(pp. 224–225)*
9. D — Palpate for chest wall deformity and for obvious deformity along the length of the spine.
   O— Inspect for open injuries, especially for open or sucking chest wounds.
   T — Palpate for tenderness.
   S — Inspect for swelling and for blood accumulation in the flanks. *(p. 225)*
10. D — Palpate the bones to feel for deformity.
    O — Inspect for open injuries.
    T — Palpate for tenderness. Palpate with less force if the bones of the pelvis are close to the skin. Palpate with more force if the patient is obese with bones under a considerable amount of tissue. Be sure to palpate the pubis bone.
    S — Inspect for swelling and discoloration around the hips. *(p. 225)*
11. D — Inspect and palpate the entire length of each bone and all joints for deformity.
    O — Inspect for open injuries.

T — Palpate each extremity for pain and tenderness.
S — Inspect for swelling and discoloration.
Note that any extremity that is painful, swollen, or deformed may be broken and should be manually stabilized until it can be immobilized. You may also wish to check pulses in each extremity, as well as for movement and sensation. *(p. 226)*

Chapter 13: Communication and Documentation

Exam Warm-up/Short-Answer Review

1. All letters should be circled. *(p. 237)*
2. b *(p. 237)*   3. b *(p. 237)*
4. a, d, e *(p. 240)*
5. Any five: Speak slowly and clearly. Push the "push to talk" button one second before you begin to speak. Talk with your mouth two to three inches from the mike. Keep a transmission brief. Listen before you transmit. Never use a patient's name or say anything over the radio of a personal or confidential nature. Never use profanities. Never speak in less than a professional tone of voice. *(p. 237)*
6. The patient's age, sex, and chief complaint. *(pp. 238–239)*
7. a—Teacher, b—Friend, c—Authority, d—Advisor, e—Advisor, f—Friend, g—Teacher, h—Authority. *(pp. 239–240)*
8. To transfer patient information from one person to another; to provide legal documentation; to document the care you provided; and to improve your EMS system. *(p. 241)*
9. Mr. Mendez was told the treatment plan, the risks of not following the plan, and that he understood those risks. *(Chapter 3)*

Vocabulary Practice

Base station is a stationary radio located in a dispatch center or hospital. A mobile radio is mounted in a vehicle. A portable radio is hand-held. Repeaters receive low-power radio transmissions and rebroadcast them with increased power. *(p. 237)*

Chapter 14: Cardiac and Respiratory Emergencies

Exam Warm-up/Short-Answer Review

1. a *(p. 250)*   2. a *(p. 252)*
3. d *(p. 252)*   4. True *(p. 254)*
5. a, b, c, e, g *(p. 254)*   6. a, c, d *(pp. 255–256)*
7. a, b, c, d *(p. 252)*
8. False. The classic symptom of a cardiac emergency is the sudden onset of chest pain. Women, elderly people, and diabetics may not have chest pain at all. *(pp. 252, 253)*
9. a *(p. 257)*   10. a, b, c, d, e, f *(p. 259)*
11. b, c *(p. 261)*
12. Any eight: physical inactivity, cigarette smoking, obesity, high serum cholesterol and triglycerides, diabetes, male gender, age, hypertension, family history of coronary artery disease under age 60. *(p. 250)*
13. Any five: chest pain or discomfort that may radiate to arms, shoulder, neck, or jaw; difficulty breathing, shortness of breath; unusual pulse; palpitations;

indigestion, nausea, vomiting; sweating; pale, gray, or cyanotic skin; a feeling of impending doom; history of heart problems or a previous similar experience. *(p. 252)*

14. O = onset, P = provocation, Q = quality, R = region, R = radiation, R = relief, S = severity, T = time. *(p. 252)*
15. **5, 3, 2, 1, 4, 6** *(p. 252)*
16. Disagree. This First Responder needs to hit the books. Cardiac emergencies can occur without any chest pain, especially in females since they sometimes have unusual signs or nonclassic signs of cardiac emergencies. If signs and symptoms indicate different illnesses or problems, always be prepared to manage the patient as if he or she has the worst one. *(p. 252)*
17. Any seven: inability to speak in full sentences without pausing to breathe; noisy breathing; use of accessory muscles to breathe; tripod position; abnormal breathing rate and rhythm; increased pulse rate; skin color changes; altered mental status. *(p. 257)*
18. **a.** Ensure adequate breathing. Carefully assess the patient's breathing to determine if it is adequate. Monitor it throughout the call. If you find respirations are inadequate, provide artificial ventilation immediately. If breathing is adequate, administer oxygen by way of a nonrebreather mask at 10–15 liters per minute.
    b. Place the responsive patient with adequate breathing in a position of comfort.
    c. Comfort and reassure the patient.
    d. If not done previously, activate the EMS system. *(p. 258)*
19. Disagree. This patient appears to be in severe respiratory distress and needs high-flow oxygen. Never deny oxygen to patients who need it. Be sure to continually assess the respiratory status of this patient. *(pp. 258–259)*

Vocabulary Practice

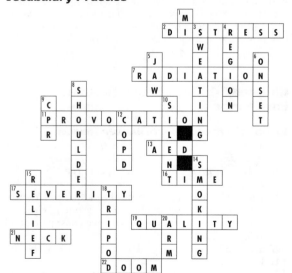

The Call
1. **d** *(Chapter 12)*
2. **d** *(p. 252)*
3. George is probably very frightened. In addition, his vital signs indicate he may not be getting enough oxygen to his brain *(p. 252)*

4. Any five: When did the pain begin? Did anything cause or start the pain? What is the pain like? Where is the pain? Does the pain begin in one place and then seem to travel somewhere else? Where? Does anything relieve the pain? What? On a scale of 1–10, with 10 the worst, how bad is the pain? How long have you had the pain? *(p. 252)*
5. **2, 5, 6, 3, 7, 4, 1** *(Chapters 8 and 9)*
6. George is in his 60s. According to his friends he was playing golf when he clutched his chest and collapsed. I arrived to find George responsive but combative. His vital signs were respirations 32, pulse 32, BP 66/32, and skin pale, cool, and moist. As I was managing George, he lapsed into cardiac arrest. I immediately delivered one shock with the AED. He now has a carotid pulse, but he still requires ventilation. George's friends say he has a history of heart problems. *(Chapter 12)*

Chapter 15: Medical Emergencies

Exam Warm-up/Short-Answer Review
1. True *(p. 267)*
2. False. To have an altered mental status, a patient must show a change in his or her normal level of responsiveness and understanding. *(p. 268)*
3. True *(Chapter 12)*
4. Every item in the list could be a cause of an altered mental status in a patient. *(p. 268)*
5. **c** *(p. 269)*   6. True *(p. 269)*
7. **b** *(p. 270)*   8. **c** *(p. 270)*
9. **a, b, c.** The first statement is careless and unprofessional. The second makes it seem that the level of care is dependent on the patient's performance, something the patient may not be able to control. The third conveys a negative, pessimistic message. The fourth is reassuring and empathetic and proposes a solution. *(pp. 272–274)*
10. **d.**   11. **c, d**
12. **d** *(p. 276)*
13. All except h are correct. *(pp. 276–278)*
14. **b.**   15. False. *(p. 280)*
16. **b.** *(p. 280)*   17. **c.** *(p. 281)*
18. **c.** *(p. 281)*
19. Monitor the patient's ABCs, making sure both breathing and circulation are adequate. if the patient is conscious and there are no suspected spine injuries, allow him to get in a position of comfort. Perform an ongoing assessment until the EMTs take over patient care. Be sure to report any changes in the patient's condition. *(p. 268)*
20. You can ask the patient's family, friends, or bystanders if the behavior of the patient is abnormal. You also can ask the patient questions such as "What is your name?" "What day is it?" "Where are you?" and "What happened to you?" to find out if he or she is responsive and oriented. *(Chapter 12)*
21. The patient's chief complaint is an altered mental status. When you have determined the scene is safe, perform an initial assessment of the patient. If possible, administer high-flow oxygen. If necessary, help the patient get into a position of comfort. Attempt to gather an accurate patient history as soon as you can. Continue to monitor the patient's airway and breathing closely until the EMTs take over care. *(pp. 268–269)*

22. A patient with an altered mental status may deteriorate rapidly. If you wait too long, the history—which could provide important clues to the cause of the patient's condition—could be lost to the EMTs and hospital staff who take over care. (p. 268)

23. Disagree. There are many reasons for altered mental status. One of the most common is a decreased level of oxygen in the patient's blood. So administering oxygen to this patient is a very good idea. All patients with altered mental status—even those suspected of having diabetes—should receive supplemental oxygen, if possible. (pp. 268–269, 271)

24. altered mental status. (p. 270)

25. a. hypoglycemia   b. hypoglycemia
    c. hyperglycemia   d. hyperglycemia
    e. hypoglycemia (pp. 270–271)

26. Any nine: sweet, fruity, or acetone-like breath; flushed, dry, warm skin or cool, clammy skin; hunger; thirst; rapid, weak pulse; altered mental status; staggering; slurred speech; frequent urination; headache; seizures; reports that patient has not taken prescribed diabetes medication. (pp. 270, 271)

27. Medical identification tag, insulin in his or her refrigerator, presence of needles and syringes, presence of special needle containers. (p. 271)

28. Have you eaten today? Did you take your insulin? Have you been ill lately? Have you been particularly stressed lately? Are you having problems with any medication? (p. 271)

29. The rule is "when in doubt, give sugar." No, it is not necessary to distinguish between hypoglycemia and hyperglycemia. Sugar can help the hypoglycemic patient and will not harm a hyperglycemic patient. (p. 271–272)

30. Patients with high blood pressure, patients with diabetes, patients who smoke tobacco. (p. 272)

31. A stroke occurs when blood flow to the brain is interrupted long enough to cause permanent brain damage. A transient ischemic attack causes only temporary brain dysfunction. A transient ischemic attack, or TIA, is a warning sign of an impending larger stroke. (p. 272)

32. The three types of signs or symptoms a patient who has had a stroke might exhibit are as follows (examples may vary): inability to communicate—the patient may either fail to speak or fail to understand what is spoken; impairment in one part of the body—loss of muscle control on one side of the face or loss of movement on one entire side of the body; altered mental status—change in personality, seizures, unresponsiveness. (p. 272)

33. a. Agree
    b. Disagree. Stroke can affect any body system or any body part, including the respiratory system.
    c. Agree. This information can help to ascertain if either side was affected by the stroke.
    d. Disagree. Generally, you should continue to talk to the patient even if he or she cannot speak. Stroke patients often can hear very well. So be reassuring, and explain to them what it is you are doing during emergency care. (pp. 272–274)

34. This First Responder is probably overreacting. While it may help the child to provide some sup-

plemental oxygen, the seizures do not appear to be status epilepticus. (pp. 274–276)

35. Any four: What did the seizure look like? Was the seizure preceded by an aura? Did it begin in one area of the body and spread? Did the patient bite his or her tongue or lose bowel or bladder control? When did the seizure start and how long did it last? How did the patient act after the seizure ended? Did the patient suffer any trauma during the seizure? Does the patient use alcohol or other drugs? Does the patient have a history of diabetes, epilepsy, stroke, or heart disease? Has the patient recently had a fever? Is the patient pregnant? (pp. 274–276)

36. 5, 1, 2, 3, 6, 4 (pp. 268–269, 276)

37. A post-seizure patient requires a calm, gentle, reassuring approach. This patient will have no memory of the seizure and needs to be oriented to where he or she is, what has happened, who you are, and what you are doing to help. Often you will need to repeat the same information until the patient becomes more alert and oriented. (p. 276)

38. Any six: abdominal pain, local or diffuse; colicky pain; abdominal tenderness, local or diffuse; anxiety; reluctance to move; loss of appetite; nausea, vomiting; fever; rigid, tense, or distended abdomen; signs of shock; vomiting blood, bright red or like coffee grounds; blood in the stool, bright red or tarry black. (pp. 276–277)

39. The four routes of exposure to poison are ingestion, inhalation, injection, and absorption. Examples of each may vary: ingestion—swallowing a handful of pills; inhalation—breathing in smoke from a fire; injection—sustaining a bite from a rattlesnake; absorption—rubbing against poison ivy leaves. (p. 278)

40. Answers will vary: When did she eat the poison? How much did she eat? What exactly did she eat? Has she vomited? Have you given her anything to make her vomit? Have you given her any kind of antidote? (pp. 279–280)

41. Disagree. All patients who have been exposed to carbon monoxide need medical care, even those who seem to have recovered. (pp. 280–281)

Vocabulary Practice

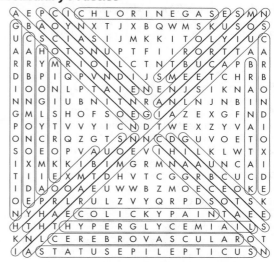

absorption
activated charcoal
altered mental status
aneurysm
brain attack
carbon dioxide
carbon monoxide
cerebrovascular
chlorine gas
colicky pain
cyanide
diabetes
embolus
glucose

guarding position
hyperglycemia
hypoglycemia
hypoxia
ingestion
inhalation
injection
insulin
mini-stroke
poisoning
status epilepticus
stroke
thrombus

The Call

1. Airway impairment. Anyone with altered mental status may not be able to protect his or her own airway. You must be especially alert to the airway of a patient who has difficulty speaking or slurred speech. If the patient has had a stroke, pressure can increase in the skull from swelling tissues and bleeding, which can cause the patient's breathing to be affected. Be prepared to provide artificial ventilation. *(pp. 268–269, 272–274)*

2. Any five (answers will vary): Can you tell me what day this is? The time of day? Where you are? What your name is? Do you have any pain? Do you remember collapsing? Do you feel any weakness or numbness? In your face? Arms? Legs? Are you having any vision problems? *(Chapter 12 and 272–274)*

3. Follow your plan for an ongoing assessment. Any time your patient's status changes, it is a good idea to perform another initial assessment, physical exam as appropriate, assessment of vital signs, and so on. *(Chapter 12)*

4. Disagree. If John did experience a TIA, it could be a significant warning sign that a stroke is imminent. He needs to go to the hospital to be evaluated by a physician. He should remain on supplemental oxygen because his brain may have suffered a temporary loss of oxygen. *(pp. 268–269, 272–274)*

Chapter 16: Environmental Emergencies

Exam Warm-up/Short-Answer Review

1. b *(pp. 288–289)*
2. c *(p. 289)*
3. False *(p. 290)*
4. d *(p. 292)*
5. a, c, f *(pp. 290–291)*
6. False. It can cause hypothermia. *(p. 289)*
7. a *(p. 290)*
8. True *(p. 293)*
9. d. The others are signs of a late or deep local cold injury. *(pp. 292–293)*
10. a *(p. 293)*
11. b *(p. 294)*
12. False. In heat stroke a patient's skin is hot and dry or hot and moist. *(pp. 295–296)*
13. a *(p. 297)*
14. a *(p. 297)*
15. b *(p. 298)*
16. a *(p. 298)*
17. a *(p. 298)*
18. b *(p. 300)*
19. b *(p. 300)*
20. b, c, d *(p. 298–299)*
21. d. Never suction a coral-snake bite. *(pp. 300–301)*
22. d *(p. 303)*
23. 2, 3, 5, 4, 1 *(p. 290)*
24. Any five: Are there any signs of head or body trauma? Any allergies to medications? Is the patient taking any medication? Is there any possibility of alcohol or drug overdose? Is there any pertinent

medical history? Any chronic medical problems that can be affected by the cold? When was the last time the patient ate or drank anything? Can the patient remember what she was doing prior to being found? How long was the patient out in the cold weather? *(Chapter 12)*

25. Medical condition of the patient (an underlying medical problem can weaken the body's responses to heat and cold); drugs, alcohol, poisons (which impede the body's ability to maintain body temperature); age of the patient (very young and very old patients are especially at risk). *(pp. 289–290)*

26. a. mild   b. mild
    c. severe   d. mild
    e. severe   f. mild
    g. severe   h. mild
    i. severe *(pp.291–292)*

27. Severely hypothermic patients are prone to ventricular fibrillation or sudden cardiac death when bounced or handled roughly. *(p. 292)*

28. a. Climate—high air temperature can reduce the body's ability to lose heat by radiation. High humidity can reduce its ability to lose heat by evaporation.
    b. Exercise and activity—each can cause a person to lose more than one liter of sweat per hour.
    c. Drugs and alcohol—either can affect heat loss in many ways including through side effects such as dehydration.
    d. Age and medical condition—very young and very old patients may be unable to respond to overheating effectively, and medical conditions, such as diabetes and obesity, can inhibit heat loss further. *(pp. 294–295)*

29. Any five: muscle cramps; weakness, exhaustion; dizziness, faintness; rapid pulse rate that is strong at first, but becomes weak as damage progresses; headache; seizures; loss of appetite, nausea, vomiting; altered mental status, possibly unresponsiveness; skin may be moist, pale, and normal to cool or it may be hot and dry or hot and moist. *(p. 296)*

30. Remove the patient from the hot environment. Administer oxygen, if possible. Cool the patient by loosening or removing clothing and by fanning the surface of the body. Position the patient with legs elevated 8 to 12 inches. Take vital signs frequently. *(p. 296)*

31. Any three: What bit or stung the patient? Where is the insect that bit or stung the patient? Is an insect nest visible in a nearby tree, under the eaves of a house, or in the ground nearby? Are there signs that the patient was engaged in activity such as clearing underbrush or gardening that might have disturbed snakes or insects? Was the patient working in a garage, basement, attic, or shed where spiders and other insects might nest? Are there dead insects on the ground near the patient? Were any insects trapped in the patient's clothing? *(p. 297)*

32. History of bites and stings; bite mark or stinger embedded in the skin; immediate pain that is severe or burning; numbness at the site after a few hours; redness or other discoloration of the skin around the bite or sting; swelling around the site, sometimes spreading gradually. *(pp. 297–298)*

33. Swelling of the tongue; tightness in the throat or chest; cough, hoarseness; rapid or labored breathing; noisy breathing, stridor, wheezing. *(pp. 297–298)*

34. 7, 5, 2, 4, 1, 3, 6 *(p. 298)*

35. a. Disagree. Never use ice on any type of bite. It can cause frostbite and local tissue damage.
   b. Agree.
   c. Disagree. A constricting band should not prevent circulation in the limb. Make sure you can feel a pulse below it. *(pp. 298–301)*

36. Take BSI precautions. Use tweezers to grasp the tick as close as possible to the point where it is attached to the skin. Pull firmly and steadily until the tick is dislodged. Wash your hands and the bite area thoroughly with soap and water. Apply an antiseptic to the area to help prevent a bacterial infection. Then have the patient document the exact time of exposure. *(p. 303)*

37. To remove a stinger, gently scrape against it with the edge of a knife or a credit card. Be careful not to squeeze the stinger. Make sure you remove the venom sac. *(p. 303)*

Vocabulary Practice

1. a. radiation   **b.** evaporation
   c. conduction   **d.** convection
   e. conduction   **f.** radiation
   g. evaporation (p. 289)

2. a. black widow spider *(p. 301)*
   b. mite *(p. 302)*
   c. scorpion *(p. 302)*
   d. fire ant *(p. 302)*
   e. brown recluse spider *(p. 301)*
   f. tarantula *(p. 302)*
   g. bee *(p. 303)*
   h. tick *(p. 303)*
   i. stingray *(pp. 303–304)*

The Call: Hyperthermia at a Structure Fire

1. This firefighter may be in trouble. It is a hot day, and he has been fighting a major fire. He appears dazed and quite hot, and his response seems inappropriate given how uncomfortable he appears to be. Do not leave this patient. Insist that he allow you to examine him and treat him as necessary. Be gentle but persistent. *(p. 294)*

2. He may be suffering from heat stroke. *(pp. 295–296)*

3. Disagree. Although this patient is probably dehydrated, he has been vomiting and has an altered mental status. If he should lapse into unresponsiveness and begin to vomit up the water you gave to him, the patient could experience a serious airway problem. Give him nothing by mouth. *(pp. 295–296)*

4. Move the patient away from the hot environment. Perform an initial assessment and administer oxygen, if possible. Place him in a supine position with legs elevated 8 to 12 inches. While waiting for an ambulance to transport this patient to a hospital, cool him by removing clothing, applying cold packs to neck, armpits, and groin, sponging with water, and fanning aggressively. *(pp. 295–296)*

The Call: Back–Country Snakebite

1. b *(Chapter 12)*

2. a *(Chapters 6 and 7)*

3. Jack will benefit from helicopter transport. This will provide him with a direct ride to the hospital. Since your dispatcher is checking on the availability of the helicopter, it probably would be a good idea to also have a ranger vehicle dispatched. The helicopter may be unavailable due to weather, location, mechanical problems, etc.; you always want a backup plan.

4. Jack appears to be going into shock and losing his respiratory drive. Since he is breathing only eight times per minute and is minimally responsive, you should probably try to insert an oropharyngeal airway or a nasopharyngeal airway. Then provide artificial ventilation via BVM or mouth-to-mask with high-flow oxygen. Keep Jack warm, and give him nothing by mouth. *(Chapters 6 and 7)*

Chapter 17: Psychological Emergencies and Crisis Intervention

Exam Warm-up/Short-Answer Review

1. a *(p. 313)*

2. a *(Chapter 3)*

3. c, d. These two quotes ask honest questions in order to determine the resolve of the patient to actually commit suicide. Do not deny the patient's feelings or become preachy (a). Never try to shock your patient out of suicide (b). This will merely heighten the patient's feelings of worthlessness. *(pp. 313–314)*

4. a, b. Safety is always the top priority. Let law enforcement handle violent, weapon-wielding patients. Stay clear of the scene—and keep others clear—until they have control of the patient. *(Chapters 2 and 10)*

5. d *(p. 316)*   **6.** False *(pp. 316–317)*

7. True *(p. 316)*   **8. b** *(p. 318)*

9. c *(p. 318)*   **10. a** *(p. 318)*

11. c, d. It is not necessary to examine this patient's vagina or anus if she tells you that she has no major vaginal or anal injuries. Minimize further emotional trauma to this patient. Encourage the patient to refrain from washing until she has been checked at the hospital. *(pp. 320–321)*

12. Situational stresses; illness or injury; mind-altering substances; psychiatric problems; psychological crises. *(p. 313)*

13. a. Probably not, but they are behaving irrationally. They are worried about their child. Every moment seems like an eternity to them in this situation. While you know that the system is doing its best for their child, they only see that you are waiting. This is a very normal response for people who feel powerless to make an ill or injured loved one better. *(Chapter 2)*
   b. Stay calm. Be sympathetic and empathetic. Explain to this child's parents what you are doing to help their child, and how the EMS system works so that they can better understand why you are waiting on scene for the paramedic ambulance. Do not be angered by their anger. Remember, they are angry because someone they love is sick. Keep your voice even and calm. In reality, you have three patients here. You need to take care of them all. *(Chapter 2 and pp. 315–316)*

14. a. Disagree. While this quote may show that the First Responder is trying to be empathetic and positive, he or she refers to the patient inappropriately as "pal" and "buddy," terms that may be perceived as condescending and phony. Call patients by their proper names.

b. Disagree. This approach is threatening and berates the patient. No one wants to spend life in a wheelchair. While the First Responder says that he or she wants to help, the tone of this quote is anything but helpful. Calmly—and without threats—explain your reasons for wanting to take spinal precautions with a patient, as well as the potential risks of refusing this care. Ultimately, however, it is the patient's right to consent or withhold consent to your treatment.

c. Agree. This is a good example of an approach that is calm, nonjudgmental, and straightforward. It informs the patient of what is happening and why.

d. Agree. This approach is also nonjudgmental. The First Responder lets her know that he or she is there to help and that it is okay if Trish does not want to talk about the incident. The First Responder also keeps things simple. While it is clear that Trish does not want to describe the incident, the First Responder wisely moves to the simple question, "Were you hurt?"

e. Disagree. This approach comes off sounding like a moralistic lecture. It is judgmental and chastises the patient for what is indeed inappropriate behavior. Avoid giving advice. *(pp. 315–316)*

15. The size and strength of the patient, the type of abnormal behavior the patient is exhibiting, the mental state of the patient, the method of restraint being used. *(pp. 316–317)*

16. Any four: unresponsiveness, breathing difficulties or inability to maintain an open airway, abnormal or irregular pulse, fever, vomiting with an altered mental status or without a gag reflex, seizures. *(p. 319)*

17. With a gloved hand, check the patient's mouth for partially dissolved pills or tablets. If you find any, remove them so they cannot block the patient's airway. Then smell the patient's breath for traces of alcohol. Ask the patient's friends or family what they know about the incident. Because signs and symptoms vary so widely and are so similar to many medical conditions, the most reliable indications of a drug- or alcohol-related emergency are likely to come from the scene and the patient history. *(p. 319)*

18. Protect your own safety, maintain the patient's airway, and manage life-threatening conditions. *(p. 319)*

Vocabulary Practice

1. behavior
2. drug abuse
3. overdose
4. withdrawal
5. positional
6. injury
7. phobia
8. reasonable

The Call

1. A few suggestions: "Hi, my name is ___. I'm a First Responder with EMS, and I'm here to treat any injury you may have. After I help you, an ambulance will take you to the hospital. I want you to know that you are safe now. Do you hurt anywhere? I've been told that you were stabbed. Were you? Could I take a look at your stab wound?" *(pp. 320–321)*

2. Your physical exam should be pertinent to her injuries only. Check her arm and any areas that are painful.

Refrain from a complete head-to-toe exam unless it is necessary, given her complaints of pain or obvious injury. Remember that detailed physical exams can often continue the trauma that a patient experienced during the rape itself. *(Chapter 12 and pp. 320–321)*

3. You may want to talk with Rachel to calm her fears and better explain what the First Responder is doing. Given the physical, emotional, and psychological trauma she has experienced, she may be too disoriented to initially understand what the First Responder is trying to accomplish. Another strategy may be to find a female First Responder to manage Rachel's injuries. After being raped by a man, it may be too difficult for the patient to allow a male First Responder to touch her. *(pp. 321–322)*

4. Your treatment plan should include emergency care for the stab wound and any other injuries as necessary. Then you should support Rachel in whatever manner she needs until the ambulance arrives. Some sexual assault patients will want to talk. Others will want to remain silent. Gently gauge what Rachel appears to need in terms of emotional support. Do not be afraid to ask her, "How can I help you now, Rachel?" *(pp. 320–321)*

Chapter 18: Bleeding and Shock

Exam Warm-up/Short-Answer Review

1. d *(p. 327)*
2. a *(p. 330)*
3. a *(p. 330)*
4. c *(pp. 321–322)*
5. c *(Chapter 4)*
6. d *(pp. 332–334)*
7. a *(p. 334)*
8. c, d *(p. 335)*
9. a, b, d *(p. 335)*
10. b, d *(p. 336)*
11. b *(p. 334)*
12. b *(p. 335)*
13. d *(pp. 335–336)*
14. c *(p. 338)*
15. b *(pp. 338–339)*
16. d *(p. 337)*
17. c *(Chapter 10)*
18. b *(Chapter 6)*

19. **a.** This injury is just below Paula's femoral pulse point. Applying direct pressure to the wound and to her femoral artery should control the bleeding. Elevating the area is really not practical as it is so close to the patient's pelvis. A tourniquet should only be used as a last resort and is rarely indicated. *(p. 330)*

20. Direct pressure, elevation, pressure points. *(p. 330)*

21. Any five: discolored, tender, swollen, or hard tissue; increased respiratory and pulse rates; pale, cool, clammy skin; nausea and vomiting bright red blood or blood the color of dark coffee grounds; thirst; changes in mental status including anxiety, restlessness, or combativeness; dark, tarry stools or stools that contain bright red blood; tender, rigid, or distended abdomen; weakness, faintness, or dizziness. *(p. 334)*

22. This patient probably died of internal injuries. Internal injuries can present with minor outward signs (in this case, minor abdominal pain). The picture becomes clear when you add up all of the elements of the call: his car was badly damaged, he complained of some abdominal pain, and his vital signs quickly deteriorated. *(p. 334)*

23. Paula's most worrisome vital signs are her level of responsiveness and respiratory rate. Both could indicate a severe head injury. She also is showing signs of

shock, but as of yet her blood pressure is within normal limits. *(Chapters 6 and 12 and pp. 335, 337)*

24. **a.** High   **b.** High
  c. Low. Pat's medical history is much less important than managing his ABCs and major injuries.
  d. Low. Cuts and bruises can wait.
  e. High. Witnesses can provide important information about how the patient landed, whether or not he initially was conscious, had a seizure, etc.
  f. High. Always think safety. **g.** Low
  h. Low
  i. High. The mechanisms of injury will help identify the patterns of injury to expect in the patient. *(Chapters 6–12)*

Vocabulary Practice

The Call

1. **c.** Remove the stinger. It can continue to inject venom for some time after the initial puncture. The more venom that is injected, the worse the anaphylactic reaction. *(Chapter 17)*
2. Respiratory and circulatory. *(pp. 338–339)*
3. Calm her down so you can properly assess her. Moving around could also make her condition worse. *(Chapter 17)*
4. Airway: Is Annie's airway patent? Are there signs of face, tongue, or throat swelling?
  Breathing: Is Annie's breathing adequate? Labored? Noisy?
  Circulation: What is Annie's pulse rate? What are her skin signs? *(pp. 338–339)*
5. Repeat the initial assessment. This should be done any time your patient has a significant status change. *(Chapter 12)*
6. Perform a head-tilt/chin-lift because there is no reason to suspect a head or spine injury. *(Chapter 6)*
7. Disagree. Allergy kits carry medicines to combat the effects of an allergic reaction, and it is the same medicine that will be given by the paramedics (a drug called epinephrine). Every moment there is a delay in administering these medications increases the chance that this will be a fatal attack. Annie's father should administer the medications as prescribed by Annie's physician. *(p. 341)*

Chapter 19: Soft-Tissue Injuries

Exam Warm-up/Short-Answer Review

1. **a, b, c, d.** All of these wounds may be easily infected. *(p. 350)*
2. **a, b, c, d** *(pp. 350–352)*   3. **d** *(p. 355)*
4. **c.** The femur. It is the largest long bone in the body, and it is surrounded by lots of tissue and blood vessels. *(Chapter 4)*
5. **c.** Cutting an impaled object should only occur if it is an unmanageable size. *(pp. 353–355)*
6. **d** *(p. 354)*   7. **a** *(p. 353)*
8. **a** *(p. 355)*   9. **d** *(p. 355)*
10. **a** *(p. 357)*   11. **a, b, c, d** *(pp. 357–358)*
12. **b** *(p. 358)*
13. **c.** Avoid materials that will easily fall apart or cling to the wound. *(p. 358)*
14. **d** *(p. 358)*
15. **b, c.** Burn pads do not absorb blood well. Petroleum gauze is only used when a non-adhering dressing is needed. *(p. 358)*
16. **b, d.** Bandages do not need to be sterile; they just need to be clean. *(pp. 358–360)*
17. **b** *(p. 360)*
18. **c.** It can be very effective to focus a terrified patient on the tasks you are going to perform. This statement also avoids judgments about the severity of the injury and whether or not the patient's response to being hurt is appropriate. *(p. 353)*
19. **d** *(p. 358)*   20. **c** *(p. 360)*
21. The patient's contusion would probably present as an area that is swollen and painful. It may exhibit ecchymosis (black-and-blue discoloration) and a hematoma (a lump with bluish discoloration). Cold compresses would help to relieve the pain and swelling. *(p. 349)*
22. **a.** Some rescuers use this term when they see signs that the patient has progressed to a more serious stage of shock.
  b. Heart rate would increase significantly; blood pressure would drop (late sign); the patient would become agitated, confused, or worse; and skin would be cool, moist, and pale, gray, or bluish and mottled. *(Chapter 18)*
23. The location of the injury, the size of the penetrating object, and the forces involved in creating the injury. *(Chapter 10 and pp. 352–353)*
24. 3, 7, 6, 2, 4, 1, 5, 8 *(pp. 355, 357)*
25. Disagree. The location of the wound indicates possible injuries to the patient's lungs and major blood vessels. A two-inch blade is plenty long enough to cause severe injuries. Wound severity should never be estimated by looking at external blood loss. Puncture wounds are rarely accompanied by significant external bleeding. Most bleeding will be internal. *(pp. 352–353)*
26. To support injured limbs, to secure splints, to form slings, and to make improvised tourniquets. *(p. 359)*
27. **a.** Disagree. If a patient tells you that the bandage is too tight, loosen it slightly. Chances are good that your bandaging job is cutting off circulation.
  b. Disagree. When bandaging wounds to a patient's arms or legs, always try to leave fingers and toes exposed so that you can assess circulation below the injury site.

c. Agree. This First Responder is concerned about cutting off circulation to the patient's forearm and hand, but all important indicators—the patient's comfort level and distal color, temperature, and pulses—indicate that this is not the case.

d. Agree. Wounds should be covered completely.

e. Disagree. Triangular bandages do not make very good pressure bandages. They are not able to provide evenly distributed pressure to the wound, and often are too tight or too loose. A roller bandage—preferably the self-adhering type—would make for a far superior pressure bandage. *(pp. 358–360, 363)*

28. Check for distal pulses. In this case, check for the presence of a pedal pulse (the pulse at the top of the foot). *(Chapter 12)*

Vocabulary Practice

1. abrasion
2. laceration
3. puncture/penetration
4. avulsion
5. puncture/penetration (bite) or laceration (scratch)
6. laceration
7. laceration
8. amputation
9. puncture/penetration

The Call

1. Take BSI precautions! If you don't have a way to protect yourself, give bleeding control instructions to the child's mother. Do not risk contamination. *(Chapter 2)*
2. (Answers will vary.) Speak in a calm but firm voice. Use the child's name and focus him on quieting his screaming and thrashing about. Praise the child when he calms down and allows you to examine him. Explain to the child the behaviors he needs to exhibit so that you can help him. *(Chapter 12 and p. 353)*
3. Running water over the wound will only serve to keep the wound freely bleeding. It will not protect the patient from getting tetanus from the rusty pipe. The only real protection against tetanus is a vaccination. *(Chapter 2)*
4. The child has a three-inch laceration to his anterior thigh, beginning midway down his thigh and ending just proximal to his knee. The laceration is about one-inch deep. *(Chapter 4)*
5. Apply direct pressure and elevation. If the bleeding still does not stop, use a pressure point. *(Chapter 18)*
6. The patient is Danny Johnson. He is four years old. He lacerated his thigh on a rusty pipe while riding his bicycle. The laceration is about three-inches long and one-inch deep. It extends down his anterior thigh, beginning midway down the thigh and ending just proximal to his knee. When I arrived, the mother was irrigating the wound with a garden hose. The patient was quite agitated. I turned the water off, calmed the child, and controlled the bleeding using direct pressure and elevation. I estimate that the child has lost about 200 milliliters of blood. *(Chapter 12)*

Chapter 20: Injuries to the Chest, Abdomen, and Genitalia

Exam Warm-up/Short-Answer Review

1. b *(p. 372)*
2. a *(p. 370)*
3. a, b, c, d *(Chapter 10)*
4. True *(pp. 374–375)*
5. b *(p. 374)*
6. c *(pp. 374–375)*
7. d, e, f *(pp. 374–375)*
8. b *(pp. 374–375)*
9. False *(p. 373)*
10. True. Remember, the chest cavity has a front, side, and back. *(p. 371)*
11. c *(p. 370)*
12. d *(p. 372)*
13. False. Pneumothorax is the collapse of the lungs caused by air in the chest. Hint: The prefix pneumo- always refers to air or gas, lungs, or respiration. *(p. 374)*
14. False. Hemothorax is the collapse of the lungs caused by blood in the chest. Hint: The prefix hemo- always refers to blood. *(p. 374)*
15. a. *(pp. 377–378)*
16. b. Plastic wrap should be applied only after a dressing has been placed directly on the wound. Never put eviscerated organs back into the abdomen. *(p. 378)*
17. c *(p. 378)*
18. a *(p. 379)*
19. c *(p. 379)*
20. a, b. Answer "a" is inappropriate because the patient states that she has no vaginal bleeding. In cases of sexual assault, field exams and treatment should be kept to a minimum. Answer "b" is inappropriate because it asks the patient to relive the assault that she has just experienced. Gather only information necessary to treat major injuries, and allow the patient to tell you as much as she feels comfortable telling you. Answer "d" is general and allows the patient to tell you where she hurts rather than what happened. Answer "c" communicates important information to the patient in a gentle fashion. *(p. 379)*
21. d. Stabilize Dave's spine before you do anything else. If he has an injured neck or back, you want him to stay very still during your assessment. *(Chapter 12)*
22. b. It appears that Dave is maintaining good perfusion by compensating for internal blood loss with an increased heart rate. *(Chapter 18)*
23. Any five: shortness of breath or difficulty breathing; pain during breathing; failure of the chest to expand normally during inhalation; cyanosis; coughing up blood; distended neck veins; rapid, weak pulse; dropping blood pressure; obvious open wounds to the chest; bruising to the chest; chest wall deformity; pain at injury site; shock. *(p. 370)*
24. 3, 4, 2, 1 *(p. 372)*
25. Both the heart and the lungs may be injured. A patient with a chest injury often requires immediate surgery. In many instances, it is not possible to even stabilize these patients in the field. *(pp. 371–373)*
26. The exception concerns a sucking chest wound. You must apply an occlusive dressing over the wound site. This helps to prevent air from being sucked into the chest cavity, which can disturb the balance of air pressure between the inside and outside of the chest. *(pp. 371–373)*
27. The dressing should be at least two inches larger than the wound on all sides. Seal the dressing on three sides, leaving the fourth side of the dressing to act as a "relief valve." *(p. 372)*
28. Any eight: open wounds, penetrating wounds to the abdomen; distended or irregularly shaped abdomen; bruising of the abdomen, back, or flanks; rigid and tender abdomen; mild discomfort progressing to intolerable pain; pain radiating to a shoulder, both shoulders, or the back; abdominal cramping; lying still with legs drawn up in a fetal position; rapid, shallow breathing; rapid pulse, low blood pressure;

nausea, vomiting; evisceration; blood in the urine; vomiting of blood; shock; weakness; thirst. *(p. 377)*

29. Perform an initial assessment and treatment, and activate EMS to arrange for transport. Maintain an open airway. Expose the abdomen and proceed with a proper assessment. Suspect and treat the patient for shock, including controlling all external bleeding. Position the patient. If you suspect a pelvic fracture, prevent movement and, if you are allowed, immobilize the patient on a long backboard. *(pp. 377–378)*

30. Disagree. It is impossible to gauge the degree of severity of an abdominal injury by looking only at external bleeding. Blunt abdominal injuries can cause severe internal bleeding. This patient received a significant blow to the abdomen. Internal injuries should be suspected, and a more thorough evaluation, including palpation, should be completed. *(pp. 375–376)*

31. 2, 6, 3, 5, 4, 1, 7 *(Chapters 10 and 12)*

32. D—Is there any hardness or rigidity of the abdomen?
O—Are there any open injuries to the abdomen?
T—Is there any tenderness?
S—Is there swelling or discoloration of the skin?
(Chapter 12)

33. Yes, maintain spinal stabilization until he is completely immobilized. The mechanism of injury suggests that you do so. *(Chapters 10 and 12)*

Vocabulary Practice

The Call

1. a. Follow your patient assessment plan. After making sure the scene is safe, always begin with an initial assessment. The other actions would be appropriate later on. *(Chapter 12)*

2. d. Correct treatment of a sucking chest wound includes covering it with an occlusive dressing. None of the other choices accomplish this. Answer "a" is particularly incorrect, because a sucking chest wound needs to be covered as soon as it is discovered. You would not delay doing so to complete your exam. *(p. 372)*

3. Air that was previously escaping through the patient's chest wall is now being trapped in the pleural space. The correct response is to temporarily release the seal during exhalation to allow air to escape. Prior to inhalation, replace the seal and closely monitor the patient for any recurrence of this problem. *(p. 372)*

4. Respirations have increased to compensate for the blood loss and as a response to the sucking chest wound and tension pneumothorax. A tremendous stress is on the respiratory system, which usually responds by increasing respiratory rate. Pulse is elevated in response to the patient's loss of blood. BP has dropped because the patient most likely has bleeding inside his chest or the build up of pressure is preventing adequate blood flow. The decrease in level of responsiveness may indicate that this patient's brain is not being adequately perfused. He may be in shock. *(Chapter 18)*

5. An ongoing assessment that allows early recognition of any changes in the patient's status; appropriate First Responder care; an accurate patient history and a physical exam; a hand-off report. *(Chapter 12)*

6. This is Hank Roberts. He is 27 years old. He was assaulted by three adult males with pool cues and probably a knife. He has a sucking chest wound just below his left nipple along with bruising to his chest. He is confused and has pale, cool, moist skin. His current respirations are 36, pulse 144, and blood pressure 82/48. The sucking chest wound has been sealed with an occlusive dressing and the patient is being assisted with high-flow oxygen. *(Chapter 12)*

Chapter 21: Burn Emergencies

Exam Warm-up/Short-Answer Review

1. c *(p. 389)*   2. c *(p. 390)*
3. d *(p. 393)*
4. a, b, d, e, f, g, h, i, j *(pp. 392–393)*
5. Depth of the burn, extent of body surface burned, which part of the body was burned, other complicating factors like age. *(p. 385)*
6. Using the "rule of nines," this patient has burned 22.5% of her body (anterior chest and abdomen, 18%; anterior arm, 4.5%). *(pp. 387, 389)*
7. a. Critical. Full-thickness burns involving the hands, feet, face, or genitals are considered critical. This patient's age also is a complicating factor.
   b. Minor. A superficial burn would be moderate only if it covered more than 50% of body surface area.
   c. Critical. Any burn complicated by a painful, swollen, deformed extremity is considered critical.
   d. Critical. The soot and cough suggest airway involvement. Any burn involving hands, feet, face, airway, or genitals in an infant or child is considered critical.
   e. Minor. Even though this patient has a partial-thickness burn, it is isolated to a small portion of a non-critical area of his body.
   f. Minor. Although burns to the hands are often deemed critical, this is a minor burn to the back of the patient's hand and would not be considered critical.
   g. Critical. Burns encompassing any body part are considered critical. All chemical burns to the eyes are considered critical, because even mild acid solutions can cause permanent eye damage. *(p. 385)*

8. Both the elderly and the very young have extremely thin skin and can sustain much deeper burns from a less severe source. People in both of these age groups have a disproportionate fluid-to-surface area ratio. Even small amounts of fluid loss can result in serious problems. In addition, both groups have weaker immune systems and are more susceptible to the infections that commonly accompany burns. (*p. 389*)

9. 3, 6, 4, 1, 2, 7, 5 (*pp. 385, 389–392*)

10. Damage to a patient's lungs is often progressive. Inhalation injuries may at first appear to be mild and then become more severe. It is important that the patient's airway and breathing be constantly reassessed in order to catch any worsening in the patient's condition. (*pp. 392–393*)

11. It is important to remove all items, such as the patient's rings and watch, which may retain heat or constrict a body part when the patient's burned skin swells. It also is important to remove any clothing near the burn sites. However, leave any clothing that is embedded in the burns. This clothing will have to be removed at the hospital by trained medical personnel. (*pp. 389–392*)

12. Tell them to stay in the car. They are safe as long as they do not complete the circuit between the car and the ground. If they try to leave the car and contact the ground with a foot while holding onto the car, they will be electrocuted. (*pp. 393–394*)

13. Altered mental status; obvious severe burns; weak, irregular, or absent pulse; shallow, irregular, or absent breathing; multiple fractures due to intense muscle contractions. (*p. 394*)

14. Provide manual stabilization of the patient's head and neck until the patient is completely immobilized. Be prepared to provide basic life support until the patient has been resuscitated. (Note that victims of lightning have been resuscitated as long as 30 minutes after a strike without any lasting damage.) (*pp. 394–395*)

Vocabulary Practice

1. Superficial burns: red skin and swelling.
   Partial-thickness burns: red skin, blisters, and intense pain.
   Full-thickness burns: charring, little or no pain.

2. **a.** partial-thickness   **b.** full-thickness
   c. full-thickness   **d.** superficial

The Call

1. You are feeling the electrical field created by the power line. This is evidence that the line is still electrified and poses a serious hazard. Pull back until the power line is disabled. (*p. 394*)

2. It is quite possible that this patient has breathing and circulation problems, spinal or other musculoskeletal injuries, external burns, and possibly internal injuries. You should have airway and breathing equipment, oxygen if possible, and burn dressings. (*pp. 393–394*)

3. Look for entry and exit wounds, in this case probably on the patient's arm or hand, leg or foot. (Imagine the farmer stepping down from the tractor, one hand on the tractor, one foot on the ground.) Cover the burns with dry, sterile dressings. (*pp. 393–394*)

4. The patient has severely compromised ABCs. His respiratory and pulse rates are too slow, and he has no measurable blood pressure. His airway should be opened with a jaw-thrust maneuver, and he needs

to be ventilated with 100% oxygen immediately. In addition to his respiratory insufficiency, he appears to be in shock, so also keep him supine and warm. His burns and broken bones can be cared for when you get more help. (*Chapters 6, 7, and 18*)

Chapter 22: Agricultural and Industrial Emergencies

Exam Warm-up/Short-Answer Review

1. a, e, f, h (*p. 402*)   2. b (*p. 406*)
3. c (*p. 406*)   4. a, b, d (*pp. 402, 406*)
5. True (*pp. 402, 406*)   6. False (*p. 406*)
7. True (*p. 406*)   8. c (*p. 406*)
9. a (*pp. 406–407*)
10. False. During any extrication, only one rescuer should give lifting instructions. (*pp. 406–407*)
11. c (*pp. 406–407*)   12. b (*pp. 407–408*)
13. a, b, c, d (*p. 408*)
14. a, b. A torch would transfer too much heat to the patient and could cause a fire. (*pp. 408–409*)
15. a, d (*pp. 409–410*)   16. a, b, c, d (*p. 410*)
17. c, d (*p. 411*)
18. a. Agricultural equipment is very complicated. The chances of injury increase as machinery becomes more sophisticated.
    b. Farmers may use old, unsafe equipment if they are unable to afford newer, safer models.
    c. Lengthy extrications can increase the severity of injuries and prolong the time before farmers can be properly treated for shock and internal injuries at a hospital.
    d. Farmers may not be missed for hours and may die from injuries that would have been nonfatal had they been discovered in time. Also, since there are often no phones, no 9-1-1, and no central dispatching service in many rural communities, there may be long delays getting the appropriate rescue and EMS resources to the emergency scene, as well as long transport times to the hospital. (*p. 402*)
19. Options for controlling bleeding include applying direct pressure, elevation, and pressure points. If the bleeding appears to be a life threat, a tourniquet may be necessary. (*Chapters 18 and 19*)
20. Red indicates combine movement controls. Yellow indicates auxiliary power controls. Black indicates miscellaneous function controls. (*p. 403*)

Vocabulary Practice

a. shear points   b. crush points
c. pinch points   d. wrap points
e. stored energy

The Call

1. d. Clearly, helicopter transport is indicated given the ground transport time. However, it is always best to dispatch a ground unit as well, in case the helicopter is unable to land due to mechanical malfunction, an unsafe landing zone, or other factors. (*Chapter 12*)

2. Mike appears to be in shock, and it is critical that he be freed as quickly as possible for transport to a hospital. Therefore, rescue should begin with the tools that are available. If the rescue is still proceeding

when the airbags arrive, a decision can then be made about whether or not to use them. *(Chapter 18)*

3. Mike's head and neck should be stabilized, and high-flow oxygen should be applied via a nonrebreather mask. External bleeding should be controlled if it is safe to do so. *(pp. 402–403)*

4. At this point, it appears that you cannot count on the helicopter to respond. If you can communicate with the ambulance, it would be appropriate to meet it since this would get Mike to the hospital more quickly. Remember, shocky trauma patients cannot be fixed in the field. They require a hospital emergency department and most likely surgery. *(Chapter 18)*

Chapter 23: Injuries to the Head, Face, and Neck

Exam Warm-up/Short-Answer Review

1. True. *(p. 419)*   2. **b, c, d** *(p. 419)*
3. True *(p. 421)*   4. **b** *(p. 421)*
5. **a, b, c, d** *(p. 421)*   6. True *(p. 421)*
7. **b** *(p. 422)*   8. **a** *(p. 422)*
9. True *(p. 423)*   10. **a, b, c, d** *(pp. 425–426)*
11. False *(pp. 425–426)*   12. **a, b** *(p. 425)*
13. False. A cold pack is okay for an eye orbit injury. But if the globe (eyeball) is injured too or if you are in doubt, do not apply cold packs. *(p. 430)*
14. **c** *(p. 430)*   15. **d** *(p. 430)*
16. **c** *(pp. 429–430)*   17. **b** *(p. 433)*
18. **a** *(Chapters 6 and 7)*
19. **d.** Severe bleeding of a wound involving a major blood vessel of the neck is a serious emergency. In addition to the possible loss of a great deal of blood, there is danger of air being sucked into a neck vein and carried to the heart. This can be lethal. *(pp. 423, 425)*
20. Any six: altered mental status; irregular breathing; open wounds to the scalp; penetrating wounds to the head; softness or depression of the skull; blood or cerebrospinal fluid leaking from ears or nose; facial bruises; bruising around the eyes or behind the ears; headache severe enough to be disabling or which appears suddenly; nausea, vomiting; unequal pupil size with altered mental status; seizure activity. *(p. 419)*
21. Disagree. Your job is not to diagnose a patient's injuries. Even if you were allowed to, there is no way to differentiate between a concussion and other head injuries in the field. While concussions are not life threatening, many signs and symptoms of concussion are identical to the early signs and symptoms of serious brain injuries. *(p. 422)*
22. You may be allowed to place a rigid item on each side of the patient's head to prevent movement. *(p. 419)*
23. Direct pressure could drive fragments of bone into brain tissue and cause further injury. *(p. 421)*
24. When the injury occurred, if the patient lost consciousness, and if the patient was moved after the injury occurred. *(pp. 420–421)*
25. If the scene is safe, enter. Take BSI precautions and establish manual stabilization of the patient's head and neck. Perform an initial assessment and treatment, including administration of 100% oxygen. Stabilize the ice pick with soft bulky dressings. Then dress the area around it with sterile gauze. *(p. 423)*

26. Any five: mouth will not open or close; drooling of saliva mixed with blood; difficulty swallowing; pain with talking or difficulty talking; missing, loosened, or uneven teeth; teeth that do not meet normally; pain in areas around the ears. *(p. 425)*
27. Any five: obvious lacerations or other wounds; deformities or depressions; obvious swelling, which sometimes occurs in the face and chest; difficulty speaking, loss of voice; airway obstruction; crackling sensation under the skin due to air leaking into the soft tissues. *(p. 426)*
28. No. Heavy direct pressure can cut off circulation to or from the brain and can slow down the patient's heart. *(pp. 426–427)*
29. 5, 4, 3, 2, 1 *(pp. 426–427)*
30. a. Eye orbits: Are there any deformities, open injuries including bruising, tenderness or pain, swelling?
   b. Eyelids: Are there any deformities, open injuries including bruising, tenderness or pain, swelling?
   c. Mucous membranes: Is there any redness, pus, foreign objects?
   d. Globes: Are there any open injuries, foreign objects, discoloration?
   e. Pupils: Are there abnormalities in the size, shape, equality, reaction to light?
   f. Eye movement: Can the eyes move in all directions? Is there an abnormal gaze or pain upon movement? *(p. 428)*
31. Eyes move together. Patching both eyes will help keep the injured eye from moving excessively. *(p. 428)*
32. Any two: One method is to flush the eye with clean water. A second method is to draw the upper lid down over the lower lid. When you let it return to its normal position, its undersurface will be drawn over the lashes of the lower lid. The lashes will "sweep" away the foreign object. A third alternative is to grasp the eyelashes of the upper lid. Turn up the lid over a cotton swab. The foreign object then may be carefully removed with the corner of a piece of sterile gauze. *(pp. 428–429)*
33. Place a rigid eye shield over the injured eye. Cover the opposite eye with gauze and arrange for immediate transport. *(pp. 428–429)*

Vocabulary Practice

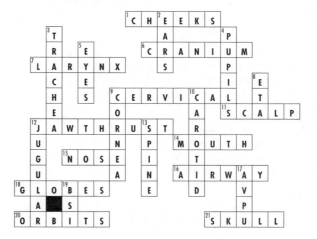

The Call

1. **d.** This patient has both the mechanism of injury and the physical findings for you to suspect spine injury. *(p. 419)*
2. **c.** The patient has serious, multiple injuries to her limbs, plus her altered mental status indicates there may be brain injury as well as skull injury. *(Chapter 12)*
3. **a** *(Chapters 6 and 7)*
4. **a, c.** This patient needs to be artificially ventilated. Her own respiratory rate is too slow and shallow to be sufficient, especially given her injuries. Her brain also desperately needs oxygen. Bag-valve-mask ventilation with 100% oxygen is the best way to meet her needs. If you are not allowed to work a BVM, then mouth-to-mask ventilation with supplemental oxygen would help this patient. *(Chapters 6 and 7)*
5. Your patient is an unhelmeted female in her 30s who was thrown from a speeding motorcycle before it wrapped itself around a tree. The driver of the motorcycle was killed. We found the female lying on the pavement, conscious but moaning. Her injuries include multiple abrasions, a large wound above her left eyebrow, some oral bleeding, apparent fractures of her left arm and leg, and bruising to her chest and abdomen. Initially, her vital signs were: respirations 16, pulse 120, and BP 116/88. Since our initial assessment and physical exam, she has become unresponsive. Her pulse has dropped to 50, and her respirations to between 6 and 8 unassisted. We are maintaining her airway with a jaw-thrust maneuver, an oropharyngeal airway, and suction. We are also ventilating her using a BVM and 100% oxygen. We have placed her on a backboard. *(Chapter 12)*
6. Every second counts for this patient. She has sustained a serious head injury and requires immediate transport to an appropriate hospital. She should be transported by helicopter. *(Chapter 18)*

Chapter 24: Injuries to the Spine

Exam Warm-up/Short-Answer Review

1. **c** *(p. 439)*
2. False. The description fits the thoracic spine. The cervical spine is made up of seven vertebrae and starts at the base of the skull where the spinal cord begins. *(p. 439)*
3. **b** *(p. 439)*   4. True *(p. 439)*
5. False. Always suspect spine injury if the mechanism of injury suggests it, even if there are no signs and symptoms. *(p. 439)*
6. **c** *(p. 440)*
7. True. Therefore, monitor the patient's airway and breathing continuously. *(p. 440)*
8. **d** *(p. 440)*   9. **b** *(p. 440)*
10. False. Stop at once if the responsive patient complains of pain or if you feel resistance in the unresponsive patient. Then stabilize the patient's head and neck in the position in which it was found. *(p. 440)*
11. False. Manual stabilization may be released when—and only when—the patient is completely immobilized on a long backboard. *(p. 440)*
12. True. Cervical collars at best restrict movement by only 70%. The remaining 30% must be achieved by manual stabilization. *(p. 444)*

13. **a, c, d** *(pp. 442, 444–445, 447)*
14. False. Manual stabilization must be maintained until the patient is completely immobilized from head to toe. The short backboard may be used to help stabilize a seated patient. It cannot replace immobilization on a long backboard. Complete immobilization on a long backboard is required to properly protect the patient's spine. *(pp. 444–445, 447)*
15. **a** *(pp. 449, 452)*
16. Any trauma severe enough to cause injury to the head can also cause injury to the spine. *(Chapter 23)*
17. Any four: motor-vehicle collision; motorcycle crash, pedestrian-car crash; falls; diving accidents; hangings; blunt trauma; penetrating trauma to the head, neck, or torso; gunshot wounds; any speed sport accident, such as roller blading, bicycling, skiing, surfing, or sledding; any unresponsive trauma patient. *(p. 440)*
18. Any five: respiratory distress; tenderness at the site of injury on the spinal column; pain along the spinal column with movement; constant or intermittent pain without movement along the spinal column or in the lower legs; obvious deformity of the spine; soft-tissue injuries to the head, neck, shoulders, back, abdomen, or legs; numbness, weakness, or tingling in the arms or legs; loss of sensation or paralysis in the upper or lower extremities or below the injury site; incontinence; priapism. *(p. 442)*
19. To assess movement, ask the patient if he or she can move hands and feet. Then have the patient squeeze both of your hands at the same time. Gauge the patient's strength and decide if it is equal on both sides. Also have the patient push his or her feet against your hands. Again, gauge strength and equality. To assess sensation, ask the patient to close his or her eyes. Then gently squeeze one extremity and then the other. As you do, ask questions such as: Can you feel me touching your fingers? Can you feel me touching your toes? *(p. 442)*
20. Apply a painful stimulus to check response. Either pinch the webbing between the toes and fingers or apply pressure with a pen across the back of a fingernail. The patient should withdraw from the pain. Note the response to pain in all four extremities. *(p. 442)*
21. A cervical collar does not immobilize the patient. The First Responder should have maintained manual stabilization of the patient's head and neck until the patient was completely immobilized. Anything less constitutes inadequate care. *(pp. 442, 444)*
22. Yes. When in doubt, take spinal precautions. That is, immediately stabilize the patient's head and neck. If you are allowed, apply a rigid cervical immobilization device and immobilize him on a long backboard. *(Chapter 23)*
23. 3, 1 ,4, 2 *(pp. 440–442)*
24. 2, 1, 3, 4, 7, 5, 6, 9, 8 *(pp. 444–445)*
25. Examples may include: when the scene is not safe, such as when there is threat of fire or explosion, a hostile crowd, extreme weather conditions; when life-saving care cannot be given because of the patient's location or position; when there is an inability to gain access to other patients who need life-saving care. *(pp. 447–448)*

Vocabulary Practice

1. The spinal cord is responsible for sending signals from the brain to the body and for receiving signals from the body and relaying them to the brain.
2. The spinal column is made up of 33 bones, one stacked on top of another. They are called vertebrae. They fit and move together, so we can bend, turn, and flex.
3. The spine is divided into five regions. They are the cervical, thoracic, lumbar, sacral, and coccygeal.
4. The cervical spine starts at the base of the skull where the spinal cord begins. It has seven vertebrae.
5. The thoracic spine is supported by the rib cage. It has 12 vertebrae, one for each rib.
6. The next group of five vertebrae make up the lumbar spine. These bones carry the weight of most of the body.
7. The last two regions of the body are the sacral and coccygeal spines. The sacrum has five fused vertebrae. The coccyx has four. Together they form the posterior portion of the pelvis.

The Call

1. In general, a calm, direct approach is probably best. There are several onlookers who need to be calmed—especially the one who is scaring your patient. It often helps to focus bystanders on a task, such as giving you the history of the event, fetching first aid materials, etc. You need to establish control and calm people down so that you can properly care for the patient. *(Chapters 2 and 10)*
2. First you need to stabilize John's head and neck. Then you need to perform an initial assessment. You will need an extra set of hands to accomplish all this. *(Chapter 12)*
3. d *(pp. 440, 442)*
4. Support John's airway, breathing, and circulation until the paramedics take over care. Be prepared to provide basic life support. *(Chapters 6 and 7 and p. 442)*
5. Disagree. Remember, John may have a spinal-cord injury. Moving him up to the roadway without the equipment necessary to properly immobilize him could further endanger John's life. It is certainly not worth the few minutes that may be saved by meeting the paramedics on the road rather than by the pool. Remember, even if John were to survive such a move, "quadriplegia is forever." *(pp. 440, 442)*
6. Your patient is a 16-year-old male named John. John dove into this pool and struck the top of his head on a rock outcropping. His friends pulled him from the water, and one shook him by the shoulders to try to get him to respond. I found him lying supine on the sand. He was awake but confused. I noted that he was breathing primarily from his diaphragm and that his pulse was 88. The only injury I found is a wound to the top of his head. Bleeding is controlled. I initially noted movement in his left arm only. Since my initial assessment and physical exam, John's level of responsiveness has worsened. He is now unresponsive. His eyes have a pronounced gaze. His pulse has dropped to 44, and his breathing appears more labored. I am

maintaining his head and neck in a neutral, in-line position. *(Chapter 12)*

Chapter 25: Musculoskeletal Injuries

Exam Warm-up/Short-Answer Review

1. a *(p. 459)*
2. c *(p. 460)*
3. True *(pp. 459–460)*
4. True *(p. 461)*
5. a *(Chapter 12)*
6. b *(Chapter 12)*
7. a *(Chapters 4 and 12)*
8. False. You may release manual stabilization of an injured limb when the limb is properly and completely immobilized. *(pp. 461–463)*
9. d *(p. 465)*
10. c *(p. 465)*
11. d. A pillow splint works best for immobilizing ankle or foot injuries. *(pp. 467, 471)*
12. False. Always take BSI precautions when you are to come in contact with a patient. A musculoskeletal injury can quickly change from a closed one to an open one. *(Chapter 2 and p. 465)*
13. The musculoskeletal system gives the body shape, protects internal organs, and provides for movement. *(Chapter 4)*
14. Direct, indirect, or twisting forces. *(pp. 459–460)*
15. Any five: deformity or angulation; pain and tenderness; crepitus; swelling; bruising or discoloration; exposed bone ends; joint locked in position. *(p. 461)*
16. A sprain, dislocation, and fracture all may present with the same signs and symptoms. It may not be possible to tell the difference among them without an x-ray. Because these injuries look so much alike in the field, they are always treated in the same way. *(pp. 459, 462–463)*
17. 5, 6, 1, 7, 3, 8, 2, 4 *(pp. 461–463)*
18. To prevent motion of bone fragments or dislocated joints; to minimize damage to surrounding tissues, nerves, blood vessels, and the injured bone itself; to help control bleeding and swelling; to help prevent shock; to reduce pain and suffering. *(p. 463)*
19. Disagree. You can't assess what you can't see. So cut away all clothing around the injury site before applying a splint. *(p. 465)*
20. Any three: compress nerves, tissues, and blood vessels under the splint; move displaced or broken bones; reduce blood flow below the injury site; delay transport. *(p. 465)*
21. STOP! Splint the injured arm in the position in which it was found. *(p. 467)*
22. Absolutely not. The elbow—and the knee—should be splinted in the position in which they are found. *(pp. 467, 470)*
23. a. Agree
    b. Disagree. When a long bone is injured, immobilize it and the joints above and below it. The splint for this patient should extend above the elbow and below the wrist.
    c. Disagree. Hands should be splinted in the position of function. Prior to splinting, a roller bandage should have been placed in the palm of the patient's hand to maintain its natural curve.
    d. Agree
    e. Agree *(pp. 465–467, 469–471)*

Vocabulary Practice

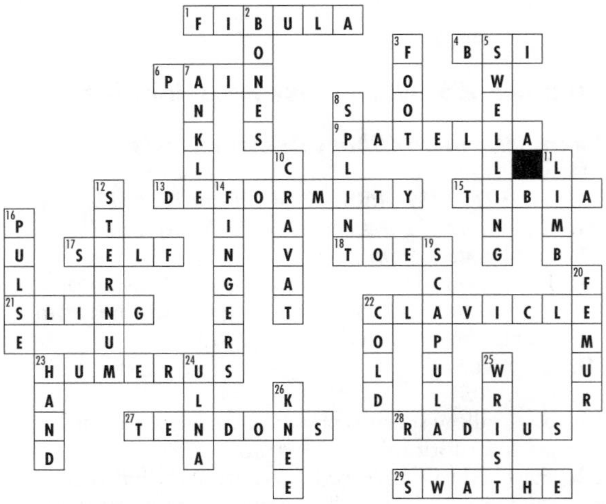

Crossword puzzle (answers):
FIBULA, BSI, PAIN, PATELLA, DEFORMITY, TIBIA, SELF, TOES, SLING, CLAVICLE, HUMERUS, TENDONS, RADIUS, SWATHE

The Call

1. **a.** Patient A: #3. He was wearing his seat belt. He has good vital signs, closed musculoskeletal injuries to one limb, and a small bump to his head. Perfusion in the injured extremities appears to be good. This patient should be treated last.

    b. Patient B: #1. He was not wearing a seat belt. This patient suffered a severe mechanism of injury. He is showing signs of shock and has an altered mental status. He has multiple extremity injuries, chest and pelvic injuries, and a large bruise to his head. He requires immediate transport.

    c. Patient C: #2. She was wearing a seat belt. She has good vital signs, but has suffered clavicle, wrist, and knee injuries. Of concern here is the lack of a pulse distal to her left knee injury. Perfusion appears to be good, except to her left foot. She needs immediate transport.

2. Agree. This EMT has recognized that Patient B is in shock and is suffering from severe injuries. This patient's broken humerus is the least of his problems. Critically injured trauma patients require immediate transport to a hospital if they are to survive. When managing this type of patient, strap painful, swollen, deformed injuries to the patient or to the long backboard. Remember, the patient's "Golden Hour" is ticking away. Prioritize.

3. Yes. Keep splinting as simple as possible. If she has immobilized the area herself (a "self-splint"), and your splinting efforts are causing her increasing pain, consider the splinting job done. *(p. 465)*

4. Splint the knee in the position found. Do not try to straighten it. *(p. 470)*

5. Apply a pillow splint to the injured ankle after removing the patient's shoe and sock. *(p. 471)*

Chapter 26: Childbirth

Exam Warm-up/Short-Answer Review

1. **c** *(p. 477)* 2. **c** *(p. 477)*
3. **b** *(p. 477)* 4. **c** *(p. 79)*
5. **a** *(p. 480)* 6. **d** *(p. 480)*
7. **a** *(p. 480)* 8. **c** *(pp. 479, 480)*
9. **d.** If the patient feels comfortable sitting, reclining, or in some other position during the first stage of labor, let her do so. *(p. 480)*

10. True *(p. 481)* 11. **a** *(pp. 491–492)*
12. **c** *(pp. 491–492)* 13. **d** *(p. 482)*
14. **b** *(p. 482)*
15. False. Meconium staining can be life-threatening. If this occurs, you must consider requesting an advanced life support team to assist. *(pp. 482–483)*
16. **c** *(p. 483)* 17. **a** *(p. 484)*
18. **a.** Rub the back gently or slap the soles of the feet. *(p. 484)*
19. **b** *(p. 484)*
20. **a, b.** Never tug on the umbilical cord. You could tear the placenta from the uterine wall and cause massive bleeding. The abdomen should be massaged only after the placenta has been delivered. *(pp. 484–485)*
21. **a** *(p. 485)* 22. **a** *(p. 485)*
23. **a, b, c, d** *(pp. 484–485)* 24. **b** *(p. 484)*
25. **c** *(p. 484)* 26. **a** *(p. 484)*
27. **c** *(p. 487)* 28. **c** *(p. 487)*
29. **a** *(p. 488)* 30. **d** *(p. 488)*
31. As labor progresses toward delivery, contractions become longer in duration, more frequent, and much more forceful. As delivery becomes imminent, contractions become extremely forceful and painful. They can last 45 to 90 seconds and may occur every 2 minutes. *(pp. 479, 480)*
32. Place your gloved hand on the mother's abdomen, just above her navel. Feel the involuntary tightening and relaxing of the uterine muscles. Time these involuntary movements in seconds. Start from the moment the uterus first tightens until it is completely relaxed. Time the intervals in minutes from the start of one contraction to the start of the next. *(p. 480)*
33. Any five: Have you had a baby before? Are you having contractions? How far apart are they? Has the amniotic sac ruptured? If so, when? Do you feel the sensation of a bowel movement? Do you feel like the baby is ready to be born? *(p. 480)*
34. By laying her on her back, you may have allowed her uterus, fetus, and placenta to press against her inferior vena cava. This can slow the return of blood to a patient's heart and decrease her circulating blood volume. You can easily remedy this problem by having her lie down on her left side. You also can treat the patient for shock if necessary. *(p. 480)*
35. Always act in a professional manner. Be calm, and reassure her. Tell her that you are there to help with the delivery. Provide as much quiet and privacy for her as you can. Get rid of distractions. Hold her hand and speak encouragingly to her. Help her concentrate on breathing regularly with contractions. Encourage the father, if present, to help. *(p. 481)*
36. Sheets and towels, sterile if possible; one dozen four-inch square gauze pads; two or three sanitary napkins; rubber suction syringe; baby receiving blanket; surgical scissors; cord clamps or ties; foil-wrapped germicidal wipes; wide tape or sterile cord; large plastic bags. *(p. 481)*
37. Any five: put on eye wear, a face mask, protective gloves, a disposable gown, and shoe coverings; handle soaked dressings, pads, and linens carefully, place them in separate bags that will not leak, and then seal and label the bags; scrub your arms, hands, and nails thoroughly before and after the delivery, even if you wore gloves. *(p. 481)*
38. Clean the area around the baby's mouth and nose once the head is delivered. Then clear the baby's

airway by suctioning the mouth first and then the nose with a rubber suction syringe. Repeat if necessary. *(pp. 482–483)*

39. The newborn is not breathing after drying, warming, and tactile stimulation or there are gasping respirations; the newborn's pulse rate is less than 100 beats per minute; there is persistent central cyanosis, or bluish discoloration around the chest and abdomen after 100% oxygen has been administrated. *(p. 484)*

Vocabulary Practice

```
                V
          2 P  L  A  C  E  N  T  A
                G
     3 C  R  4 O  W  N  I  N  G
       O     V        5 B  S  I
       R     A     7 A  B  8 C  U
       D        9 S     E     P  10 U
          11 A  F  12 T  E  R  B  I  R  T  H
                C     O     V     N     E
      13 B  14 T     X     I     E     R
       R     W     E     X     15 T  U  B  E  S  16
     17 M  E  C  O  N  I  U  M     18 C     S     H
       E        I        P           O
       C        19 L  A  20 B  O  R        W
     21 T  H  R  E  E        B
```

The Call

1. It would probably be a good idea to see if one of the rescuers can move the station wagon to a safer location, preferably off the expressway. You need to work with the mother to calm her and reassure her and to help her focus on her labor. Her husband needs to be calmed and reassured as well. A rescuer should help him to support his wife by placing him by her head or somewhere else close to her. *(p. 481)*

2. Since this is her first baby and her contractions are still 6 minutes apart, there is probably time for transport to the hospital. *(p. 480)*

3. Recheck the contractions. See if they have changed in any way. If her contractions are two minutes apart or less and she feels the urge to push, birth may be imminent. Check to see if the baby's head is crowning at the vaginal opening. *(p. 480)*

4. The patient's amniotic sac, or bag of waters, has broken. This indicates that her labor is indeed progressing. Once the amniotic sac is broken, labor usually accelerates. *(p. 479)*

5. The labor has progressed. The baby's head will appear at the opening of the birth canal very soon. *(pp. 479, 480)*

6. This baby needs to be ventilated. Provide the baby with small, controlled puffs to oxygenate her at a rate of 40–60 per minute and continue to stimulate her to breathe. *(p. 484)*

7. Disagree. The mother and baby should be transported by an ambulance. Both patients need to be monitored closely until they reach the hospital. It is important for both to have their ABCs reassessed, especially the baby's. In addition, the mother still needs to pass the placenta. Caregivers will have more room to work in the ambulance, and it is better equipped should the mother or baby require any additional care.

Chapter 27: Infants and Children

Exam Warm-up/Short-Answer Review

1. b *(pp. 497–498)*
2. e *(pp. 497–498)*
3. b *(pp. 497–498)*
4. d *(pp. 497–498)*
5. c *(pp. 497–498)*
6. False. *(p. 498)*
7. a *(p. 498)*
8. False. Infants and young children would not be able to communicate that information to you, even if they knew it. A better way may be to ask the caregiver what is normal. *(p. 499)*
9. True *(p. 500)*
10. a *(p. 501)*
11. b *(p. 501)*
12. True *(pp. 499, 500)*
13. c *(p. 505)*
14. False. It can indeed be significant. Monitor pediatric patients carefully, record any change, and be prepared to provide basic life support if necessary. *(p. 505)*
15. d. Low blood pressure is a late sign of shock. *(p. 505)*
16. False. These vital signs are generally not normal for a four-year-old. The child's pulse and respirations are elevated and the blood pressure is low. *(p. 505)*
17. True. Reportedly, more than 90% of pediatric deaths from foreign body airway obstructions occur in children under five years of age. Of those, 65% are infants who might have been saved by early detection. Always suspect an FBAO in any short-of-breath or unresponsive infant or child. *(pp. 509–510)*
18. d *(p. 511)*
19. a, b *(p. 512)*
20. True *(p. 512)*
21. b *(p. 513)*
22. False. It cannot be predicted or prevented, and no one yet knows what causes it. *(p. 513)*
23. b *(p. 513)*
24. Infant: birth to 1 year
   Toddler: 1–3 years old
   Preschooler: 3–5 years old
   School Age: 6–12 years old
   Adolescent: 13–18 years old. *(p. 497)*
25. Any one: explain to the caregivers what is being done; tell them why it is being done; ask them to assist, if appropriate. *(p. 498)*
26. The First Responder's approach is guaranteed to alienate and upset Katie's parents. He lacks any empathy for Katie's mother and does little to hide the fact that he sees her as a nuisance, a barrier to caring for Katie, rather than a resource. An appropriate response would be to empathize with Katie's mother. A seizure is scary to watch, especially when someone you love is convulsing in front of you. After reassuring her that the worst is probably over, focus on tapping Katie's mother for important patient history information. In addition, there is no one better qualified to calm Katie than her mother or father. Generally, allow parents to stay with their children, but it is not appropriate to have the mother hold the child while enroute to the hospital. Both the mother and baby must be properly seat belted in for the transport. *(p. 498)*
27. Had the child been moved and, if so, where did the incident occur? *(p. 499)*
28. Any five: noisy breathing; cyanosis; flaring nostrils; retractions; use of accessory muscles to breathe; breathing with obvious effort; altered mental status. *(pp. 500–501)*
29. a. Palpate the infant's brachial pulse.
   b. Palpate the unresponsive child's carotid or femoral pulse.

c. Palpate the responsive child's radial or brachial pulse. *(p. 504)*

30. Responses should include the following: When did the signs and symptoms develop? How have they progressed? Is the problem a recurring one? If so, has the child been seen by a physician? If so, is the specific diagnosis known? What treatment was received? *(p. 504)*

31. It is difficult to assess pain in infants and children. They may lack the body awareness and vocabulary necessary to describe it. Children also may not be able to separate the fear they feel from their physical condition. *(p. 504)*

32. b. When an infant's tongue relaxes, it can easily block the airway. Carefully position the airway in any infant with an altered mental status to avoid this problem.

c. Because of the larger head, the airway is more easily closed off when the patient is on his or her back. It may be necessary to place a thin pad under the shoulders in order to keep the patient's head in a neutral position and the airway open. Because of their larger heads, infants and children are more likely to suffer head and neck injuries, too. Always take spinal precautions for any infant or child who has suffered a mechanism of injury that suggests a possible head or spine injury.

d. Loss of even a small amount of blood may cause shock in an infant or young child. Carefully monitor the vital signs of any infant or child patient who has experienced even slight external blood loss or who may have internal bleeding.

e. This makes pediatric patients more susceptible to hypothermia and dehydration, and more adversely affected by burns. Keep your pediatric patients warm.

f. Make sure that cervical collars fit correctly. Many children will not fit into even the shortest ones. Be prepared to use a rolled up towel in these cases. *(p. 501)*

33. Any five: altered mental status; apathy, lack of vitality, inability to recognize a parent; delayed capillary refill; rapid or weak and thready pulse; pale, cool, clammy skin; rapid breathing; falling or low blood pressure (a late sign); absence of tears when crying. *(pp. 508–509)*

34. First Responder care of a pediatric patient who is having an asthma attack is the same as for any respiratory emergency. Be sure to monitor the airway and breathing constantly. Arrange for transport to the nearest hospital as quickly as possible. *(p. 511)*

35. Increased or decreased heart rate; unequal central (femoral) and distal pulse rates; poor skin color and delayed capillary refill; altered mental status. *(p. 511)*

36. Provide CPR for two minutes, and then call out for help. *(Chapter 8)*

37. Any five: How often? Was this seizure the same as the others? Have the previous seizures been associated with fever? Or do they occur when the baby is well? Did others in your family have seizures in childhood? How many seizures has the child had in the last 24 hours? What was done for them? Is the child taking seizure medication? What did this seizure look like? Did it start in one part of the body and progress? Did the eyes go in different directions? *(p. 512)*

38. Sudden infant death syndrome. *(p. 513)*

39. Any six: When was the baby put in the crib? What was the last time the parents looked in on the baby? What were the circumstances concerning discovery of the infant? What was the position of the baby in the crib when found? What was the physical appearance of the infant and the crib? What else was in the crib? What is the appearance of the room and the home? Is there any medication present? What is the behavior of the people present? What is the general health of the infant, recent illnesses, medications, or allergies? *(p. 513)*

40. Any five: multiple bruises in various stages of healing; injury that is not consistent with the mechanism of injury described by the caregivers; patterns of injury that suggest abuse, such as cigarette burns, whip marks, or hand prints; fresh burns such as scalding in a glove or dip pattern; burns not consistent with the history presented by the caregivers; untreated burns; repeated calls to the same address; caregivers seem inappropriately unconcerned or give conflicting stories; the child seems afraid to discuss how the injury occurred. *(p. 513)*

41. Lack of adult supervision; appearance of malnourishment; unsafe living conditions; untreated chronic illness, such as no medication for asthma; delay in reporting injuries. *(p. 513)*

42. It is not appropriate. When at the scene of a suspected child abuse emergency, a First Responder should deal with the child's immediate medical emergency. This is not the time to be accusatory or confrontational. *(pp. 513, 515)*

43. Who must report the abuse; what types of abuse and neglect must be reported; to whom the reports must be made; what information you are required to give; what immunity do First Responders have granted to them; criminal penalties for failing to report. *(p. 515)*

44. Critical incident stress debriefing. *(p. 515)*

Vocabulary Practice

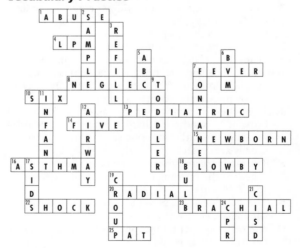

The Call

1. Lateesha's respirations, pulse, and blood pressure are all higher than normal. Normal ranges would be respirations 12–26, pulse 80–100, and blood pressure 96–98/70. *(p. 505)*

2. Any five: Is this the first time you have ever had trouble breathing? Is your breathing getting better? Is it getting worse? Do you have any pain in your

body? In your chest? In your back? In your stomach? Do you take any medicine for your breathing? Do you take any other medicine? How is your breathing right now? What were you doing when you began to have trouble breathing? *(Chapter 12)*

3. 7, 1, 6, 3, 4, 5, 8, 2. Note that the order of steps a (7), c (6), and g (8) may vary. *(Chapter 12)*

Chapter 28: Geriatric Patients

Exam Warm-up/Short-Answer Review
1. **b** *(p. 521)*   2. True *(p. 524)*
3. **d** *(p. 524)*   4. **c** *(p. 526)*
5. **b** *(p. 526)*
6. Any of the changes included in the chapter are acceptable responses. *(pp. 521–524)*
7. **a.** Any three: They may fear leaving home, going to a hospital, or losing independence. They may have concerns about the cost of medical care, ambulance transport, and possible admission to a hospital. They also may be afraid to leave behind a spouse or sibling or pet for whom they provide care. *(p. 527)*
   b. Arrange for a family member to care for the spouse or pet. Ask a spouse or adult child to talk to the patient to convince him or her to accept care and transportation. Take time to explain and discuss alternatives with the patient. Show empathy or concern and tell the patient that the problem will not go away, may worsen with time, and, if it is nothing, then the hospital will not admit them.
8. Any three: requires assistance with daily activities; has lost bladder control; has bizarre behavior due to Alzheimer's disease or another progressive dementia; has difficulty sleeping. *(p. 524)*
9. The most common mechanisms of injury in the elderly are falls, burns, and vehicle crashes. *(p. 525)*
10. Speak slowly and clearly. Face the patient and speak in a voice that is louder than normal conversation but not shouting. Get down to the patient's level. *(p. 526)*

Vocabulary Practice

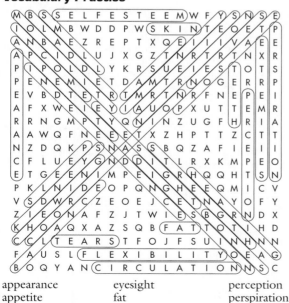

appearance   eyesight   perception
appetite   fat   perspiration

arteries   flexibility   prostate
balance   hearing   self-esteem
bladder   immunity   skin
bones   income   sleep
chewing   independence   smell
circulation   kidneys   strength
coordination   mobility   taste
digestion   nerves   tears
extremities   nutrition   teeth

The Call
1. Yes. Elderly patients can have poor circulation and decreased body fat. Lying on a cool surface outside overnight would clearly be enough to cause hypothermia. Existing conditions such as heart or breathing problems can be worsened by the fall and prolonged inactivity. *(Chapter 16)*
2. Shoes with non-slip soles; eliminating throw rugs and other slippery items in the home; installing railings near all stairs. *(p. 526)*
3. Determine if the patient remembers the fall. Ask if there was any incidence of dizziness, fainting, respiratory problems, or chest pain prior to the fall. Furthermore, examine the area for evidence of tripping such as a bunched-up rug, and so on. *(Chapters 10 and 12)*

Chapter 29: EMS Operations

Exam Warm-up/Short-Answer Review
1. **a** *(pp. 533–534)*   2. **b** *(pp. 533–534)*
3. **c** *(pp. 533–534)*   4. **a, d, e** *(p. 534)*
5. **d** *(pp. 533–534)*   6. **e** *(pp. 533–534)*
7. **a** *(p. 535)*   8. **a** *(p. 535)*
9. False. Too many emergency responders are injured because they have done this. Keep your seat belt on until the vehicle has come to a full stop. *(p. 536)*
10. True *(p. 536)*   11. **b** *(p. 536)*
12. True *(p. 536)*   13. False *(p. 537)*
14. **c** *(p. 538)*
15. Airway adjuncts, suction devices, pocket masks, or other artificial ventilation devices. *(p. 532)*
16. Dressings, bandages, materials to stabilize impaled objects, sterile saline, scissors, adhesive tape. *(p. 532)*
17. Any three: nature of the call, caller's name and exact location, patient's exact location, severity of the patient's problem, number of patients, call-back number of the caller, and special problems or considerations that may be pertinent. *(p. 534)*
18. Any four: know all local and state guidelines related to driving emergency vehicles; when possible, travel in pairs; when backing up, do so slowly and carefully, use all available mirrors, and have your partner take a position in the rear to act as spotter; know the territory and take alternative routes to avoid potential problems; avoid sudden braking at high speeds; practice special caution on curves and hills. *(p. 535)*
19. Keep the windows closed while the siren is on; wear ear plugs or ear muffs; move the siren speakers from the top of the cab to the front grille. *(p. 536)*
20. He should put on an impact-resistant protective helmet with reflective tape and a strap under the chin. *(pp. 537–538)*
21. Check to see how much traffic is following from behind. Wait a few minutes, if possible, to let traffic clear. *(p. 537)*

22. Open the door slowly to alert traffic that he or she is exiting. *(p. 537)*

23. They should exit the rear door because it does not discharge into traffic *(p. 537)*

Vocabulary Practice

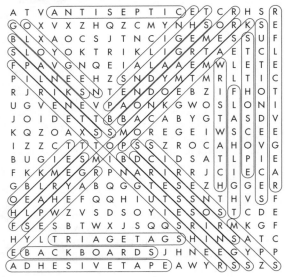

adhesive tape
antiseptic
backboards
bandages
batteries
blankets
body armor
dressings
eye wear
fire extinguisher

flares
flashlight
gloves
helmet
maps
OB kit
oxygen
penlight
pocket masks
reflective gear

saline
scissors
sirens
sphygmomanometer
splints
stethoscope
suction devices
triage tags
wrist watch

The Call

1. Any five: know the location; plan a route; wear seat belts; exercise due regard for safety of others; use lights and siren; use a spotter to back up the vehicle; avoid excessive speed; park on the shoulder or in a driveway. *(pp. 535–537)*

2. To channel traffic around the scene to avoid additional collisions; to minimize disruption of traffic flow when possible; to clear the scene for safe arrival of additional emergency vehicles. *(p. 538)*

3. Have all responders wear reflective equipment; place the cones or flares 10 to 15 feet apart and approximately 100 feet into traffic; place them at the beginning of a curve or the crest of a hill. *(p. 538)*

Chapter 30: Hazardous Materials Incidents and Emergencies

Exam Warm-up/Short-Answer Review

1. d *(p. 547)*   **2.** a *(p. 547)*

3. c *(p. 548)*

4. d. The NFPA 704 system is used on fixed structures, not trucks. *(p. 547)*

5. a, b, c, d *(p. 549)*

6. a. The first step is always to take a position from a safe distance and then assess the situation. If you do this prior to contacting EMS, you will have more information to give them regarding the specific nature and circumstances of the incident. *(p. 549)*

7. c *(p. 549)*   **8.** a *(p. 549)*

9. b *(p. 550)*   **10.** c *(p. 550)*

11. Toxicity, flammability, and reactivity. *(p. 545)*

12. Any three: explosives, compressed and poisonous gases, flammable solids and liquids, oxidizers, corrosives, radioactive materials. *(p. 545)*

13. Department of Transportation (DOT). *(p. 547)*

14. Material safety data sheets. *(p. 548)*

15. a. First Responder Awareness—learns how to recognize a problem and how to call for the proper resources.

   b. First Responder Operations—learns how to keep at a safe distance and how to stop the emergency from spreading.

   c. Hazardous Materials Technician—learns how to plug, patch, or stop the release of a hazardous material.

   d. Hazardous Materials Specialist—learns to provide command and support activities at the site of a hazardous materials emergency. *(p. 548)*

16. Identify the emergency as a hazmat incident; identify the hazardous materials; establish command and control zones; establish a medical treatment sector. *(p. 549)*

17. Take command of the situation by moving everyone away from the truck. Access the EMS and fire services so that trained personnel can respond to the incident and actually deal with the hazmat threat. Assume that the truck is carrying compressed gas that is dangerous. *(pp. 549–550)*

18. Any three: smoking or self-igniting materials; extraordinary fire conditions; boiling or spattering of materials that have not been heated; wavy or unusual vapors over a container of liquid material; colored vapor clouds; frost near a container leak; unusual condition of containers. *(p. 549)*

19. The nature and exact location of the incident; a description of the incident, including any potential for fire or explosion; the number of patients involved; a request for additional help, such as fire, police, EMS, and hazmat support; suggestion for the way rescuers can approach the scene; if possible, identify the hazardous materials and the severity of the situation. *(p. 550)*

20. You can alert the responding hazmat team as to the type of substance leaking from the truck and the approximate area of contamination. You can deny entry to the scene and possibly set up a medical treatment sector. However, you should not enter the scene to render aid to the driver or other injured people because you lack the equipment and training to do so. While it is difficult to stand by while an injured patient is unattended, you must not risk exposure to the acid. *(pp. 549–550)*

Vocabulary Practice

1. labels   **2.** placards

3. shipping   **4.** numbers

5. OSHA   **6.** awareness

Scrambled letters: L B C S I N U O A R
Unscrambled letters: BINOCULARS

The Call

1. b *(pp. 549–551)*

2. Never deviate from your EMS system's hazmat response plan. Never discontinue it based on partial or sketchy information. Cutting corners in an emergency response to a hazardous material can lead to lost lives and bungled operations. Stick to the plan no matter what the material turns out to be. *(pp. 549–551)*

3. Deny them access. A search of the shed requires rescuers equipped with self-contained breathing apparatus and specialized training. Your job is to protect those who have escaped. *(pp. 549–551)*

Chapter 31: Multiple-Casualty Incidents and Incident Command

Exam Warm-up/Short-Answer Review

1. c *(pp. 558–559)*
2. b, e, f, h *(p. 541)*
3. c *(p. 559)*
4. a. The triage officer supervises patient assessment, tagging, and removal of patients to a designated treatment area.
   b. The treatment officer sets up a treatment area and supervises treatment.
   c. The transportation officer arranges for ambulances and tracks the priority, identity, and destination of all patients leaving the scene.
   d. The staging officer releases and distributes resources when they are needed and sees that gridlock does not occur in the transportation area. *(p. 557)*
5. Establish command, size up the scene, request additional resources, and begin triage. *(pp. 558–559)*
6. Is the scene safe? How many patients are involved? What are the needs for extrication? How many ambulances will be needed? Are there any other factors that affect the scene and resources (such as weather or terrain)? How many sectors will be needed? Where is the best place to stage resources? *(p. 559)*
7. Nature of the problem, potential hazards, number of patients, time elapsed since the emergency occurred, what already has been done. *(p. 559)*
8. Simple Triage and Rapid Treatment. *(p. 559)*
9. *(pp. 541–542)*

a. priority 1	j. priority 1	s. priority 2
b. no care	k. priority 1	t. priority 1
c. priority 3	l. priority 1	u. priority 1
d. priority 2	m. priority 3	v. priority 1
e. priority 2	n. priority 1	w. no care
f. priority 2	o. priority 1	x. priority 1
g. priority 2	p. priority 1	y. priority 1
h. priority 1	q. priority 1	z. priority 1
i. priority 3	r. priority 3	

10. a. Priority-1 Red   b. Priority-0 Black
    c. Priority-1 Red   d. Priority-1 Red
    e. Priority-2 Yellow *(p. 543)*
11. Rescuers often feel fearful about their personal safety. They may feel frustrated, fatigued, guilty, depressed, angry, and preoccupied with death. *(pp. 564–565)*
12. One of the best ways to deal with the stress from an MCI is to go through the process of a critical incident stress debriefing (CISD). *(pp. 543–544)*
13. Any three: make sure rescuers are fully aware of their exact assignments; assign rescuers to tasks

according to their skills and experience; tell rescuers to rest at regular intervals away from the disaster; have counseling available for those who need defusing; have several workers circulate among rescuers to watch for signs of physical exhaustion and stress; provide plenty of nourishing drinks and food; encourage rescuers to talk among themselves; make sure that rescuers have a chance to talk with trained counselors after the incident. *(pp. 564–565)*

Vocabulary Practice

1. Triage Officer—supervises patient assessment, tagging, and removal of patients to a treatment area.
   Treatment Officer—sets up a medical treatment area and supervises treatment.
   Transportation Officer—arranges for ambulances and tracks the priority, identity, and destination of all patients.
   Staging Officer—releases and distributes resources when they are needed
   Safety Officer—identifies potential danger on scene and takes action to prevent it from causing injury to patients and rescuers.
2. Priority-1 Red—immediate-care category
   Priority-2 Yellow—urgent-care category
   Priority-3 Green—delayed-care category.
   Priority-0 Black—no-care category

The Call

1. How many patients are there? What priority are these patients? What type of extrication effort do they need? How many ambulances are needed? Where should the incoming resources be staged? Are there any other factors affecting the scene? Are there any other resources needed to manage the incident? *(p. 559)*
2. a. immediate   b. immediate
   c. delayed   d. delayed
   e. immediate   f. delayed
   g. immediate *(pp. 541–542)*
3. Patient "a," the unresponsive 18-month-old with head and chest injuries and signs of shock, should be the top priority patient. The other "immediate" patients are older. (Remember that the very young and the very old are at a higher risk for serious trauma.) They are also conscious. Unresponsive patients are unable to manage their own airways. All of the "immediate" patients should be tended to as quickly as possible, however.
4. At least four ambulances should be dispatched to this incident. You are faced with four critically injured "immediate" patients. Each one should be allocated an ambulance. The one viable "delayed" patient— the driver of the bread truck—can be transported with one of the critical patients since he appears to be quite stable and will probably only require monitoring en route to the hospital. Mortally injured patients are given a delayed status and are often left at the scene. (Follow local protocols.)
5. When confusion and disorder set in, take the time to pull rescuers into a meeting. If the incident is large enough, you may want to just meet with the various officers. If the incident is relatively small, you may want to pull everyone together to focus them on their specific tasks and to coordinate the various jobs that need to be done. No matter how

bad the incident, you must take the time to reorganize people if it appears that the scene is becoming unsafe and ineffective.

6. This rescuer is letting out some of the pent-up emotions generated by this incident. Be gentle. Reassure him that his feelings are normal and appropriate. Let him talk out these feelings if he so wishes. Be empathetic. This rescuer definitely should participate in a critical incident stress debriefing (CISD), which should be held soon after the incident is over. *(pp.564–565)*

Chapter 32: Water Emergencies

Exam Warm-up/Short-Answer Review

1. **a** *(p. 572)*
2. **a, b, c, d** *(pp. 572–573)*
3. **c** *(p. 572)*
4. **a** *(p. 574)*
5. **d** *(p. 574)*
6. **e** *(pp. 573–574)*
7. **a.** True
   b. False
   c. True
   d. True *(pp. 572–573)*
8. **d** *(p. 576)*
9. **a.** Ventilation of a near-drowning patient must begin as soon as possible. If necessary, start ventilations in the water. *(p. 574)*
10. False. The force of moving water is measured by its depth, width, and velocity. *(p. 576)*
11. **a** *(p. 577)*
12. False. *(p. 578)*
13. **a** *(pp. 578–579)*
14. **c** *(pp. 578–579)*
15. **b** *(pp. 579–580)*
16. **d** *(pp. 579–580)*
17. **c** *(p. 580)*
18. Drownings that occur in cold water have resulted in successful resuscitations, even up to an hour after submersion. *(pp. 571–572)*
19. You are a good swimmer; you are specially trained in water rescue; you are wearing a personal flotation device; and you are accompanied by other rescuers. *(p. 573)*
20. **a.** Reach—Hold out an object for the patient to grab and then pull the patient to shore.
    b. Throw—Tie a rope to an object that floats, throw the object to the patient, and pull on the rope to tow the patient to shore.
    c. Row—Use a boat to get closer to the patient. *(p. 573)*
21. **a.** Strainers—These are obstructions that allow water to pass through but catch people and other objects. If a strainer catches a swimmer, the force of the water can hold him or her there until hypothermia sets in and he or she tires and drowns.
    b. Obstructions—A swimmer can get pinned against any type of object and be held there by the force of the moving water, again until he or she drowns.
    c. Recirculating currents or "holes"—When water flows over a large object, a "hole" may form.

The current can keep recirculating a swimmer in its backwash until he or she tires and drowns.

d. Low-head dams—These dams are wide and difficult to see from upstream. They create a recirculating current across the width of the water below the dam. This "boil line" is capable of trapping swimmers, boats, and other large objects. *(pp. 576–577)*

22. **a.** Reach and Throw—A hypothermic patient will find it more and more difficult to hold on to anything small. So throw a fire hose, if possible, which can be inflated quickly and pushed out to the patient.
    b. Row—A conventional boat may not be able to break the ice as it moves, so an option is to use a small inflatable craft with ropes to tether it and pull it from shore.
    c. Go—When patients are too hypothermic to hang on, rescuers must go get them. This usually means wearing a "dry" neoprene ice-rescue suit that is tethered to shore. The rescuer then crawls, shuffles, or swims out to grab and pull the patient in. *(p. 578)*

Vocabulary Practice

The Call

1. Establish who will be responsible for functions such as assessing the patient, ventilating the patient, gathering a patient history, and so on. You can also review your plan for controlling the scene and interfacing with the other responding agencies. *(Chapters 10 and 12)*
2. Establish a command presence on calls where emotions are running high. In this instance you have a patient that requires immediate resuscitation. You need to move the crowd away to keep them from inadvertently interfering with rescuer efforts. Move this group away from the child, and focus them on giving you helpful information about the incident. Explain that the best way they can help the child is to allow the rescuers the space necessary to help her. Be empathetic but firm. Call for law enforce-

ment if it appears that the crowd is becoming unmanageable or dangerous. *(Chapter 10)*

3. Relieve the exhausted lifeguard. Reassess the patient's ABCs, readjust her airway while maintaining spinal precautions, suction if needed, assess breathing, ventilate, check her pulse, and proceed with ventilations and, if necessary, CPR. Use the AED according to your protocols. *(Chapters 6 and 7)*

4. Any three: reposition her head and re-attempt to open her airway using a jaw-thrust maneuver; reinsert the oropharyngeal airway after checking that it is the correct size; evaluate the patient for a foreign body airway obstruction; check that your ventilation equipment is not faulty (holes in the BVM, etc.); check that the BVM fits her face correctly. You also may try a different device, such as a pocket face mask with oxygen. If after all of the above you are still unsuccessful, consider trying a head-tilt/chin-lift maneuver as a last resort. While it is important that you protect her spine, it is more important that you ventilate her enough to keep her alive. *(Chapters 6 and 7)*

5. It is important that you be honest with the parent about the condition of his or her child. It is also important that you reassure the parent that you are doing everything you can to help. In this instance you may want to say the following: "Your daughter's heart is beating, but she is not breathing, so we are concentrating on breathing for her, using 100% oxygen. We are also suctioning her mouth to keep it free of water and food from her stomach. We are holding her neck and back to protect them from any possible injuries. She isn't awake right now, but we are doing everything we can to help maintain her breathing and heartbeat. The paramedics will be here any minute, and they will be transporting her to the closest hospital." Do not pronounce any judgments about the child's final outcome. It is best not to hypothesize about whether or not the child will survive. Leave this up to the medical team at the hospital. *(Chapter 27)*

6. 5, 3, 1, 2, 4, 6, 7 *(Chapter 12)*

Chapter 33: Vehicle Stabilization and Patient Extrication

Exam Warm-up/Short-Answer Review

1. c, d *(p. 587)*
2. a, b, c, d *(p. 587)*
3. b *(p. 587)*
4. c *(p. 587)*
5. c. Never crib a vehicle underneath its wheels or tires because it will tend to roll. *(pp. 587–588)*
6. a, b, d, g *(pp. 587–588)*
7. False. Simple access is access by which no tools are needed. Complex access is access that requires tools and specialized equipment. *(p. 588)*
8. b, c. Even if the proper equipment were immediately available, removing the windshield or cutting off the roof of the car will take too much time, given how injured the patient appears to be. *(pp. 588, 590)*
9. True *(p. 588)*
10. b, d *(p. 590)*

11. a *(Chapter 24)*
12. Since you are alone, you will not be able to extricate the patient. Make sure the scene is safe. Set out flares to warn oncoming motorists. Make sure that the car's ignition is turned off and that there is no threat of fire. Make sure that the vehicle is stabilized. If possible, gain access to the patient and assess his ABCs. Support his ABCs, if necessary, and apply oxygen, if it is available. Attempt to keep his head and neck in a neutral position. *(pp. 590–591)*
13. When assisting with a vehicle extrication, you should wear safety glasses or other eye protection; protective gloves; a flame-retardant turnout, brushfire garment, or other protective clothing; and protective boots. *(p. 586)*
14. Any five: ask a responsive patient to tell you how many others were involved in the crash; question witnesses to see if a patient walked away from the scene; in case of a high-impact crash, search the surrounding area carefully; look for tracks in the earth or snow; search the vehicle itself carefully (under the dashboard, for instance); look quickly for items that give clues to unaccounted for patients (lunch box, diaper bag, jacket, etc.). *(p. 586)*
15. It is on a tilted surface such as a hill; part of it is stacked on top of another vehicle; it is on a slippery surface such as ice, snow, or spilled oil; it is overturned; it rests on its side. *(pp. 587–588)*
16. 1, 3, 2, 6, 5, 7, 4 *(pp. 588, 590)*
17. Remove a shoe or other piece of clothing that may be pinning the patient. *(p. 590)*

Vocabulary Practice

1. Unstable. Any vehicle on a tilted surface such as a hill should be considered unstable until stabilized with cribbing or blocks at wheels to prevent rolling.
2. Unstable. Any vehicle that is stacked or partly stacked on top of another vehicle should be considered unstable until you have made it stable.
3. Stable
4. Unstable. Any vehicle on a slippery surface, such as ice, snow, or spilled oil, should be considered unstable.
5. Unstable. Any vehicle found on its side should be considered unstable until you make it so.
6. Stable

The Call

1. a. Chris—immediate, 1
   b. Jim—immediate, 2
   c. Sherri—delayed, 5
   d. Michael—delayed, 4
   e. Holly—immediate, 3
2. Your top patient-care priority should be the driver, Chris. He is unconscious, with snoring, gurgling respirations and major injuries. He needs airway management with spinal stabilization. You should also check to make sure that the other four patients have no immediate, life-threatening airway, breathing, or circulation problems, including any massive bleeding. Instruct them to remain calm and still. The major

problem with providing care at this point is a lack of access to these patients. Most treatment will have to wait until your patients are extricated. (pp. 590–591)

3. The patients should be extricated in the following order: Sherri, Michael, Holly, Chris, Jim.

4. While Chris and Jim are being extricated, support their ABCs and maintain spinal stabilization. Watch Chris carefully. Communicate closely with the extrication team so that you can stay clear of their work space while still maintaining Chris's airway and breathing. (pp. 590–591)

5. Apply a cervical collar, if you have not already done so. Secure Chris to a short board and then place him on a long board. (Chapter 24)

Chapter 34: Special Rescue Situations

Exam Warm-up/Short-Answer Review

1. a (pp. 597–598)
2. e (pp. 597–598)
3. b (p. 598)
4. b (p. 598)
5. c (p. 598)
6. a (p. 599)
7. a, e (p. 600)
8. d (pp. 602–603)
9. A confined space is a place with limited access and egress, which is not designed for human occupancy. (p. 597)
10. Any three: silos, storage bins, underground vaults, wells, culverts, cisterns. (p. 597)
11. Any three: normal ground travel to the appropriate medical facilities would take more than 30 minutes; extrication will be prolonged; location of the emergency is at a remote site; patients need paramedic-level emergency care. (p. 601)
12. Any five: fall of 15 feet or more; blow from a vehicle traveling over 20 mph; ejection from a vehicle; a vehicle rollover without restraints; major deformity to the passenger compartment or to the vehicle's front end; a death of one of the car passengers. (p. 601)
13. It must be free of obstructions, free of traffic, have no loose objects, and have scene lighting. (pp. 602–603)
14. Answers should include the following: If the pilot or crew chief signals you to approach, maintain eye contact, approach only from the front, stay low, avoid carrying anything above your head, avoid wearing anything loose that can be blown away by the rotor wash. (p. 603)
15. Yes. The high-angle rescue team is needed because the terrain carries great risk of injury or death if a rescuer slips, the rescuer cannot climb without using his or her hands for support, and it may be necessary to rappel to Andrew. (p. 600)
16. About 18 or 20 people are needed for a litter relay. Form groups of 4–6 members each, keeping group members about the same height. As the move proceeds, rotate members from side to side and finally replace them with rested members. (pp. 599, 600)

Vocabulary Practice

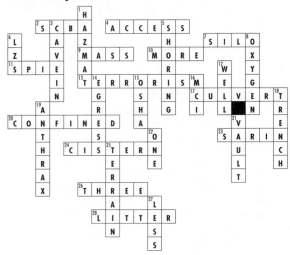

The Call

1. You will need appropriate rescue units to stabilize the tree and extricate the victim from the vehicle. If a helicopter is available, place it on standby as ground transport will be lengthy, extrication will be prolonged, the site is remote, and the patient will need advanced-level care (chest trauma is evident and the mechanism of injury is serious). (Chapter 10 and p. 601)

2. Establish a site that is 100 by 100 feet without obstructions. Be sure there are no loose objects that can be caught up in the rotor wash and blown at rescuers. Keep the emergency light on but not aimed at the helicopter. Mark off each corner of the site with light sticks or small strobes. Keep all traffic at least 100 feet back from the landing zone. (pp. 602–603)

3. Perform an initial assessment with attention to the chest injury. Maintain an open airway. Be sure of adequate breathing. Add oxygen by way of nonrebreather mask, if you are allowed. Control any obvious bleeding by direct pressure or pressure points. Monitor vital signs as allowed and level of responsiveness. Keep the patient warm, and offer emotional support.

Appendix 1: First Response to Terrorist Incidents

1. b (p.609)   2. a (p. 609)
3. Become familiar with likely targets. Learn what hazardous material could be involved. What type of protective equipment would be needed? (p. 609)
4. a (p. 610)   5. c (p. 609)
6. c (p. 610)
7. Number of patients and their injuries (p. 610)
8. People running in and out of the scene will create chaos. (p. 610)

The Call

Yes, a terrorist attack should be suspected because of the facility involved and the number of patients with symptoms. (p. 609)
Have a plan of action. Know how many people could be affected and what hazards may be present. (p. 609)
Additional EMS, fire, police, public works. (p. 610)